Figure 1. Housewrights sawing joists for a new building.

THE
COLONIAL
CRAFTSMAN

CARL BRIDENBAUGH

DOVER PUBLICATIONS, INC., New York

For
Roberta

This Dover edition, first published in 1990, is an unabridged republica-
tion of the work originally published in 1950 by New York University
Press, New York.

Library of Congress Cataloging-in-Publication Data

Bridenbaugh, Carl.
    The colonial craftsman / by Carl Bridenbaugh.
        p.   cm.
    Reprint. Originally published: New York : New York University
Press, 1950. Originally published in series: Anson G. Phelps lectureship
on early American history.
    Includes index.
    ISBN 0-486-26490-4
    1. Artisans—United States—History—18th century. I. Title.
II. Series: Anson G. Phelps lectureship on early American history.
HD2346.U5B7   1990
331.7'94—dc20   90-3472
                                                                      CIP

Manufactured in the United States by Courier Corporation
26490405
www.doverpublications.com

PREFACE

WHO HAS NOT in the course of his reading, at some time or other, determined to write a book because he could not find out what he desired to know about a given subject? For many years I have wanted to read a work about the colonial craftsman, but no such treatment existed. Everything on the subject was written from an antiquarian point of view. As time permitted, I gradually accumulated over a period of years a mass of data about the artisan and his place in the colonial community; and the invitation to prepare the Anson G. Phelps Lectures on Early American History provided both the ideal opportunity and the necessary incentive to assemble it in a form that I believe to be entirely different from previous works on early American craftsmen. From the latter, however, I have learned much, although I have ventured frequently to disagree with their findings.

The following chapters are printed exactly as they were written for oral delivery. I see no reason to alter their form or content. Consequently, I have placed the notes, which are merely references to authorities, at the end of the volume where they will not annoy the casual reader. The illustrations have been selected with great care and are referred to at appropriate places in the text.

To Dean Joseph H. Park, Professor Wesley Frank Craven, and the Stokes Foundation, I am deeply indebted for the privilege of delivering the Anson G. Phelps Lectures; and to Miss Jean B. Barr and the officials of New

York University Press I am grateful for their co-operation in bringing them to publication.

CARL BRIDENBAUGH

*Institute of Early American History and Culture
  at Williamsburg, Virginia*
September, 1949

CONTENTS

LIST OF ILLUSTRATIONS

NOTE: All of the illustrations in this book have been taken from the great French *Encyclopédie*, which includes a twelve-volume *Receuil des planches* (Paris, 1762-1777). M. Diderot's engravers drew heavily from English examples for illustrations of the work of the several crafts, and thus they are much nearer to colonial practice, which closely imitated the English, than might at first appear. They are, moreover, unusually faithful representations, for each piece was designed for the head of a plate explaining the nature of a given craft. Here they are reproduced exactly as they appeared in the *Encyclopédie*, because collectively they mirror the style of book illustration in the eighteenth century and are superb examples of the important engraver's art.

Illustrations (continued)

THE CRAFTSMAN
OF THE RURAL SOUTH

INTRODUCTORY

C RAFTS—and the artisans who practiced them—played a
     most important part in early American life; even more
than historians have generally supposed. Next to husbandmen, craftsmen comprised the largest segment of the colonial population; whereas the former made up about eighty
per cent of the people, artisans constituted about eighteen
per cent. In these lectures I propose to discuss the artisan
or craftsman (for the terms are interchangeable) rather than
the things he produced or the processes he used. It is the
fundamental importance of the contribution this man and
his fellows made to colonial society that interests me rather
than the antiquarian quaintness of a Betty lamp or the exclusiveness attaching to the possession of a unique Revere
creamer or a block-front desk by Goddard. We have too
long been blinded by the crowded displays of antiques in the
Fifty-seventh Street shops and the "Ye Olde" emporiums
of New England and Pennsylvania. It is the actual people,
real living human beings, who made the artifacts needed
both for the existence and the embellishment of eighteenth-
century living that I wish to pass before you.

When they spoke of a *craft,* our forefathers and their
English and German ancestors thought of a skill, an art, an
occupation. Or they meant a calling requiring special training and knowledge; or possibly, even, the members of a
given trade or handicraft taken collectively. But the word

craft always suggested a trade or occupation, the "Art and Mistery" of which was acquired only after a long period of tutelage by a master craftsman.

In considering a craft, we must not fall into the common error of assuming that the term always implied handwork. It might, or it might not, according to conditions in a given trade. Clothworkers employed the spinning wheel, loom, and fuller's mill; the potter had his wheel, the turner his lathe, the ironworker his tilt hammer and mechanical bellows, and the printer had his press. Not infrequently, too, wind, water, and horse power were harnessed to the machine to save labor. As early as 1622 the word *manufacture* was generally understood to include the making of articles by mechanical as well as by physical labor.

The craft system, then, was a method of producing articles used in daily life, and this activity, by its very nature, was at the same time artistic. "The sight of a skilled workman plying his trade is one of the experiences that sweeten life," a modern scholar tells us, and with him we look back, with nostalgia, across two centuries at the man who, with apparent ease, skillfully synchronized mind, eye, and hand in fabricating a piece of handicraft. We envy his opportunity to be "creative"; we praise his "pride in his work." Yet we must beware of surrounding the artisan with the haze of romance. Labor performed principally by hand is hard—very hard—and so long did it take to finish a good job that the workman must often have yearned to drop it and seek greener pastures.

We must also remember that only the best of the eighteenth-century craftwork has survived to be dignified by inclusion in our museums or private collections. Although craftsmanship stimulated the creativeness of the individual, many inferior articles were produced—inferior in utility, inferior in finish, inferior even in design and appearance. English and colonial laws passed to enforce high standards of workmanship and materials offer abundant evidence that sleazy products were often palmed off on an unsuspecting colonial public. That an article is "handmade" and "antique" is no guarantee of its excellence.

Like us, early American artisans were human beings and their output was both good and bad. Something can be said for the machine. I would far rather have my modern wrist watch and the shoes I am wearing than the finest products from the shop of an eighteenth-century watchmaker or cordwainer.

Among the thousands who went out to the Continental colonies in the seventeenth century was a large proportion of skilled artisans who took with them the medieval English craft tradition as part of their cultural baggage. According to immemorial custom a master craftsman presided over his household unit, which consisted of one or more journeymen and apprentices. He not only personally supervised their work and training, but he also dealt with the consuming public, either producing goods upon order or making articles that he expected would find a purchaser. Within the shop, such organization offered certain artistic possibilities that, given an able workman, sometimes favored the emergence of a creative craftsman—a daily chance to use one's hands and tools, ample leeway for the expression of individual judgment and taste, free play for the imagination, and an opportunity to experiment—yet all properly circumscribed by the comments and criticisms of customers. Although division of labor and quantity production were not unknown to Europeans, and capitalistic control had become widespread in several fields of endeavor, craft organization was not corporate; it was predominantly personal.

The villages that dotted the English countryside in the two centuries of our colonial period were centers of industry as well as of agriculture; they pulsed with the activity of trades supplying either the needs of the neighborhood or catering to the demands of a distant market. Daily the members of the several crafts met on the streets, at the market place, or in the taverns and rubbed shoulders and exchanged ideas and amenities. Village artificers were indeed simple folk, but there was nothing of the rustic boor about them. They dwelt not apart but in the midst of life and, with the vanishing yeomanry, they shared the attributes and dignities of the lower middle class. It is of profound significance that in the development of a class of colonial artisans many English craftsmen bred in Old England during its great age of village life shared in a migration to the New World, which beginning in 1607 continuously mounted throughout the whole colonial era.

In the seventeenth century, craftsmen and husbandmen who came to America faced the compelling problem of hewing a living out of the forest; they had little time and less energy for fashioning artifacts beyond absolute necessities. These each individual made for himself.

All along the Atlantic coast, save in a few seaports, the struggle to survive eventually made farmers out of immigrants. In the rural and frontier areas, which constituted ninety-five per cent of the English settlements, skills transplanted from the Old World deteriorated as the artisan struggled at becoming a farmer. Wilderness circumstances dictated that the needle, the awl, and the chisel give way to the axe, the hoe, and the gun. The pioneer's dilemma was trenchantly expressed by a Bostonian: "The Plow-Man that raiseth Grain, is more serviceable to Mankind, than the Painter who draws only to please the Eye. The hungry Man would count fine Pictures but a mean Entertainment. The Carpenter who builds a good House to defend us from the Wind and Weather, is more serviceable than the curious Carver, who employs his Art to please his fancy. This condemns not Painting or Carving, but only shows, that what's more substantially serviceable to Mankind, is much preferable to what is less necessary." [1]

Figure 2. Moravian potters at Salem, North Carolina, found in this ancient craft a source of community profit.

Figure 3. The shoemaker, or cordwainer, was a familiar artisan in both town and country.

In Virginia and Maryland, prospects of a quick cash crop and easily acquired land lured free workers into tobacco culture. Nearly every artisan who came over as an indentured servant was channeled by his master into the same course and, at the end of his service, also set up as a farmer. Moreover, a sparse population and a poor market for goods tended to force him out of his craft. Every attempt at establishing manufactures proved abortive. Placing the blame for the discouraging outlook as much on the people as on the environment, Robert Beverley caustically arraigned his fellow Virginians at the end of the century:

"They have their Cloathing of all sorts from England, as Linnen, Woollen, Silk, Hats, and Leather. Yet Flax and Hemp grow no where in the World, better than there; their Sheep yield a mighty Increase, and bear good Fleece, but they shear them only to cool them. . . . The very Furs that their Hats are made of, perhaps go first from thence; and most of their Hides lie and rot, or are made use of only for covering dry Goods, in a leaky House. Indeed some few Hides with much adoe are tann'd, and made into Servants Shoes; but at so careless a rate, that the Planters don't care to buy them, if they can get others; and sometimes perhaps a better manager than ordinary, will vouchsafe to make a pair of Breaches of a Dear Skin. Nay, they are such abominable Ill-husbands, that tho' their Country be overrun with Wood, yet they have all their Wooden-Ware from England; their Cabinets, Chairs, Tables, Stools, Chests, Boxes, Cart-Wheels, and all other things, even so much as their Bowls, and Birchen Brooms, to the Eternal Reproach of their Laziness." [2]

In the colonies north of Maryland, a similar situation that conspired to reduce the craftsman to a farmer was measurably relieved by the growth of such little villages as Newcastle, Burlington, Milford, Providence, Plymouth, Ipswich, and Hampton, where artisans could settle and where grist and saw mills, smithies, breweries, cooperages, and tanneries began to make their appearance. Moreover, in these colonies the rise of Philadelphia, New York, Newport, and Boston to the status of small cities provided a congenial atmosphere in which a nascent colonial craftsmanship was nurtured. Here some division of labor actually occurred before the turn of the century. At Boston both the coopers and the shoemakers were numerous enough to petition successfully "about being a company" with authority to dictate rules for the trade in 1648. Each group was made a gild for three years, "and no longer." [3]

Notwithstanding favorable portents, no craft, not even shipbuilding, had progressed beyond the household stage by 1700. The medieval gild system, based as it was on restriction of the labor supply, could not survive under colonial conditions where labor was always at a premium; hence American arts and crafts entered the new century wholly devoid of organization beyond the basic family unit. Such organizations as eventually came to fill this vacuum were fated to vary considerably from those prevailing in the mother country.

The great age of the colonial craftsman began with the eighteenth century. By 1700 English civilization had become firmly planted in America. The population of the twelve colonies numbered over 220,000 persons, and, as Benjamin Franklin was to point out, it doubled every twenty years. A burgeoning society like this provided a constantly expanding market that could never be exhausted by English importations alone. In fact, despite rapidly growing purchases of British manufactures—one-third to two-fifths of the whole output of English cloth after 1760, for example— it is clear that in each successive decade they represented a progressively smaller proportion of the goods needed by colonial society as more and more settlers moved inland away from the sources supplying European articles.

Sensing that they could demand higher real wages than

were their lot in their homelands, numerous native and immigrant English, Scottish, Irish, German, and French artisans grasped the opportunity to cross the ocean and set up establishments in colonial centers. There, where wealth was increasing at an amazing rate and was fairly widely diffused, they participated in the ever-rising standard of living. This, plus a greater complexity of existence that proved favorable to the crafts and the very normal human desire for the refinements of life, brought them steady American patronage.

I have chosen, in these lectures, to chronicle the colonial craftsman's years of apprenticeship and maturity in the eighteenth century rather than to examine minutely his early beginnings in the first century of settlement in America.

The Craftsman of the Rural South

Colonial society was based upon agriculture. We will do well, therefore, to discuss the rural artisan and then proceed by logical steps from the simple handicrafts of farm and frontier to the more complex industrial activities of the seaboard urban centers. Let us first turn to the colonial craftsman of the rural South.

In 1775 slightly more than 1,400,000, or over half of the American people, lived in the colonies below Mason and Dixon's line. Population density was very low, for then, as now, the inescapable fact about the South was its *ruralness*. This rural quality, taken with certain striking geographical features of the region and the colonial policy of the mother country, provides the key to its peculiar development. There were two Souths along the Atlantic seaboard in the eighteenth century. The Chesapeake Society, which grew up along the shores of the great bay and its numerous navigable tributaries, was composed of the colonies of Maryland, Virginia, and the Albemarle region of North Carolina. The other South may be called the Carolina Society and embraced the water-broken coast of North Carolina below

Cape Fear, sea-island and low-country South Carolina and Georgia, as well as the Savannah River settlements.

In the Chesapeake region, tobacco, the most important staple, was raised in ever larger quantities. For over a century and a quarter after 1612, production of the weed on relatively small plantations absorbed the energies of a growing population. By 1750, however, the culture had passed its peak in the Tidewater, and low prices and soil exhaustion, coupled with luxurious living, had combined to produce a debt-ridden, declining economy for which the only salvation seemed to lie in expansion and diversification of crops. Some planters sought new lands to the westward; others forsook Sweet Scented and Oronoco for the culture of corn and wheat.

By means of an unrivalled system of easy water carriage, nearly every plantation below the falls of the rivers emptying into the Chesapeake was in direct communication with the mother country. At least once a year when the tobacco fleet came in, one or more of its ships came up to the planter's wharf with goods ordered directly from Bristol or London. I may observe that such articles were both better and cheaper than any that could have been fabricated locally. And we all are aware of the magic effect of the word "imported." So long as the planter maintained a favorable balance with his London merchant, or so long as he could command a long-term credit, he preferred to purchase what he and his family wanted from England. This habit embraced his entire needs—from luxuries all the way to tools and cloth for slaves' clothing—and was further battened down by British laws to discourage manufacturing in the colonies.

Easy and ready communication by water from Europe, the inclinations of the planters, and governmental policy effectively discouraged the development of towns where crafts might have flourished and even deterred local manufactures everywhere. The problem of the craftsman has no-

where been better stated than in the joint report of three
Virginians made at the opening of the century:

"For want of Towns, Markets, and Money, there is but
little Encouragement for Tradesmen and Artificers, and
therefore little Choice of them, and their Labour very dear
in the Country. A Tradesman having no Opportunity of a
Market where he can buy Meat, Milk, Corn, and all other
things, must either make Corn, keep Cows, and raise Stocks,
himself, or must ride about the Country to buy Meat and
Corn where he can find it; and then is puzzled to find Car-
riers, Drovers, Butchers, Salting, (for he can't buy one Joynt
or two) and a great many other Things, which there would
be no Occasion for, if there were Towns and Markets. Then
a great deal of the Tradesman's Time being necessarily
spent in going and coming to and from his Work, in dis-
pers'd Country Plantations, and his Pay generally in straggling Parcels of Tobacco, the Collection whereof costs about
10 per Cent, and the best of this Pay coming but once a
Year, so that he cannot turn his Hand frequently with a
small Stock, as Tradesmen do in England and elsewhere,
all this occasions the Dearth of all Tradesman's Labour, and
likewise the Discouragement, Scarcity and Insufficiency of
Tradesmen." [4] And the Chesapeake Society continued
throughout the colonial period to be predominantly rural.
In the French and Indian War scarcely one in ten of the
Virginia troops was an artisan.

The other important section of the seaboard South, the
Carolina Society, was a more recently developed area than
the tobacco colonies. Prosperity began with the rice culture
about 1700 and was vastly augmented after 1745 by the
introduction of indigo as a staple, which doubled its resources and intensified the system of great plantations.
Whereas the customary number of men working under the
master and his family during the growing season on a Chesapeake tobacco plantation ranged from five to ten, of whom
frequently part were white, a typical estate of the Carolina

Society was one with about thirty Negro slaves, who cultivated rice in the inland swamps or indigo on dry fields
throughout the year under the direction of a white overseer.
Here the large, slave-operated unit prevailed; a small farm
was seldom seen in the Low Country.

Harsh conditions and the pitiless routine of rice and
indigo cultivation proved too trying for white indentured
servants who, furthermore, faced a discouraging future
when they came to freedom. The region was thus deprived
of a potential supply of artisans. On the other hand, although the waterways of the Low Country were not navigable
for ocean-going ships, they did converge toward one spot
where Charles Town rapidly rose to be the South's one large
city, the entrepôt of the rice and indigo traffic. Similarly,
Savannah catered to the needs of the Georgia plantations.

In addition, the planters and merchants of the Carolina
Society were even more wedded to things English than
Marylanders and Virginians. Mounting prosperity made
the acquisition of British manufactures possible and the
nature of their economic organization made it inevitable.

The economic character of each of the southern seaboard
areas was dictated by the prevalence of plantations operated
for the production of a single cash crop, be it tobacco, rice,
indigo, or some other staple. Plantations varied widely in
size according to the region and the wealth of the owner.
On the largest, the great estates of the Chesapeake and the
Carolinas, there developed certain crafts necessary for the
maintenance of the inhabitants or auxiliary to the prepara-
tion of staples for market. These were usually the simple,
unspecialized industries of a rural society. In general, they
were conducted in the same manner in the two regions, save
that there were more craft activities in the Chesapeake and
in the Carolinas the overwhelming majority of artisans were
Negro slaves.

On every plantation, housing for both the master and his
servants and slaves was of prime concern. "The Virginia

planters readily learn to become good Mechanicks in Building, wherein they are capable of directing their Servants and Slaves," observed the Reverend Hugh Jones in 1724.[5] Half a century later a Georgia planter wrote of building a house, barn, stable, and outhouses at a cost of only £174 and the labor of ten Negroes for three months; "this was done by hiring carpenters and paying them by the month; and two of the slaves learnt so much of that art in that time, that by working since with them occasionally, they are become good carpenters enough to raise a shed, or build any plain out house." [6]

As the planters grew more prosperous they desired to emulate English country gentlemen by erecting mansion-houses, and soon on the banks of the James, Ashley, and other streams rose those beautiful homes which attract so many American tourists of our own day. There was not, either in England or America, any profession of trained architects before 1750; most mansionhouses were planned by their owners in conjunction with a master builder, or housewright, and the liberal use of current builders' manuals (Figure 1). Henry Carey who superintended the erection of the Governor's Palace at Williamsburg and "the ingenious Samuel Cardy" who built beautiful St. Michael's Church in Charles Town were two such master workmen who attained real eminence in their craft; but the total number of skilled housewrights in the South was never large or adequate for its needs.[7]

More indicative of prevailing conditions are the advertisement of Robert Waller of Norfolk in 1752 that he "is much in Want of House-Joiners" and a letter of the same year from Robert Jerdone of Lancaster County to a sea captain requesting him to procure in London "a house carpenter, . . . that is a good Tradesman, withall sober and industrious, . . . and . . . get him indented for four years. I to pay him seven pounds sterling yearly wages and find him bed, room, board and washing and all tools." [8]

Nearly all of the really capable master builders of whom we have record in the southern colonies before the Revolution were brought over by gentlemen for specific jobs and then remained to work at their mysteries. Ezra Waite, "Civil Architect, House-Builder in general, and Carver, from London," completed the exquisite interiors of Miles Brewton's house at Charles Town in August, 1769, but died before he could undertake other commissions. One of the outstanding colonial "architects," William Buckland, aged twenty-one, crossed to Virginia under a contract of August, 1755, to serve Thompson Mason for four years at an annual salary of £20 sterling with board and lodging and "had the entire Direction of the Carpenters and Joiners work" for Gunston Hall, seat of George Mason, which was completed by November 8, 1759. Skipping the journeyman stage, he worked in northern Virginia and built several houses and other structures before settling down at Annapolis in 1772. There he became the favored architect-designer of mansions for the Maryland gentry and had his portrait painted by the former saddler and shoemaker, Charles Willson Peale. In like manner, Governor William Tryon brought William Hawks with him to North Carolina in 1764 to design and superintend the construction of the governor's mansion at New Bern. Having completed the "palace" late in 1770, Hawks designed a few other buildings in the neighborhood, but failing further commissions he finished out his life as clerk of the upper house of the North Carolina Assembly.[9]

The building of gentlemen's great houses provided, perhaps, the greatest opportunity in the South for a display of artisans' skills. There were some joiners and housewrights who were able and willing to rise to the challenge because fine, careful work had been taught them as apprentices; yet they were few in number, and it is probable that most of the great plantation houses were the fruit of plans made in England or by craftsmen brought from there for that purpose. As a result, only the bigwigs could afford such luxuries, and the homes of the general run of small planters continued to be such structures as the master, his neighbors, and his servants or slaves were able to raise.

In the marketing of southern staples, containers of various kinds were absolutely necessary—kegs, barrels, hogsheads, and casks of many sizes. When it is realized that 116,231 barrels and 460 hogsheads of rice, tar, turpentine, resin, beef, and pork were shipped in 1754 from Charles Town alone, and that 68,000 hogsheads of tobacco were exported from the Chesapeake colonies, not to mention 37,000 barrels of wheat, corn, and flour—totalling nearly a quarter of a million casks of all types—it is evident that not only was the mystery of cooperage the most important but it was also the largest single craft in the South.[10]

Many coopers in the larger towns supplied planters with casks. At Annapolis, William Hewitt employed several good hands who made "Bathing-Tubs, Coolers, Casks, and Kegs of all Sizes, Butter Churns, Pails, Piggins, Ships Buckets, Nun Buoys, Mess Cans, Etc.," in much the same fashion as Thomas Rose, who worked with his apprentices in one of Mr. Mazyck's tenements on Bedon's Alley, near the Bay in Charles Town. In the 1760's several coopers at Wilmington began to supply barrels for the planters along the Cape Fear River.[11]

Most substantial planters kept men continually at work fashioning staves, heads, and wooden hoops against shipping time. At Nomini Hall on the Potomac in 1774, Robert Carter contracted with Hugh Burnie, a Scottish cooper, to "get up 10 good flower Caskes per day" for an annual salary of £30. Many white indentured servants worked as coopers on Virginia and Maryland estates and also, as at Nomini Hall, instructed slaves as apprentices in the craft. On the other hand, Negro coopers appear to have been used almost exclusively on the rice and indigo plantations of the lower South, where it was not infrequently the custom to hire out a slave craftsman who might be advertised as "a good

Cooper, likewise a Corker, and . . . a sensible fellow." What William Tatham said of the tobacco business sums up effectively the situation for all southern commodities requiring casks: "The cooperage, in respect to tobacco hogsheads is not a professional performance, as in other branches of the cooper's trade, but is generally an employment taken up by a cooper or carpenter upon the plantation, of which there are commonly one or two upon each estate of tolerable size, who serve the occasion; or in default of such, by persons of sufficient ingenuity, who are to be found in the respective neighbourhoods where tobacco is cultivated, and who occasionally take up such an employment, rather as a matter of rural accommodation." [12]

Despite repeated attempts by immigrant cordwainers to market quality shoes, southern gentlemen, save at Annapolis, insisted upon purchasing imported English footwear for themselves and their families. Consequently, when many a freed servant set up as a maker of fine shoes, he experienced the plight of Thomas Steptoe who was thrown in gaol for debt by the sheriff of Calvert County, Maryland, and after languishing there ten months was reduced to advertising himself as willing to be bound out as a servant "on reasonable terms." [13]

This was not the case with the fabrication of common leather shoes (Figure 3). "The Virginians have most of their shoemakers in their own families, and have no occasion for any but stuff [cloth] shoes from Britain" was the lament of a Lancaster County merchant in 1748. Abundance of leather and a ready labor supply obtainable from the servant ships made this possible. We find, for example, that in 1737 Isham Randolph of Goochland agreed to exchange the remainder of the servitude due him from "John Newland, cordwainer and indentured servant," for 250 pairs of shoes for his slaves. Cordwaining was one of the few trades in which journeymen craftsmen could earn a living, and there is ample evidence of their activities in Tidewater Virginia.

As population spread westward beyond the "fall line" toward the mid-century, a great demand for white shoemakers arose, and even the Reverend Robert Rose of Tye River, in Albemarle County, scrupled not to write in his diary: "My Boy Francis Dean, went to John Parks to learn Shoemaking (to serve 3 years). He had a Hammer, Pincers, 2 Doz. Tacks, and 2 Doz. Awls, also ½ Doz. knives." A striking climax to all this enterprise came in 1775 with the opening at Petersburg of "a manufactory of men's boots and shoes, women's Leather, Cloth, Calimanco, Silk and satin shoes," by John Blaney and Company, which announced that "many of the hands have worked with *Didsbury* and other capital [London] Tradesmen in that Branch." When a southern colony offered sufficient encouragement, a craft like shoemaking could flourish, but when, as in South Carolina, even the bulk of slaves' shoes was imported, it was bound to wither and die out.[14]

Any large plantation had need of artificers skilled in several other crafts. Carpenters were always in demand to make the crude furniture used in the slave quarters and barns, fashion wooden implements, erect small outhouses, and perform the repairs that were constantly called for. More and more such work was turned over to Negro slaves who had been trained in the craft, and in the Carolinas planters frequently hired out their "Rough Carpenters" by the week or month. Blacksmiths, bricklayers and masons, tanners, millers, weavers, and often tailors were at work on large southern estates, and always the same conditions existed—the gradual but relentless replacement of white by Negro labor. When a Palatine weaver named Held proposed to move from Pennsylvania to South Carolina in 1747 to earn a better living, a friend predicted that "his service in Carolina will last probably no longer than until two negro slaves shall have learned the weaver's trade from him and can weave themselves. So it goes through all Carolina; the negroes are made to learn all the trades and are used for all kinds of business. For this reason white people have difficulty in earning their bread there, unless they become overseers or provide themselves with slaves." [15]

The presence in Maryland and Virginia of easily mined surface deposits of iron ore led to the erection of many furnaces, bloomeries, and forges. Eventually bar and pig iron became a minor Chesapeake Bay staple, especially in Maryland. Although the iron industry could not be classed as a typical activity of the South and its product never counted heavily in the commerce of the Empire, it is worth examination if only for its intrinsic interest and because it gave employment to artisans of many skills.

Stimulated by Governor Alexander Spotswood in Virginia and by the formation of the famous Principio Company of Maryland, the Chesapeake iron manufacture made a good beginning in the early twenties. In 1737 the *London Daily Post* expressed deep concern over the discovery that England consumed annually more bar iron than the 18,000 tons she produced and avowed satisfaction that a new source had arisen—"In our American colonies are now erected several Forges and Bloomeries for making Bar-Iron"—which was equal to the British product. High transatlantic freight charges, it was feared, might discourage exportation of American iron and force the colonials to creep into the manufacture of ironware themselves. That this was not to be the case with Maryland and Virginia became evident when, in 1751, these provinces shipped 2,950 tons to the mother country, one-sixth as much as England produced.[16]

The iron industry required a heavy investment of capital in land, buildings, equipment, and slaves as William Byrd II learned in his progress to Spotswood's furnaces at Fredericksville, Virginia, in 1732. That fine brick furnace, with "2 Mighty pair of Bellows" operated by a water wheel twenty-six feet in diameter, charcoal house, 15,000 acres of land, and slaves, cost £12,000. Experts agreed that at least two square miles of woodlands were needed to supply fuel for making charcoal. Well might Mr. Byrd have paused before he proceeded to set up an ironworks on his James River estate.[17]

The largest iron manufacture in the colonies was conducted by the Principio Company, which opened two furnaces and a forge in Cecil County at the head of Chesapeake Bay about 1720. By 1751 the English investors in this enterprise had either constructed or acquired two additional furnaces in Baltimore County and Captain Augustine Washington's Accokeek Furnace in King George County, Virginia. But later ironworks did not command as much capital as these first undertakings. The Baltimore Iron Works was established on the Patapsco in 1731 with an investment of £3,500, and "altho in its infancy" in 1765 each of its five proprietors drew an annual profit of £500 from its products.[18]

By its very nature, the iron industry was easily adapted to plantation economy: a large tract of undeveloped woodlands was needed to supply charcoal for a furnace; a farm had to be operated to furnish food and other necessaries for the labor force—altogether, the services of from one hundred to one hundred and twenty slaves were needed for such a business; and housing had to be provided for all. Care of the wagons, tools, machinery, and other equipment required the work of carpenters, blacksmiths, wheelwrights, cartwrights, millers, and sawyers to such an extent that an iron plantation was probably the most self-sufficient large economic unit in America.

Slave labor was well fitted for the heavy work, simple operations, and intense heat at a furnace or a forge. Intelligent blacks readily learned the techniques of refining, forging, chafering, and casting under the direction of an ironmaster, who was usually brought over from the British Isles to manage the works. At his forge and "geared Grist-Mill" near Todd's Warehouse on the Mattaponi, Bernard Moore had a trained group of Negro workers which he advertised to dispose of by a lottery in 1769: Billy, aged twenty-two, is an "exceeding trusty good forgeman as well at the finery as under the hammer, and understands putting up his fire"; Mungo, twenty-four, is a good firer and hammer man; Sam, twenty-six, a capable chafery hand; Abraham, twenty-six, a reliable forge carpenter; while Bob, twenty-seven, thoroughly understands the duties of a master collier. The roster of this forge included seventeen skilled slave artisans and is typical of the comparatively small ironworks of the area.[19]

After 1751 the amount of iron shipped to England by the Chesapeake colonies decreased. In Virginia the pig and bar iron industry declined, and small forges sprang up to take off Maryland's bar iron and manufacture it into much-needed ironware. In 1770 ten Negro slaves were turning out axes, broad hoes, and grubbing hoes for local use at Providence Forge in New Kent County. These establishments, however, failed to fill the colony's wants, and such items as hoes, axes, and nails were always prominent in lists of merchants' importations. As late as 1784, Dr. Johann Schoepf was astonished at the vehicles he saw in Tidewater Virginia—"wagons made of wood throughout, not the smallest bit of iron to be found in the construction."[20]

The alarming decline of the tobacco yield in the Chesapeake area brought about by soil exhaustion, as well as the low price of the staple, directed the planters' attention after 1740 to other crops, in particular corn and wheat. The extent of the shift, even by the mid-century, has not been sufficiently recognized. In the year of Braddock's defeat, Virginia, alone, exported 408,373 bushels of Indian corn, principally to the West Indies and southern Europe. By 1770 wheat production had also increased, and the total grain shipments of the Old Dominion soared to the surprising figure of 660,049 bushels, while those of Maryland, totalling 388,109, greatly overshadowed the 198,683 bushels exported by the province of Pennsylvania.[21]

Most of the corn and wheat was exported in bulk, but the demand for flour and ship's bread induced a multiplication of mills throughout the whole Tidewater, especially from the Rappahannock up to the head of the Bay. For the first time, millwrights became recognized artificers, and a skilled craftsman like William Hansbrough of Charles County, Maryland, advertised that he had "performed many fine pieces of work" in both his own colony and in Virginia. Small mills suited to local needs had always existed in the plantation country, but the growing flour trade called for a larger enterprise known as the merchant's mill. Instead of grinding for a toll or percentage of the grains brought to him, the miller purchased wheat, stored it in his granaries, ground it into flour, bolted it, and barreled it for shipping or, perchance, baked batches of ship's bread out of it. The merchant mills of Pennsylvania and Maryland have long been celebrated; those of Virginia less so, but they were nevertheless important to her economy.[22]

John Ballendine, enthusiastic entrepreneur of the Northern Neck, constructed a merchant mill at the Falls of the Potomac in the sixties which was the equal of any in America. It consisted of a wharf with a crane, a three-and-a-half-story store building (151 feet by 36 feet) containing a mill with two pairs of stones, bolting mills, and fans for blowing away chaff, which required the services of four men and two boys and could grind 50,000 bushels of wheat per year. Adjoining the mills were a three-oven bakery, two large granaries, a neat retailing store, and a two-story stone dwelling for the miller. By means of the crane, barrels of flour could be swung directly from the storage loft into the holds of vessels lying at the wharf. At the beginning of the War for Independence, Robert Carter counted twenty-three gristmills within twelve miles of Nomini Hall capable of grinding 30,000 bushels of grain annually, enough to meet the local demands of Westmoreland County. Small wonder then that the millers gradually became prosperous and much-sought-after artisans.[23]

In every southern colony "inferior planters," whom Governor Dinwiddie grouped with "tradesmen" and regarded as "the lowest Class of our People," leaned heavily on the great planters for many services. Living back from the river fronts, they used the planter's wharf, bought clothing and European goods through him before the advent of the Scottish factors about 1750, had their corn ground at his mill, and not infrequently acquired their tobacco hogsheads from his cooperage. The large planter's economic importance in his locality was as great as his political and social prestige, and the combination assured him the preferred status of an English aristocrat.

The needs of a small planter or tobacco farmer were actually few. Except for rum, sugar, and molasses, a little cloth, and a few iron implements, he and his family could get along without purchases from the outside world. Crude furniture was fashioned in the home, and a clever man could cooper his own hogsheads and peg shoes for the family during off seasons. Corn meal was ground in hand mills at many small plantations.[24] In an agricultural society where gentleman planters maintained their own craftsmen and lesser folk had no great need of them, it was not strange that the mechanic arts languished.

Here and there, however, an artisan or two managed to hang on, and their numbers appear to have increased somewhat as the eighteenth century wore on. In Maryland the rural craftsman was better off than anywhere else, but as one went southward prospects for the free artisan faded rapidly. Twenty-five miles east of Richmond in New Kent County, Virginia, lived the Jarratt family. The father, Robert Jarratt, had been "brought up to the trade of a carpenter, at which he wrought till the day he died" in 1739, although much of his time must have been absorbed by a 1,200-acre farm that his son tells us supplied everything the family

Figure 4. Bells were needed for New England's many meetinghouses.

Figure 5. Most of Germantown's noted stockings were woven in workers' homes.

needed but sugar, which rarely appeared on the table. There were no slaves. Mrs. Jarratt made all the clothing worn by the family except hats and shoes, "the latter of which we never put on, but in the winter season." It is fairly amazing that such primitive conditions of life prevailed in the midst of the famed plantation country between the York and the James and only twenty-five miles from the provincial capital at Williamsburg in the middle of the eighteenth century; but it is undeniable proof of the immutable rural character of the colonial South. Although two of Robert Jarratt's sons learned carpentry and a third became a millwright, it is clear that tobacco planting steadily encroached on their trades. Occasionally, of course, a cooper or a blacksmith pursued his trade, but the combination of an enervating climate, Negro competition, an uncertain market for his handicrafts, cheap land and the social status its possession afforded nearly stifled the crafts in the Old Dominion.[25]

Conditions for the emergence of the artisan to prosperity were even more unfavorable in the Carolinas and Georgia. At Edenton in 1752, Bishop Spangenberg, the Moravian leader, found only one tailor, one cobbler, and one blacksmith. With dismay he confided to his diary that "of handicrafts I have seen practically nothing in the 150 miles we have travelled across this Province. Almost nobody has a trade." Yet within two decades, as North Carolina filled with people and the Revolution approached, the crafts began to gain a foothold. A Frenchman noticed in 1765 that "there is plenty of saw mills in this Country set up at little Expense." In the province where there had been only three water-powered gristmills in 1737, Granville County, alone, could boast of at least forty-one between 1749 and 1776, and it also enjoyed the services of numerous carpenters, joiners, blacksmiths, wheelwrights, coopers, a haberdasher, a weaver, a tailor, a bricklayer, and, most notable of all, a silversmith. Far removed from a deep water port and the artisans of large plantations, the inhabitants of inland North Carolina were forced to develop their own handicrafts. Their southern neighbor, however, continued in thralldom to the mother country, and such free craftsmen as the Low Country possessed centered in Charles Town.[26]

As settlements appeared beyond the limits of navigation, a series of little villages sprang up along the "fall line" to act as trading centers for the "large, populous and extensive back country, west and south of them." Among them were Upper Marlborough on the Patuxent, Falmouth and Fredericksburg on the Rappahannock, Petersburg at the Falls of the Appomattox, and Wilmington on the Cape Fear. Serving as entrepôts for the upcountry traffic, these communities were able to support a limited number of shoemakers, tailors, blacksmiths; perchance also a saddler or wheelwright and more rarely a cabinetmaker or silversmith.[27] George Buckner of Port Royal, Virginia, earned a living as a smith, making and repairing adzes, axes, hoes, chariot wheels, plows, and knives for people in Caroline and King George counties, while at Wilmington, Thomas Brown, coppersmith from Philadelphia, made and sold "Stills, brew-kettles, wash kettles, and tea kettles, also other kinds of copper work."[28] Rapid though this multiplication of villages proved to be, it did not materially relieve the deficiency of skilled workers, and the South continued to be a rural area without any significant town life.

During the second quarter of the eighteenth century when the Chesapeake and Carolina societies were reaching their maximum, the back country of the South began to attract large numbers of settlers whose origins and mode of living made for a different and often separate form of life. After 1730, native English Quakers, Palatine Germans, and Scotch-Irish Presbyterians began to stream southward from York, Pennsylvania, through Frederick, Maryland, into the Valley of Virginia and eventually debouched on to the Carolina Piedmont as far south as the Savannah River. Concurrently, native Virginians of the Anglican persuasion were moving westward through the mountain gaps to meet and fuse with Germans and Scotch Irish in the Shenandoah Valley. Others pushed southward and westward from the neighborhood of Petersburg into the parts of North Carolina lying along the Nottaway, Roanoke, and their tributaries.

Details of this migration are well known to readers of American history, but its relation to the colonial craftsman needs to be singled out for emphasis. The farther south the settlers went, the greater distance they were from sources of supply and markets. Communication with Lancaster and the Delaware Valley, even by the "Great Philadelphia Wagon Road," was slow, hazardous, and unsatisfactory. Only such articles as the pioneers could not do without were loaded into Conestoga wagons for the trip south, for weight was always a consideration. Contact with the eastern seaboard of the South was so difficult that the two areas developed without much interchange. Among these western folk, fortunately, the Pennsylvania craft tradition was strong, and necessity drove them into the making of their own manufactures; it was a simple case of "root, hog, or die." Few people had any cash, and it was to be many years before the upcountry developed a money economy.

South of York along the "Great Wagon Road," which was open as far as Opequon in the Valley as early as 1734, settlement was not as dispersed as we sometimes imagine. A series of hamlets grew up along the route—Frederick, Martinsburg, Winchester, Strasburg, Hamburg, and Staunton in the Valley of Virginia. In the Carolina Piedmont, in time, arose such tiny centers as Guilford Court House, Salisbury, Salem, Mecklenburg, Orangeburg, and Ninety-Six, although permanent settlements in this country were really just beginning when the Revolution broke out. Under free labor, the arts and crafts of a simple agricultural society soon began to develop. Deer hunting and cattle raising supplied materials aplenty for tanners and shoemakers; tailors also prospered, for the region became known as the land of buckskin breeches.[29] All-around blacksmiths came to mend pots and pans, repair guns, and hammer out farming implements and crude tools. Mills were constructed on every available stream to grind the corn and wheat that grew in such abundance, but even so there were never enough. "We are assured that there is now a very considerable Crop of Wheat made in the Back-Settlements," remarked Peter Timothy of the *South Carolina Gazette* on April 18, 1759, "and that if the Planters there had Mills erected amongst them early enough, they would be able this Year to supply the Charles Town Market with near the Quantity of Flour Annually imported from the Northern Colonies." Sometimes spring freshets swept away these laboriously erected enterprises: "last night my Mill dam on Hat Creek blowd up after 20 days with a great many hands. Such are the Profits of Mills," bemoaned a Tye River planter in 1751.[30]

Village crafts were never able to satisfy the demands of the southern back country in the colonial period. In remote spots from Pennsylvania to Georgia, families of farmers were forced to develop mechanical skills in order to do their own milling, tan their own leather and make their own shoes and breeches, fashion their own furniture, and perform all the operations from shearing sheep to tailoring their own clothing. From the Old Cheraws in South Carolina in 1769 came the report that "many of the Inhabitants of the North and Eastern Parts of this Province have this winter clothed themselves in their own manufacture; many more would purchase them if they could be got." [31]

Two back-country enterprises command our attention as being of special significance and interest; one because it was a triumph of pioneer individualism, the other because it provided a unique example of co-operative endeavor. The Shenandoah Valley was the most prosperous section of the inland South and attracted some of the ablest settlers. Isaac

Zane, Jr., son of a wealthy and prominent Philadelphia Quaker craftsman and a man who would be disowned by the Meeting for behavior "contrary to discipline," in 1767 purchased a share in an ironworks that had been erected on Cedar Creek, a few miles south of Winchester, Virginia, in 1763. Before long he bought out his Quaker partners and moved out to the Valley to operate the Marlboro Iron Works, as he now named it. By 1771 he was producing weekly at Cedar Creek four tons of bar iron and two of castings, consisting of middling and small kettles, bake plates, pots, pestles and mortars, and farming implements. The enterprise was a success from the beginning, and in addition to the furnace and forge at Cedar Creek a second furnace called "Bean's Smelter" was placed in operation near Stephensburg—the whole employing 150 hands of whom only one was a slave. Zane sold some of his bar iron and ironware locally, but the bulk of his output was sent down by wagon to Georgetown or Alexandria for shipment to Philadelphia, or he disposed of it to William Allason of Falmouth on the Rappahannock for export to England.[32] When the State of Virginia needed ordnance, cannon balls, salt pans, and other ironware to supply the revolutionary armies, the former Quaker promptly came to his country's rescue.

The manifold activities of Isaac Zane were blanketed by the titles of "gentleman and merchant." He was not only an ironmaster, but he also conducted a great farm to feed all his workers, a retail store, a distillery, and both saw and grist mills. Few Tidewater estates outshone this elaborate 20,000-acre iron plantation. Its roomy stone mansionhouse, filled with superb furniture made by Benjamin Randolph of Philadelphia, was surrounded by a garden with fountains, two orchards, a fishpond, bathhouse, icehouse, stables, three barns, quarters for servants and slaves, a forge, two furnaces, a stillhouse, a sawmill, a smithy, warehouse, countinghouse, liquorhouse, springhouse—nearly all of stone construction.

Colonel Isaac Zane was a man of culture, equally at home with the savants of the American Society for promoting and propagating useful knowledge, held in Philadelphia (of which he was then a member), and with the tobacco gentry of Williamsburg or the simple farming folk of the Valley. His library contained four hundred volumes, to which in 1778 he added one of the largest and finest collections in the colonies, which he purchased from the widow of William Byrd III for £2,000. At first "a Quaker for the Times," then a "Patriot of Fiery Temper," this flamboyant bigwig, who lived in baronial splendor with "Miss Betsey McFarland, his kept and confessed Mistress, and their young son," as shocked Philip Fithian tells us, was a fine specimen of the little-studied frontier capitalists who were such vital leaders in opening the American West.[33]

No greater contrast to the individual enterprise of Isaac Zane can be found than the settlement at Wachovia in North Carolina where, in 1753, a picked band of Moravians founded a community in the wilderness wherein farming and the crafts would be judiciously combined in a planned economy for members of their sect. In their first settlement, Bethabara, it became necessary to set up certain artisans, such as smiths, millers, tanners, and sawyers, to support the agricultural work for a time. There workers were temporarily located in log huts, and we learn with amusement as well as surprise that one day in 1755 "the shoe-maker took down his house to kill the rats, which have done much damage. Many were found. By evening the logs were nearly all laid up again."[34]

Situated near the Yadkin in Anson County on the upper road to Pennsylvania three hundred miles from Charles Town, the same from the James River, and one hundred and fifty miles from Cross Creek on the Cape Fear River, the Moravians were truly isolated. Yet with careful economy their semimonastic system flourished, and after fifteen years Bethabara could report to Bethlehem that "we have established, at least in a small way, all the really necessary businesses and handicrafts, which are greatly missed in other localities here. In addition to our farm of about two hundred acres of cleared land, we have a grist and saw mill, which can also be used for breaking tan-bark and pressing oil; a brewery and distillery, a store, apothecary shop, tanyard, pottery, gunsmith, blacksmith, gunstock-maker, tailor-shop, shoe-maker, linen-weaver, saddlery, bakery, and the carpenters, joiners, and masons, who do our building, and there is also our tavern. Even if these businesses are not particularly profitable they are indispensable, and with them we can provide ourselves with most necessaries of life." [35]

At first Wachovia consisted of two agricultural villages, Bethabara and Bethania, but in 1766 the Brothers decided that it was time to begin work on the principal town, Salem. One of the leaders told church authorities at Bethlehem: "This town is not designed for farmers but for those with trades." Forty-six master craftsmen and ten apprentices formed the nucleus of the Moravian industrial center, and by 1772 all trades had been moved there from Bethabara. Constantly recruited from Pennsylvania, the inhabitants of the Wachovia communities numbered 792 in 1776. Exactly half of these were members of the United Brethren. As Salem grew, more and more crafts were introduced, including such refinements as silversmithing, hatmaking, cabinet-making, wood turning, and organ building. Following the lead of their great center at Bethlehem, the North Carolina Brethren in 1773 constructed one of the earliest American waterworks.

Because they had perfected a well-knit organization, the Moravians succeeded in establishing the European craft system with all its ramifications in a wilderness region. When two or more men worked at a trade, one was recognized as master, the others as journeymen. Apprentices came from distant Pennsylvania; in 1764, states the record, twelve boys walked all the way from Bethlehem "to learn trades from one of our master workmen." Their terms of service were ordinarily five years, or until they came of age, during which time they were given to understand that they must work hard and faithfully and "must yield obedient service." The Moravian settlements were conducted on a wage-earning economy; they were not communistic as some people have supposed. Master craftsmen customarily received 4s.6d. per day and journeymen 16s. a week. An eager spirit of useful endeavor permeated the village of Salem—"I made the top of a table for myself, and . . . cut wood for feet on the table," wrote an aged inhabitant. "They shall be Lyons Claws, is not that too much? One day I am a Joiner, the next a Carver; what would I not learn if I was not too old?" [36]

The craftsmen of Wachovia made not only the articles needed by their own people but provided services for neighboring folk and in some lines a surplus for sale at Cross Creek (Fayettesville) or Charles Town. So much wheat was brought in for grinding in 1775, it was decided that Brother Bulitshek, the millwright, should plan the construction of a merchant mill. Tanneries processed deerskins and oxhides from places as far north as the James Valley, while tailors made buckskin breeches for men throughout the back settlements.

The most interesting, and certainly one of the most useful, of the craft activities was the pottery opened by Brother Gottfried Aust at Bethabara on December 1, 1755 (Figure 2). He made earthenware and clay pipes at his initial firing. The following August he attempted his first glazed pottery. Word of the enterprise circulated rapidly, and at a sale in June, 1761, "people gathered from 50 and 60 miles away to buy pottery, but many came in vain, as the supply was exhausted by noon. We greatly regretted not being able to supply their needs," wrote a Moravian diarist. A year later people came from both Virginia and South Carolina to attend the sale. Soon wagonloads of milk crocks and pans were being sent to Fort Dobbs, Pine Tree, and other Piedmont villages. The arrival from Charles Town in 1773 of a journeyman potter named Ellis, who understood the mystery of glazing and burning of Queen's Ware, led to the construction of a new kiln at Salem. The Brothers provided Ellis with food, clothing, and "a douceur for his work," hoping that Aust could learn the processes. Ellis' work was most successful, but, says the diarist, "the good man found our Town too narrow for him," and soon "bid us a friendly farewell." Brother Aust had indeed acquired the technique since the next year Bethlehem officials were told that "for some time our pottery has been turning out a good product not very different from Queensware" and also "tortoise shell, that is, a fine pottery resembling porcelain." [37]

So successful was this unique community industrial experiment that throughout the South it gained fame from its products and, as we have seen, attracted the services of journeymen who were not Moravians. With real satisfaction Brother Marshall could record that, when the Provincial Congress at Hillsborough offered awards for home manufactures in 1775, one member sought unsuccessfully "to debar the Moravians, for they would win all the premiums." [38]

From this survey of economic conditions in the rural South during the eighteenth century, it is obvious, I think, that beyond basic needs almost no crafts developed. Quality goods for general sale were not produced. All observers agreed that this was so. What an astonished French traveler said of the Old Dominion was equally true of the other provinces: "From England, the Virginians take every article for Convenience or ornament which they use, their own manufactures not being worth mentioning." [39]

The few cases to the contrary that I have mentioned serve only to emphasize this truth. What could be more striking than the need for a quarter of a million containers for southern exports in 1754, which grew to about 300,000 on the eve of the Revolution, and the complete failure of the region to develop coopering into an established craft! In 1772 John Hobday of Gloucester County, Virginia, invented a "cheap and simple Machine for separating Wheat from the Straw" that would daily beat out 120 bushels with the aid of three horses. He announced in the newspapers that any tolerable carpenter could easily make the machine and that he would attend at several places on the York and James to demonstrate it while his brother performed the same services on the Rappahannock. Despite enthusiastic endorsements from prominent gentlemen like Jaquelin Ambler and John Page, Virginians appeared indifferent to the device.[40]

The dearth of artisans was deplored by thinking men of the South from the beginning. From about 1680 to 1720 serious, though fruitless, efforts were made in all provinces to establish towns to provide a favorable environment for the development of trade and crafts. Frustrated by local conditions and discouraged by British policy, these attempts failed. Decades later, speculators sought in vain to people their holdings with tradesmen. There is something genuinely pathetic about an advertisement that appeared in a *Maryland Gazette* of 1734: "This is to give Notice to all Artificers, viz. Joyners, Carpenters, Mill-wrights, Smiths, Tanners, Shoemakers, Taylors, Improvers, and Dressers of Hemp and Flax, or any other Tradesmen whatsoever, that the Manor commonly called My Lady's Manor, . . . on the North Falls of Gun-Powder River, in Baltimore County, consisting of 10,000 Acres, will . . . be divided into Lots or Farm[s], and will be let out either upon Lease or Life." We know that the proprietor had as few inquiries as did Daniel Carroll in 1760 when he sought to attract craftsmen to Upper Marlborough.[41]

There was no encouragement, other than such appeals, for the young men to go into crafts. The apprentice system was negligible in the South, save in the case of orphans who

were bound out until they came of age that they might become "inured to useful Labour," and as a result there were
no accepted standards for artisans to live up to. Nearly all
craftsmen were inexorably drawn into planting or farming,
because they could not gain a living from their trades. Pay
was bad and slow coming in. Poor Nicholas Norman announced in 1767 that Marylanders had taken so little notice
of repeated requests for payments due him for currying and
shoemaking that he was being forced to go to the law to
collect on accounts that had run for over twelve months.[42]
And, finally, there was the undeviating reliance of planters
on English importations, which it must be granted sometimes went to absurd extremes, as when William Reynolds
of Yorktown, in 1774, sent two pieces of Mantua silk all
the way across to London to be dyed because they were
spotted.[43] Not infrequently the goods shipped by London
merchants to colonial customers proved to be inferior in
quality, or the wrong size, or something that had not been
ordered at all. Inasmuch as it took at least a year to rectify
the error, planters usually accepted whatever came over and
contented themselves with letters of reproach and complaint.
Any way it was viewed, the system was costly and unsatisfactory, but it was also inevitable. In fact all the deterrents
to the development of crafts have their origins in the topog-
raphy of the South and its distinctive agricultural economy.

At the time of the nonimportation movements when it
became not only patriotic but necessary to enter upon American manufactures, energetic and ambitious Southerners like
John Ballendine, George Washington, and Robert Carter
took up the cause, but because there were so few craftwork-
ers available the movement petered out after a delusive flush
of activity. No class of "mechanicks" emerged to meet the
South's wants except the crude artisans of the back country.
When the fight for freedom came, and the South was cut off
completely from trade with England, every colony found

itself poorly equipped to meet the emergency, and in the
long run suffered acutely from its inability to nourish a
middle-class group of craftsmen, whose skills and solid
worth as citizens would have contributed greatly to the
common weal.

THE VILLAGE CRAFTSMAN
OF THE RURAL NORTH

NORTH OF Mason and Dixon's line, the rural aspects of eighteenth-century society seemed as pervasive and universal as in the plantation South. Yet it must be emphasized that, although there were many features common to both sections, certain points of divergence presented striking and far-reaching contrasts. Throughout the North, a rigorous, changeable climate kept the inhabitants housebound for long periods in the winter, but nevertheless generated an abundance of human energy. Furthermore, neither New England nor the Middle Colonies ever produced an exotic staple to exchange for the manufactures of the mother country. In order to acquire the money to make returns for imports, Northerners had to enter into commerce, and ultimately they came into competition with Great Britain instead of fitting neatly into the commercial system like the planters of the tobacco, rice, and sugar colonies.

The eight northern provinces may be conveniently separated into the New England and Middle Colonies because of important regional variations. The eve of Independence found their society growing; with nearly 1,300,000 people, of whom only 57,000 were blacks, they almost equalled the South in numbers. Population was comparatively dense in Massachusetts, Rhode Island, and Connecticut. Here lived the famed Yankees, a stock about seventy per cent English with a liberal infusion of recently arrived Scots, Scotch Irish, Celtic Irish, and some Germans, dwelling in a land containing few Negro slaves or indentured servants. Theirs was fundamentally a free society.

The presence of a bewildering variety of nationalities in the population of the Middle Colonies impelled J. Hector St. John Crèvecoeur to propound his famous question: "Whence came all these people? They are a mixture of English, Scotch, Irish, French, Dutch, Germans, and Swedes. From this promiscuous breed that race now called Americans have arisen." [1] English, Scotch Irish, and Germans predominated in these provinces where, although slavery was relatively unimportant, the institution of indentured white servitude furnished the principal source of labor for both farm and shop.

A village society evolved naturally in this land of small farms, just as it failed to appear in a plantation region. The New England system of land grants predetermined that there would be a center with a village green, destined to be as effective for economic as for religious and social purposes. Small communities also appeared with the spread of settlement in New York, the Jerseys, and the Quaker Colonies, although they exhibited few of the planned characteristics of their Yankee counterparts.

Agricultural life in the North was indubitably rural, but it was never isolated, and it therefore proved congenial to the development of handicrafts. Many an artisan who emigrated from Old England found in these little northern hamlets many resemblances to the village he had just left behind him.

Although villages grew up to serve local needs, the predicament of the small farmer living inland was everywhere the same. It was well analyzed by Governor William Keith in a report on New Jersey manufactures to the Board of Trade in 1728: having no local sale for his surplus grain or means of transportation to a distant market, the husbandman could not get the wherewithal to purchase European goods and had perforce to manufacture for himself. Any stock and grain farm could support a few sheep whose wool could be spun into yarn and woven into cloth during the winter when performance of outdoor chores was difficult. Flax was easy to raise, and the linen made from it was twice as serviceable as English cloth. Besides, hemp-string bags and plough traces wore longer than the boughten kind. Many of the operations in the making of cloth could, moreover, be performed by old women and children, thereby saving much expense to the family. Countrymen almost universally wore breeches made of home-tanned leather.[2]

The extent of household manufactures is surprising. In 1743 a leading Philadelphia merchant, Samuel Powel, commented significantly on the cloth industry in a letter to a London correspondent: "A vast deal of linen and woolen is made within the Province; so much linen by the back Irish inhabitants that they not only hawk a great deal frequently about both town and country but they carry considerable quantities away to the Eastward by land, quite away as far as Rhode Island." By 1750 nine-tenths of Pennsylvania's farmers fabricated their own wearing apparel. A survey of the clothing worn by servants and slaves who ran away from New Jersey masters, 1704-1777, shows that, of 822 cases, 227 had clothes from homemade Osnaburgs or linsey-woolsey, 276 wore leather, buckskin, or bearskin breeches, and 245 were partially clothed in garments of home manufacture. A similar report could probably have been compiled in New York, for according to Governor Moore "every house swarms with children, who are set to work as soon as they are able to Spin and Card, and as every family is furnished with a Loom, the Itinerant Weavers who travel about the Country, put the finishing hand to the work." Prior to 1765 the average family was forced into making fabrics for its own use simply because it did not have the money to buy them, and in 1772 David Valentine of Suffolk, Long Island, solicited subscriptions for *A Treatise on Weav-*

ing, Consisting of near 300 different Draughts with full and plain Directions for the use of such countryfolk.[3]

The same situation existed in rural New England where, as early as 1704, it was predicted that some towns which formerly had less than a hundred sheep would soon raise a thousand. In 1718 an official at Boston thus described the progress of Massachusetts manufactures: "Scarce a Country man comes to town, or woman, but are clothed in their own spinning. Every one Incourages the Growth and Manufacture of this Country and not one person but discourages the Trade from home, and says 'tis pitty any goods should be brought from England; they can live without them." [4]

Inability to purchase European goods, which were customarily marked up from one hundred to three hundred per cent, had the effect of keeping alive throughout the whole population much-prized skills and of engendering a wholesome respect for the man who made things. In every colony most husbandmen strove to live like the Connecticut Valley farmer who never bought anything to "wear, eat, or drink," and only spent a little over £2 per year for salt and nails, which he could not make at home.[5] To this could be added rum, sugar, tea, or coffee for those living on a slightly higher scale. At all events, young lads who grew to manhood on a northern farm had the tradition of English or German craftsmanship inculcated equally with the lore of husbandry. Indeed, we will do well to think of these people as farmer-craftsmen who could turn a hand either at husbandry or a trade. It is wrong to call them Jacks-of-all-trades because the phrase implies master of none. Tench Coxe well understood this distinction and reported that the farmer-craftsmen of America "often make domestic and farming carriages, implements, and utensils, build houses and barns, tan leather, and manufacture hats, shoes, hosiery, cabinet-work, and other articles of clothing and furniture, to the great convenience and advantage of the neighborhood." [6]

In comparison with the South, the North had few navigable rivers that could serve the inland towns and provide means of transportation to the seaports. As the century progressed, overland routes and facilities for travel improved so conspicuously, particularly along the seaboard, that in 1732 Daniel Henchman of Boston published a guidebook, *The Vade Mecum for America: Or a Companion for Traders and Travellers,* which described the highroads and listed taverns from Maine to Virginia. Beginning about 1740, a regular network of roads traversed interior New England over which peddlers and stagecoaches made their way with increasing frequency. A highway ran westward to the Susquehanna from Philadelphia after 1733, and many other passable tributary roads connected the largest colonial city with the rest of Pennsylvania and New Jersey. "The roads for communication are good," was the opinion of one familiar with English highroads of the day. Postal service steadily improved, and gradually mail-order services as well as newspaper deliveries became available in many parts of the country.[7]

German farmers of Bucks, Lancaster, Northampton, and York counties in Pennsylvania maintained from eight to ten thousand great covered freight wagons to haul their produce, and often dispatched them in convoys of a hundred or more over the Lancaster Road to the Philadelphia market. When one immigrant from the Hebrides first glimpsed some Conestoga six-horse teams, he wanted to know "what was the use of these huge moving houses, and where those big horses came from?" He had never seen anything like them in Scotland.[8]

A thriving coastwise traffic carried passengers and freight in small vessels from port to port in New England and up the Hudson and Delaware. Lumber, shingles, and barrel staves from the Atlantic side of West New Jersey, for example, were shipped directly to New York. Beyond the limits of ocean-borne navigation, moreover, much use was made of water transportation; on the Delaware a shallow-draft boat, named Durham after its inventor, made its appearance for use above Trenton Falls, and on Massachusetts and New Hampshire streams the gundelow and Moses boat served a similar purpose. Thus, by land and by sea the colonists doggedly persevered in improving modes of travel and communication, and with each decade, as inland villages grew into sizable towns, connections with their markets grew steadily better.

The towns of interior New England were basically farming communities, but most had long since passed through the pioneer stage. By 1776 there were 566 of them, each with its small village formed around a green and meeting-house, and each numbering among its inhabitants a little coterie of artisans and craftsmen—the blacksmith, the wheelwright, the weaver, the cobbler, the carpenter, the housewright, and other tradesmen needed to render the town self-sufficient. Compact settlement and relative ease of communication made a division of labor and an exchange of local services both possible and practical.[9]

Towns lacking the services of certain artisans often made efforts to secure them. "The Trade of a Currier is very much wanted in Middletown, the Metropolis of Connecticut," reads an attractive advertisement of 1758; a master of the business "may get a pritty Estate in a few Years." The importance of the village craftsman is brought home to us as we learn that when a house burned at Preston, Connecticut, in 1749, John Avery, a weaver, and his family lost their looms and £400 "worth of cloath of their own Manufacture." One of the weaver's fifteen children was shortly to conduct a goldsmith's and clockmaker's business on his farm at Preston, rear a family of fourteen, and rise to the rank of lieutenant in the militia. In spite of this last attainment, with its attendant prestige, John Avery's prosperity enabled him to hire a substitute when the call to duty came in the War for Independence.[10] The Averys were obviously successful, but it may be observed that they followed the general practice of most village tradesmen and combined farming with their crafts to supplement their incomes. In this respect they merely duplicated the custom of contemporary English village artisans.

Perhaps it was the long, cold winters which confined the craftsmen and farmers indoors that encouraged them to meditate on and experiment in their skills. While traditionally the average farmer whittled wooden nutmegs, many a Yankee artisan tinkered. At any rate, long before 1776, some of these craftsmen had developed specialties that came to enjoy more than a local vogue—they served adjacent towns and ultimately became known throughout the country. All of these small-town northern tradesmen worked for a larger market than plantation artisans.

The decades of the forties and fifties witnessed a stabilization of New England society; wealth accumulated, and the standard of living mounted and kept pace with it. Many middle-class families lived in solid comfort and, occasionally, in affluence. An outward and visible sign of the new dispensation can be detected in the high quality of domestic and ecclesiastical architecture achieved by the builder-architects of the period as they replaced old utilitarian structures of the seventeenth century (Figure 1). Employing designs found in current English builders' manuals, they produced satisfying results. Most of the lovely, frame New England meetinghouses were designed and constructed by local carpenters, masons, and other artisans, who were usually members of the Congregational Church. In the diary of Joshua Hempstead, versatile craftsman and dignitary of New London, we can follow his work on the meetinghouse step by step when he was able to spare time from his farm and shipyard. One of the finest of these carpenters was Captain Judah Woodruff, who not only designed and built the church at Farmington in 1771 but carved its handsome pulpit and sounding board with his own hands. Now and then success with one structure brought a commission from a neighboring town, as in the case of Kilbourn, builder of Litchfield, who became master workman "in the frame" along with Eaton of Pittsfield, joiner, in the erection of Christ Church at Great Barrington in 1764.[11]

Enough bells were needed for the towers of the new edifices to support several founders (Figure 4). In 1753 John Witear, clockmaker, began casting church bells at Fairfield, and, long before Paul Revere entered the trade, Caleb and Robert Barker, ironmasters of Hanover, Massachusetts, announced that they could cast "Bells for Meeting Houses and other Uses, from a smaller to a greater, even to one of two Thousand Weight; cheaper than they can be imported." Twelve years later Robert Barker cast bells at two shillings the pound. Near the Air Furnace in Abington, Massachusetts, Aaron Hobart opened a bell foundry in 1770, and four years later the famous Isaac Doolittle "erected a suitable building" for casting bells at New Haven, advertising that he paid cash for old copper.[12] Certainly New Englanders can be pardoned for the pride and satisfaction they took in being summoned to divine worship on the Sabbath by bells made in their own country.

New meetinghouse and private dwellings had to be furnished in keeping with the dignity and beauty of their exterior and interior finish, with the result that the services of new and specialized craftsmen were soon in great demand. Local joiners could now add the fabrication of decorative furniture to the serviceable products they had been turning out for farm and village homes. Doubtless the inhabitants of Braintree, including possibly the Adamses, were as proud of the cabinetwork of James Allen as were the good people of Colchester of that of the skilled Pierpont Bacon—the latter unfortunately lost his shop, tools, and £100 worth of furniture in a fire of 1760 (Figure 10). At Enfield after 1754, Eliphalet Chapin began evolving a Connecticut style of furniture based on designs in Chippendale's *Director* and executed it in native cherry instead of mahogany. His workmanship was highly valued in Enfield and Windsor and soon influenced fashions throughout the Land of Steady Habits.[13]

"Remember that time is money," was Poor Richard's advice to a young tradesman, and Connecticut Yankees acted as if the adage had been directed at them. Everybody wanted to know what time it was, and a host of skilled clockmakers came to their assistance. Although Connecticut clockmaking is usually regarded as a postrevolutionary development, wooden clocks are believed to have been made at New Haven as early as 1715 and had become an article of commerce by 1750. Certainly by the mid-century a small but definite beginning had been made in the industry. Ebenezer Balch forsook his native scene at Boston to serve Hartford and Weathersfield as a clockmaker and silversmith, training his son Joseph to succeed him, and there is ample evidence that at East Hartford, Benjamin Cheney, who had apprenticed to Seth Young of Hartford in 1739, was making both brass and wooden clocks at his own shop in 1745 and had commenced training his four sons and "Poor John Fitch" of steamboat fame as apprentices. In 1764 Benjamin Willard, a last maker, came down from Massachusetts to learn clockmaking from Cheney, a craft he later taught to his brother, the great Simon Willard, and it is interesting that it was Cheney's brother Timothy who trained the famous Eli Terry.[14]

In the city, craftsmen worked with imported tools; village artisans had to buy up old brass and construct their own lathes and cutting engines. In the tiny rural communities of New England, where the demand for clocks or for watch repairs was small, the workman was forced into versatility

—a condition that in the long run had profound effects on the course of American invention.

Closely allied to the clockmakers were the silversmiths (Figure 8). Not infrequently, in fact, country artisans combined the two trades. The multiplication of silversmiths in the New England countryside was a sure index of prosperity, for in the days when there were no banks country squires put their savings into plate and jewelry for safekeeping and because they coveted the amenities of life. The so-called Narragansett Planters patronized four silversmiths of the hamlet of Little Rest (South Kingston), Rhode Island. Chief among them was Samuel Casey, a capable worker, who moved down from Exeter to open a shop in 1763. Despite a forge fire the next year that burned his house down and with it "a great Quantity of Furniture" and stock worth £2,000 sterling, he continued to produce some beautiful tankards, cups, and teapots in the six years before he misapplied his skill in "Money-Making" and was sentenced to be hanged for his crime. On the night of November 3, 1770, however, a masked mob forced the Little Rest gaol and freed all the prisoners, including the counterfeiter. From that time on little more is heard of Samuel Casey.[15]

Yankee thrift and pride, as well as skills, are revealed by the record that at least seventy-six silversmiths worked in twenty-six different Connecticut towns before 1776. Prior to 1680 when Job Prince began work at the trade in Milford, worthies of that town had procured their silver from New York or Boston. The craft began to center in New London and Norwich, however, particularly after the Huguenot René Grignon settled at the latter in 1708. Hartford became active in the mystery with the arrival of John Potwine in 1737, but after the last French war New Haven ranked as the leading town in silversmithing.

The work of the village artisans did not compare with the silver or jewelry produced in the cities, either in design or craftsmanship; it was attractive, simple, and competently performed however. A good idea of the kind of commissions they undertook may be had from the account of the pieces stolen from John Jennings' shop at Norwalk in 1763: "a Silver Cream Pot, 6 large Spoons, 2 or 3 Dozen Tea Spoons, a great many pair of Stone Buttons, Gold Studs, Jewels and other Silver Buttons, several Pair of Silver Buckles, some with Fluke and Tongs, and some without, and sundry other Articles, to the Value of £100." [16]

The presence at Boston of many of America's finest silversmiths acted as a deterrent to any widespread practice of the trade in the country towns of Massachusetts. Near the common at Concord, however, John Ball worked with silver in a small brick shop, and at such places as Newbury, Salem, Taunton, and Worcester occasional silversmiths wrought for the local trade and managed to contest successfully with the master craftsmen of the metropolis. [17]

In like fashion, Bay Town coach and carriage makers enjoyed a monopoly of the country gentry's custom until the year of the Stamp Act, when August Plumb of Middletown started to manufacture vehicles of every type and provided competition for Paul Verstile of Weathersfield, who sold riding chairs and chaises "made in Boston" by the famous Adino Paddock (Figure 13). In 1768 Jonathan Brown returned to Hartford from the West Indies and advertised that his "compleat set of Hands" would construct a plain riding chair of the finest quality for £13. After 1774, he was able to outstrip his principal rival, Consider Burt, by bringing down coach trimmings in his Boston stagecoach at no charge to himself. [18]

Other specialized trades appeared in certain towns of rural New England, particularly as the economy matured after 1750. Potteries opened at Roxbury and Concord, and wigmakers set up shop in remote places like Londonderry in New Hampshire (Figure 2). The *Boston Evening Post* for July 14, 1752, reported that a ship had just arrived from Holland with 300 Germans "skilled in the making of Glass, of various Sorts" and that "a House proper for carrying on that useful Manufacture, will be erected at Germantown [Braintree] as soon as possible." So many curious folk went out from Boston to inspect the new factory that they retarded the work and, like tourists in any period, did so much damage to the premises that in 1753 a shilling entrance fee was charged (Figure 6). The principal products of the Germantown works were window glass and bottles, which were marketed in Boston by Thomas Flucker and Jonathan Williams. Although the Germans could blow daily five gross of bottles worth £55, Massachusetts currency, the profit lay in window glass. Despite apparent success the enterprise did not really prosper. After the loss of the main building by fire in 1755, Jonathan Williams and Joseph Palmer carried on the project, making bottles of all kinds, chemical retorts, pickle and conserve pots, with indifferent success until about 1761 when the factory seems to have closed. Perhaps it was in the glasshouse that Richard Cranch opened his Germantown spermaceti-candleworks in 1762.[19]

The growth of metal trades in New England was stimulated by the manufacture of pig and bar iron in both Massachusetts and Connecticut. From 1715 on the iron industry flourished in the Bay Colony, tending to locate south and east of Boston in Suffolk, Plymouth, and Bristol counties. According to a report drawn up by Andrew Oliver in 1758, there were forty-one forges, fourteen furnaces, four slitting mills, and one steel furnace in the province. The country about Stoughton, Middleboro, Raynham, Norton, and Taunton was appropriately styled "the Land of the Leonards," for Nathaniel, Elkanah, George, Ephraim, Elijah, Zephary, James, and Eliphalet all owned and operated eight forges, and Seth had a furnace. Wealth dug from the iron bogs enabled the Leonard family to live in near-baronial style and to dominate, nay rule over, the social and political life of southern Massachusetts until the coming of the Revolution.[20]

Of very great importance, although not so widely known, was the establishing of secondary iron manufactures in eastern Connecticut between 1732 and 1748. At plating mills in Woodstock, Norwich, Plainfield, Stonington, Groton, New London, Saybrook, and Killingworth, enterprising Yankee ironmasters hammered out sheet iron for cooper's hoops and tin plate for whitesmiths. Connecticut's eight plating mills, outnumbering by two all those of the twelve other colonies, procured their supply of bar iron at considerable expense from Pennsylvania, New York, and Massachusetts furnaces, as well as from "sundry" refining forges and a furnace situated in the colony.[21]

Near the New York border at Salisbury in Litchfield County lay a deposit of rich ore first exploited in 1734 by Philip Livingston, when he, the Reverend Jared Eliot, and others built a works at Lime Rock. This furnace had its ups and downs, probably on account of its inaccessibility. In 1765 the *Connecticut Courant* of Hartford told its readers that it was a matter of great moment that a road be cut and kept open through the Green Woods to Canaan and Salisbury, especially since there was an iron furnace in the latter from which the principal refiners in the colony were supplied. Before long, Salisbury Furnace was turning out a variety of products useful in many crafts—forge hammers, blacksmith's anvils, potash kettles, hatter's basons, clothier's plates, chimney backs, gristmill hardware, smoothing irons, and carriage boxes. This ironworks was completely rebuilt and improved in 1771 on the 600-acre tract containing a mansionhouse and two buildings for workmen, and at nearby Colebrook a fine double forge was constructed, along with a blacksmith's shop and sawmill, and placed under the management of a Mr. Ogden. At Hartford William Tiley, merchant and goldsmith, who was also part owner, marketed the products of Salisbury Works and advertised that his partner, Jared Lane, would make "Castings to any particular Pattern left at the Furnace." When in 1773 Tiley and Richard Alson of Middletown undertook to sell the "Blistered and Faggot Steel, manufactured by Aaron Elliott & Co., in Killingworth [and] warranted equal to the best English Steel," the metalworkers of the colony were well served.[22]

These simple, finished metal trades that produced ironware, clocks, and silver plate were the village precursors of the great industries located today at Bridgeport, New Haven, New Britain, Wallingford, and Meriden. Their line of descent is clear and unbroken from the late 1730's to the present, and by the time the difficulties with the mother country became critical they were well rooted.

A situation had been developing in eastern Connecticut for several decades that ensured hearty co-operation in the intercolonial effort to promote American manufactures to bring economic pressure on England. Agriculture had never really prospered in this region, and its shallow soil was nearing exhaustion so that large segments of the increasing population were looking for other means of gaining a living. Many sought out fertile lands in Pennsylvania and elsewhere, but others turned with marked success to the arts and crafts. Patriotic and political motives, engrafted on existing economic needs and desires, stimulated a growth already in process. Moreover, when the nonimportation movements collapsed in the early seventies, Connecticut's craftsmen, as contrasted with the incipient manufacturing efforts of the rural South, not only continued to flourish but were destined to play a vital role in the industrialization of the United States in the nineteenth century.

The movement for colonial manufactures provided Connecticut with an opportunity, not only to achieve a measure of independence from English manufactures, but also to free herself from the necessity of purchasing them at considerable advance in prices through Boston, New York, and Philadelphia merchants. It is evident that hope of release from the economic imperialism of these cities figured prominently in the plans of local merchants. Ambitious Yankees met the new challenge with vigor, intelligence, and resourcefulness as the activities of two of their towns abundantly indicate.

Norwich, situated where the Yantic and the Quinebaug join to form the Thames River estuary, had in 1756 a population of 5,540, of which the majority lived in the settled area around Norwich Landing. Eighteen years later the number had risen to 7,327; Norwich was the leading town east of the Connecticut and second only to New Haven in the colony. Much of this growth can be attributed to the driving energy and foresight of its leading merchant, Christopher Leffingwell. In 1764 he hired John Bliss, "said to be one of the most curious mechanicks this age has produced," to design and construct a toll bridge across the Shetucket River to connect Norwich Landing with the interior country. Contemporaries regarded the structure as "the most curious and compleat piece of architecture of that kind, ever erected in America." Two years later Leffingwell introduced a new industry to the colony at his "Norwich Paper Manufactory" in Yantic. It was not long before Connecticut newspapers were being printed on Norwich paper and local printers were purchasing rags for the mill. Using skilled labor procured from Philadelphia and New York, the enterprise was immediately successful and supplied a fillip to Yankee pride. "It is a curiosity," remarked one gentleman, "that they mould and make ready for the Press about ten sheets per minute, by the watch." In 1766 also, Leffingwell brought William Russell from England and soon had him working at a stocking loom. In time this undertaking had to be enlarged in order to meet the local demand for hosiery.[23]

Christopher Leffingwell was an early prototype of the Yankee entrepreneur. The prosperity of his fulling mill and dyehouse, opened in 1770, led Simon Huntington to build others in 1772, and he gained fame from the fact that "a single workman could produce annually nearly 5,000 pounds of chocolate" at the water-powered chocolate mill erected in 1770. Joining with Thomas Williams the following year, he planned a "new earthenware manufactory" at Norwich and advertised in the New York papers for two skilled throwers or wheelmen [24] (Figure 2).

Others, like the Huntingtons, followed Leffingwell's lead, and during the two decades before the War for Independence the metal trades began to flourish with the establishment of two ironworks, an agricultural implement manufacture, a brass foundry, several gunsmiths, Nathaniel Niles's iron wire and card manufacture, and Edmond Darrow's shop for making cut shingle-nails from old iron hoops, one of the first attempts to improve the nail industry. Ten silversmiths also worked regularly at their crafts. When Thomas Harland came over from England in 1773 to set up as a clock and watch maker, Norwich acquired a superior craftsman who was, for years, Connecticut's leading trainer of apprentices. He also is said to have made the first American watch.[25]

A similar, if less spectacular, development occurred at Hartford. Clockmakers, nailmakers, wigmakers, and leather-breeches makers were among the craftsmen whose enterprise was notable. Tradesmen of the river town were thoroughly aware of the need to compete with established urban artisans. Because Philadelphia's leather breeches enjoyed an intercolonial repute and were sold by Stephen Austin, who had come from the Quaker City with skilled workers, local craftsmen advertised that their skins were dressed and made up "in the same Manner as those from Philadelphia." Epaphras Bull pointed out that his copper stills and kettles, his brass and irons, and stirrups were as good and as cheap as those brought in from New York. Cotton Murray, former Boston tailor, may have succeeded in attracting Hartford custom for his "Men's Cloaths, both Leather and Cloth," but shoemakers like Moses Smith found hard going in competing with Benjamin Morris and Caleb Bull who carried "Lynn Shoes" in stock [26] (Figure 3).

"Lynn Shoes" owed their fame to the skill and energy of a single person, whose craftsmanship enabled this Massachusetts village to specialize narrowly and wrest the lion's share of the shoe manufacture from the adjacent city of Boston. John Adam Dagyr, a Welsh cordwainer who concentrated on women's shoes, found only three masters with enough business to employ journeymen when he arrived at Lynn in 1750. He not only began making women's shoes equal to any imported, but he initiated his fellow workers into the secrets of quality cordwaining. By 1764 the *Boston Gazette* could proudly report, yet not without a touch of envy, that "it is certain that women's shoes, made at Lynn, do now exceed those usually imported, in strength and beauty, *but not in price.*" Production rapidly increased as the market broadened to include all New England, and even New York and Philadelphia. The output for 1767 was put at 80,000 pairs. So reliable was the quality of this footwear that shoemakers who set up shop in such New Hampshire towns as Exeter and Portsmouth announced that they had served their apprenticeship at Lynn.[27]

After the end of the French and Indian War, colonial society advanced with startling rapidity—a fact of which the mother country was totally oblivious and which the colonists themselves came only gradually to realize. Among artisans and craftsmen, this maturation had reached a point where it was about to express itself in the now famous Yankee ingenuity. For example, Edward Pattison of Kensington Parish, Berlin, Connecticut, was not content to be a pioneer in the making of tinware; looking beyond his locality he also devised and inaugurated a remarkably effective system of marketing when he hired peddlers to hawk his wares in other towns. By adding scissors, buttons, brassware, and other items to his pack, the ubiquitous Connecticut peddler became a familiar American institution of the next century.[28]

That spirit of inventiveness which seems so outstanding among our national characteristics had its beginnings not after the Revolution, as is so often stated, but in the late colonial period. Significantly the phenomenon developed even more in the rural villages than in the larger towns. It first appeared in eastern Connecticut, and not inappropriately a clergyman of the standing order was its patron saint.

The Reverend Jared Eliot of Killingworth (now Clinton) practiced what Cotton Mather dubbed the "angelic conjunction," for he was both a noted minister and a much-sought-after physician. He also evinced a great interest in agriculture and iron mines, investing in 1734 in the undertaking at Salisbury. When his son, Aaron, erected a works for refining pig iron into steel at Killingworth, the parson's active mind turned to the problem of finding a cheaper source of supply than that offered by New York. A black sand on the beach attracted his attention in 1761. After contriving an "Engine to separate the sand ore from ordinary sand," he succeeded in having it smelted at the Killingworth furnace and in extracting an excellent iron. At New York the following year, he published his findings in *An Essay on the Invention, or Art of making very good if not the best Iron, from black Sea Sand*. Dedication of this well-written piece to the Society of Arts in London, of which he was a corresponding member, brought him the Society's gold medal in appreciation of his achievements.[29]

Interest in Jethro Tull's new horse-hoeing husbandry stimulated Jared Eliot to experiment with a seed drill that would be less cumbersome than the Englishman's. Aided by the "mathematical Learning and Mechanical Genius" of the Reverend Thomas Clap, President of Yale College, and the skill of Benoni Hylliard, Killingworth's master wheelwright, he contrived a simpler and more efficient machine which, drawn by three oxen, would open furrows, drop seeds and fertilizer, and cover them in a single operation. At the time of his death the apparatus still had "bugs" in it, but

Eliot's son-in-law, Benjamin Gale, made further improvements until it deposited the seeds and manure in the soil
simultaneously. A model of the plough and drill was sent
to the Society of Arts. This not only brought him the gold
medal for invention but also a lawsuit by Benoni Hylliard,
who alleged that he was the real inventor and that Gale was
only his agent in dealing with the London body. The General Assembly, however, exonerated Gale.[30]

As a matter of fact, no colonist, not even Benjamin
Franklin, was more active in encouraging American inventors and manufactures than Benjamin Gale. He operated
the Killingworth steel mill with Aaron Eliot and kept in
touch with every new development. It was he who, as a
Connecticut member, forwarded to the American Society for
promoting and propagating useful knowledge, held in
Philadelphia, a set of polished crystals executed by Abel
Buell, jeweler and lapidary of Killingworth, "who by force
of a natural Genius, has invented a Machine to grind and
polish Crystals of every Kind, without having Instructions
from any one skilled in that Art." [31]

Abel Buell was a Yankee with clever fingers who, in
1764, earned notoriety before fame by misusing his newly
acquired engraving technique to raise five-shilling currency
to five-pound notes. "From a compassionate regard and
pity for his youthful follies," the court released him with a
slightly clipped ear, a faint brand, and an even lighter gaol
term, and he went straight thereafter. In April, 1769, the
Reverend Ezra Stiles of Newport received a letter from
Saybrook containing news that: "Our American Genius,
Abel Buell, is now manufacturing type for printing. Dr.
Gale thinks they will be equal to any European ones; the
Dr. designs a present of enough of them to print an advertisement, to your American Society." Ere long, Gale
sent some samples of the type to Stiles, who had Solomon
Southwick, the Newport printer, set them and pull the first
proofs. At Boston the Reverend Charles Chauncy expressed

astonishment, on seeing Edes and Gill print with some of Buell's type, "that such a specimen shd be made without instruction, from the mere force of Genius." Suggestions from the Boston printers and the members of the American Philosophical Society, sent through Dr. Gale, assisted the inventor in improving his types and encouraged him to seek support from the Connecticut Assembly for a type foundry which he erected at New Haven in 1770. As a friend remarked: "This Buell is Rich in Genius, poor in Purse." Like many inventors, he lacked business acumen, and financial mismanagement was responsible for the failure of the earliest undertaking of this kind.[32]

There were other Yankees who served their country by tinkering and inventing. In New Haven lived one of the most versatile of Connecticut's craftsmen, who was also one of its principal manufacturers. Trained as a clockmaker, Isaac Doolittle followed that business and also made surveyors' instruments and mariners' compasses, and in time became a bell founder. In 1769 he received widespread popular acclaim for the first American printing press, made of mahogany and "of the most approved construction," for William Goddard of the *Pennsylvania Chronicle*. About this time, too, the newspapers announced that two years previously a machine had been built "for cutting iron screws for clothier's presses, . . . and is still occupied by Abraham Brownson, its inventor, in Litchfield gaol-yard, where . . . screws and boxes" are made. In nearby Dutchess County, New York, Cornelius Atherton was making fullers' shears in "a new invented manner," while over in East Bridgewater, Massachusetts, Scottish Hugh Orr produced the finest edged tools to be had anywhere, and as early as 1753 had invented a machine to clean flaxseed.[33]

Fired by patriotic zeal in 1775, David Bushnell, a young graduate of Yale, reached the heights of Yankee inventiveness when he completed at Saybrook a man-propelled submarine, called the American Turtle. On the outside was

Figure 6. Windowpanes and bottles were the principal products of colonial glassworks.

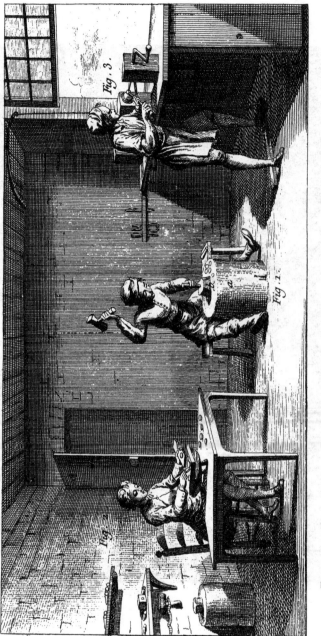

Figure 7. The "Famous Philadelphia Brass Buttons" of the Wistars were all fabricated by hand.

fastened a wooden bomb containing a clockwork detonating mechanism that could be attached to the hull of an enemy warship. This amazing engine of destruction performed satisfactorily in trials, but when an attempt was made to blow up Admiral Lord Howe's flagship in New York harbor in 1776 his secretary merely recorded in his journal: "The Rebels fired two Bombs this Evening, probably as an Experiment. They seemed poorly made, and not calculated to much Execution." In Operation Turtle, Bushnell had the "cordial and intelligent assistance" of Dr. Benjamin Gale.[34] Surely an inventive spirit was abroad in the land!

When we come to the Middle Colonies, we discover a vast area of unrivalled soils, rich with natural resources. Save in the valley of the Hudson where great proprietors engrossed the best lands, small and prosperous farms characterized the region. Here English, Scotch-Irish, and German farmer-craftsmen, as we have noted earlier, not only produced great quantities of wheat, Indian corn, meats, and lumber, but entered widely into household industries.

As the interior country was settled after 1730, local needs forced the founding of numerous inland villages along routes of travel or by the rivers' sides. New Jersey and Pennsylvania towns became essential units of society as communication with the seacoast slowly but surely improved. Contemporaries clearly appreciated their importance, and such land speculators as Chief Justice William Allen, Edward Shippen, and the Reverend William Smith established Allentown, Shippensburg, and Huntington to enhance the value of their holdings. Hearing of Provost Smith's proposed town on the Juniata in 1769, "Anglus Americanus" regretted that "Towns are pretty much wanting in America," yet their role in furnishing a market to the farmer, employment to the artisan, man power for the wars, and revenue to the state is acknowledged by all. Admitting that a healthy site, abundant water power, and an inland location in the midst of a fruitful countryside were most desirable, he contended that, since "employment is the very soul of a great town," the prime necessity is manufacturing. "Philadelphia is by no means the most proper place for such purpose; our hands are sufficiently busied in maritime and other employments; wood and provisions are dear, rents high, and the methods of living, if not luxurious, are at least elegant." Manufactures will prosper in rural surroundings, such as on the banks of the blue Juniata, where the cost of English goods goes up fifty per cent each hundred miles you journey inland from Philadelphia and farmers' lads are eager to enter into trades.[35]

Such impulses caused many villages in the commercial domain controlled by the cities of Philadelphia and New York to outgrow their localism and develop prominently as centers for particular crafts whose products found their way to intercolonial markets. A brief examination of the economy of four of them will indicate the variety and extent of handicrafts and manufactures in the rural communities of the Middle Colonies.

In the seventeenth century, Francis Daniel Pastorius and a group of Dutch and German artisans founded a village near the Wissahickon Creek, nine miles from Philadelphia. The arts and crafts always thrived at Germantown. There, in 1738, a former tailor and clockmaker, Christopher Sower, began a notable career as the first German printer and publisher in all America. A year later he brought out the first issue of his *Hoch Deutsch Pensylvanische Geschict Schreiber*, a newspaper that enjoyed a long existence under various titles, and in 1743 he published, for the Ephrata Brethren, the first Bible in a European tongue to be printed in the New World. Returns show that, out of 481 persons who were taxed in Germantown in 1774, there were 106 master artisans engaging in twenty-seven different crafts. The leather trades employed thirty-one (including fourteen cordwainers and five saddlers); fourteen coopers made casks for the flour and meat export trade; and, despite its nearness to the colonial metropolis, specialty crafts provided a living for two coachmakers and several clockmakers, bookbinders, chairmakers, and turners.[36]

Notwithstanding the importance of its paper and flour mills, which I will discuss later, its leather trades, and its diversified crafts, the industrial fame of Germantown stemmed from the stocking manufacture (Figure 5). Five master stocking weavers, employing a host of women and young girls, carried on "a very great Trade in Making Stockings, Etc., both of thread and Woolen yarn wch is Milled and thereby made very warm and Suitable to their weather." As early as 1762 New Jersey servants were running away wearing Germantown stockings. The output in 1768 was estimated at 6,000 dozen pairs.[37]

The Moravian town of Bethlehem, situated on the Lehigh River in Northampton County, was but the elongated shadow of Bishop Augustus Spangenberg, a man combining remarkable executive ability with great piety. "Though this place ... seems but small," observed a visitor of 1751, "you can scarcely mention any trade which is in the largest city in this country, but what is at this place and carried on after the best manner." Several years later, a meeting of master artisans declared that more than one hundred of the commodities sold at the store could be fabricated in the community. The Moravian "Economy," as it was called, lasted until 1762 when individuals were permitted to purchase the stock and fixtures of the several handicrafts and to lease shops from the Church. Mills of all kinds, erected by ingenious mechanics like Henry Antes and Hans Christiansen, potteries (Figure 2), wagonmaking, woolen and linen weaving, smithing, hatmaking, and other crafts were operated upon an even larger scale than at Wachovia, but after the "Economy" was terminated more and more artisans seem to have turned to farming, for in the returns of 1774 only nineteen master craftsmen representing eleven trades were listed among the village's 145 taxpayers.[38]

Two achievements by skilled artificers of Bethlehem command our attention. Hans Christiansen, millwright, undertook to bore hemlock trunks to make water pipes in 1754. Next, he designed three self-acting pumps, which were cast at the Durham Iron Works, and fitted them with a triple crank forged by Brother Blum, Bethlehem blacksmith. Then he erected a water tower, built tanks, and laid the pipes in the ground; so that on May 2, 1755, water was successfully forced up to the tower, which was seventy-five feet high, and on June 27 it began to flow into the tank in the public square. This was the first municipal waterworks in the English colonies. No less striking was the career of John Klem, a wayward Moravian, who arrived in 1746 with a portable organ he had made in Philadelphia (Figure 15). Deciding to settle in Bethlehem, he passed the remainder of his days there making and repairing organs as well as teaching his craft to David Tannenberger, joiner, who came over from Germany in 1749. Tannenberger established an organ workshop at nearby Nazareth in 1758, then moved to the other Moravian center at Lititz, and, after Klem's death in 1762, made a genuine contribution to American musical life as the country's foremost piano and organ builder until his own death in 1804.[39]

Built in 1741, on the banks of the Codorus Creek, the town of York had a population of about 2,500, overwhelmingly German, when the Revolution came, and fulfilled a very real need for a borough town in the midst of a prosperous farming country. Dr. Schoepf observed that at York "shopkeepers and craftsmen come together and supply the other scattered and sporadic settlers with conveniences, clothing, utensils, and articles of luxury (giving these in exchange for the products of their land and flocks)." Thirty-nine separate trades employed over half the town's 385 taxpayers in 1779. Seventeen shoemakers, as many tailors, eleven blacksmiths, nine hatters, nine weavers, and seven hosiers made up the roster of the leading crafts, but breeches makers, cardmakers, locksmiths, turners, blue dyers, silversmiths, potters, tinmen, and other artisans also contributed to the town's activities. The Updegraffs were York's premier artisan family—three were hatters, two were heelmakers, and one each was a breeches maker, a tanner, and a lastmaker. Schoepf noted as he rode along the "Philadelphia Wagon Road" that nearly every farm contained a wall or standing clock made at York.[40]

Its situation near the Maryland boundary line made York the gateway to the Shenandoah Valley and the South, and added not a little to its prosperity. Among those engaged in fitting out wagon trains moving southward were ten master saddlers and four saddletree makers. No artisan of the western country was more enterprising than William Bailey, coppersmith. He made and sold stills, brewing coppers, wash and fish kettles, tea kettles, saucepans, coffee and tea pots, and mended any article made of copper or brass. With apparent reason he claimed that his wares were known from Pennsylvania to the Carolinas as "far superior to any made in these parts," and, "to prevent disputes," he stamped his name on all his work and warranted it "to be good." He decided to expand his trade and opened a branch shop at Hagerstown, Maryland, in 1773, "for the conveniency of the inhabitants of the back part of this country" and also announced that he would attend all court meetings during the year at Frederick and Carlisle.[41]

The village of Trenton in West New Jersey rose early to prominence because of its strategic location at the Falls of the Delaware. All goods coming up the river had to be transshipped at Trenton Landing to Durham boats. There, wheat, iron, and lumber from New Jersey and the valley of the upper Delaware converged for transport to Philadelphia; there the highroad to New York crossed the ferry; there stage routes terminated; there abundance of water power and iron ore ensured industrial activity. Men of vision and energy like George Thomas and Dr. Thomas Cadwalader of Pennsylvania joined with Colonel Lewis Morris and Dr. Daniel Coxe of New Jersey to promote the development of an entrepôt for Hunterdon and Somerset counties.

About 1719 Chief Justice William Trent, who gave his name to the community, built on the Assunpink Creek near the Falls of the Delaware "a fine water mill . . . with a pretty cascade" that fell "over the dam like a transparent sheet over 30 yards wide." His mill was the nucleus around which settlement clustered, and it became a very lucrative enterprise. In time saw and fulling mills were erected; Dr. Coxe's paper manufactory, a tannery, a pottery, and an establishment for pickling and packing sturgeon were opened. In 1758 the town contained about 150 houses, mostly occupied by artisans who worked in the mills. Passing through various hands, "Trenton Mills" ground wheat and corn for both domestic and merchant custom. When Robert Lettice Hooper advertised them for sale in 1765, the equipment consisted of a great stone millhouse with three pairs of stones, four bolting reels, and two large screens for cleaning wheat. His twenty-two-acre estate also included a new cooper's shop, a dyehouse and press, and a water-powered fulling mill. The dam had been repaired recently and new waterwheels and shafts had been installed in the mill. All in all it was one of the finest colonial flour mills. Many other millers were attracted by the Delaware's falls, and the Trenton district was an important flour-milling center before the more famous Brandywine mills came into competition in the lower Delaware Valley; a daily sight at Trenton Ferry was the passing of narrow-beamed Durham boats carrying fifty to sixty casks of flour on their way downstream to Philadelphia.[42]

Iron ore of excellent quality cropped out in spots on both shores of the upper Delaware, and Trenton naturally became the center to which it was sent by wagon or boat for shipment to Philadelphia. In 1723, the village got its own ironworks, located near the mill on the Assunpink, and eleven years later Isaac Harrow began to operate a planing and plating mill that turned out frying pans, dishes, axes, shovels, and saws. Bar and pig iron were brought in from neighboring forges and furnaces, and in 1745 at Harrow's mill Benjamin Yard began producing "Trenton Blistered Steel," which found a ready market with Philadelphia iron-mongers like Owen Biddle. When John Zane ran these works in 1772, John Pemberton at Philadelphia took most of his steel, "either in the blister or neatly faggoted," although Zane advertised that he could supply any merchant or shopkeeper with small bars for carriage springs, mill and crosscut saws, and, on order, for scythes. His "American Steel," warranted as good as any made in England, was also sold at New York along with Newark potash, kettles, and hollow ware.[43]

In the Middle Colonies, soil and easily obtainable sub-surface deposits combined to foster a third type of arts and crafts, clearly differentiated from those of village or plantation. It was in this region that large-scale industries requiring a heavy capital investment made their first American appearance. Among these, flour milling provides an interesting illustration of an industry in which two different stages of development existed side by side, often under the same roof.

Wheat was the grand staple of New York, New Jersey, and Pennsylvania, and much of it was exported in the form of flour and bread. Any map of the middle regions was dotted with gristmills. As fast as new lands were cleared, millers set up their stones by the nearest streams. Most of the mills served local farmers, the proprietor taking a fixed proportion of the grist as his toll. In addition, after 1750 many large merchant mills were erected. Philadelphia was the greatest exporting center, shipping off five million pounds of flour in 1771. Consequently merchant mills tended to concentrate along streams that could be easily dammed up, but that also flowed into navigable waterways affording ready access to the metropolis.

Although there were 107 mills in Philadelphia County in 1773, the eleven noted "Wissahickon Millers" of Roxborough and Germantown ground a very large proportion of its flour. In the upper Delaware Valley, at Trenton and on such Pennsylvania and West Jersey creeks as the Neshaminy, Pennypack, Crosswicks, Rancocas, and Pensauken, there were many merchant mills, and below the city on Chester and Brandywine creeks the flour trade enjoyed a mushroom growth on the eve of the Revolution as Wilmington became the leading milling town of the colonies.[44]

A merchant mill represented a sizable investment, as we noted in the case of those on the Potomac. Richard Brown's new mill was in Upper Freehold Township on Crosswicks Creek in West Jersey, not far from Bordentown. The stone mill, measuring 55 feet by 26 feet with a 12-foot lean-to, housed two pairs of stones, three bolting cloths, and a hoisting jack, all driven by water power; also a scale, a wire screen for cleaning wheat, and numerous other utensils. A fulling mill and dyehouse, with a large furnace and press screw, a sawmill, and a cooperage completed the layout on a large farm of 180 acres. Although water transportation was excellent, local farmers usually sold their wheat to Brown for a penny a bushel less than to mills nearer the Delaware. Across the river at Buckingham, Pennsylvania, John McKinley maintained a medium-sized merchant mill much like Brown's.[45]

The colonial iron industry reached its zenith in New Jersey and Pennsylvania because these provinces not only possessed superior deposits of iron ore, but also because of the presence of two other essentials in great abundance— limestone for a flux and timber for conversion into charcoal.

The number of ironworks established before 1776 is fairly astonishing; eighty-one bloomeries, forges (Figure 17), furnaces, slitting mills, plating mills, and steel furnaces were set up at one time or another in Penn's colony, and in 1767 New Jersey had eight furnaces, forty-two forges, one plating mill, one slitting mill, and one steel furnace. I may leave the detailed story of the great ironworks at Durham, Pine Forge, and Cornwall to Professor Arthur Bining, who has told it so well, with merely the comments that iron plantations flourished in the middle even more than in the southern provinces, and that the total colonial output of iron in 1775 amounted to one-seventh of the production of the entire world. Colonial iron was largely consumed in America, and we must not overlook the fact that the deliberate building of this great industry in the face of British restrictive legislation made independence possible. Had it not progressed to such a high degree of industrialization, the revolutionary armies would have been helpless indeed.[46]

Another industry of great consequence owed its rise chiefly to the efforts of a single colonial businessman. The first three American paper mills had been built in the environs of Philadelphia before 1730, but it was Benjamin Franklin who succeeded in placing paper manufacture on a sound and profitable basis. First and last, he was concerned in setting up eighteen mills during his active career as a printer, although he never entered the craft himself. Rather did he purchase rags in large quantities and sell them to the paper mills and, in turn, take off a large share of their output of paper and pasteboard, which he disposed of to the many printing houses up and down the coast in which he had an interest. Between 1739 and 1747, for example, he sold 166,084 pounds of rags to seven paper mills near Philadelphia, and from these same establishments purchased 2,935 reams of paper, much of it for resale. In the light of the development of paper manufacturing across the Atlantic, it is extremely doubtful if any Englishman was as large a paper dealer as Poor Richard in these years.[47]

From 1690, when William Rittenhouse built the first paper mill on a branch of the Wissahickon in Germantown, Philadelphia County was the seat of the colonial paper industry. In 1773 it contained fifteen of the province's seventeen paper mills. The largest annual production at a single mill, however, was claimed by the German Baptist Brethren, who had operated their paper manufactory at Ephrata since 1736. A few mills appeared in the other Middle Colonies. In 1728 William Bradford of New York opened one at Elizabeth Town, New Jersey, and by 1772 there was another at Perth Amboy. Hugh Gaine, Manhattan printer, erected a mill at Hempstead, Long Island, in 1768. Colonial paper could be made and sold cheaper than that imported from England, and since the expanding printer's craft provided a good outlet the industry prospered.[48]

The colonies offered an excellent market for glass, but skilled workers and sufficient capital to promote the manufacture were hard to find (Figure 6). We are all familiar with the grandiose efforts of "Baron" Stiegel to make glass as well as iron at Manheim, Pennsylvania, and with the beautiful work his glassmen achieved from 1765 to 1774. His efforts to persuade the colonists to buy "American Flint Glass" through his Boston, New York, Philadelphia, and Baltimore agencies petered out, perhaps as much from the high cost of the pieces as from Stiegel's extravagant style of living.

Another German succeeded where the "Baron" failed. Caspar Wistar, wealthy manufacturer of the "Famous Philadelphia Brass Buttons," acquired a two-thousand-acre tract of land along a branch of Alloway Creek, near Salem, New Jersey, in 1737. Here on a little plantation known as Wistarburg, a number of experts from Rotterdam built a glass factory, and by 1740 they were producing glass. During the next forty years the business added two furnaces, two

flattening ovens in separate buildings, a storehouse, pot-
house, cuttinghouse, a stamping mill, rolling mill, a mansionhouse, ten dwellings for workmen, a bakery, and a
retail store in addition to farm buildings. Caspar's son Richard owned the works after his father's death in 1752, but
they were managed for him by Benjamin Thompson.[49]

Richard Wistar pushed sales of his products by advertising in Philadelphia, Lancaster, and New York newspapers.
The profits of his glassworks came almost wholly from the
sale of window glass, which was made in all "common sizes"
or to order. In addition, the manufactory produced lamp
glasses, snuff canisters, preserve jars, and many other articles
as technical skills increased. Not the least significant of the
special products of Wistar's works were retorts of several
sizes, "electerizing globes and tubes," and bottles for
Leyden jars that Franklin had urged him to attempt in the
early fifties. Some of the Wistar glass, though utilitarian in
purpose, possessed real beauty and a striking individuality.
At his factory, too, the first American flint glass probably
was made, and also the first successful fusing of different
colored glasses. Many glass blowers received their training
at Wistarburg, and two of them, Jacob Stenger and his
brother, started a rival factory in 1775 which is still operat-
ing today at Glassboro, New Jersey, as the Whitney Glass
Works.[50]

From this survey of the state of the arts and crafts in the
rural regions of the American colonies, it should be evident
that in the South conditions beyond human control frustrated their progress everywhere except in the back country,
whereas in the northern provinces a different environment
nourished them and caused them to proliferate. The principal explanations of this profound contrast lie in the staples
produced and the nature of the settlement of each area.
Where a village society could emerge, there the crafts could
take hold and grow; there artisans might dwell together

and specialize, each in his trade, certain of a demand for his
wares. Given ample resources, a maturing economy, and
an expanding market, men's minds would eventually turn
to ways of increasing production and even to invention.

The American colonists were unable to increase their purchases of European manufactures from 1700 to 1775 in
proportion to the needs of a population that doubled itself
every twenty-five years. With each decade the differential
became greater and was made up by manufacturing in the
colonies. "By manufactures," wrote the author of *American
Husbandry*, "are not to be understood the fabrics of private
families who work only for their own use, but those that are
wrought for sale, and which are the only or principal livelihood of the person concerned and employed in them." [51]
It was his opinion that the northern colonies alone manufactured for sale nearly £1,000,000 worth of goods a year, and
nothing is more certain than that a goodly portion of these
articles was produced by village craftsmen. If, to this sum,
we add the market replacement value of colonial household
manufactures, it seems certain that the Americans of 1775
were producing more goods than they imported from the
mother country.

In 1772 General Thomas Gage effectively summed up
the colonial manufacturing situation in a letter to Lord Barrington: "I [think it would] be for our interest to Keep the
Settlers within reach of the Sea-Coast as long as we can;
and to cramp their Trade as far as it can be done pruden-
tially. Cities flourish and increase by extensive Trade,
Artisans and Mechanicks of all sorts are drawn thither, who
Teach all sorts of Handicraft work before unknown in the
Country, and they soon come to make for themselves what
they used to import. I have seen this Increase." [52]

THE URBAN CRAFTSMAN
(1)

IN THE YEAR 1756 a Manhattan artisan insisted that the only suitable place for the crafts to locate was in a city or town; the proper role of the countryman was agriculture. And, continuing somewhat querulously, he pleaded that "it should not be permitted for one man to carry on the Business of Tanning, Currying, and Shoemaking; much less ought a Farmer to do one, or all those occupations within himself. . . . A Farmer also ought to employ himself in his proper occupation, without meddling with Smiths, Carpenters, Coopers, or any other mechanical Arts, except making and mending his Plow, Harrow, or any other Utensil for Farming." [1]

In the previous lectures I have discussed those rural artisans who undertook the trades "in all their branches." In a village a man was not often called upon to subdivide a craft or to develop minute, specialized skills. A carpenter could perform all the operations involved in woodworking, building a house, making a chair, or turning a rolling pin; likewise, a blacksmith could cut nails, forge a hinge for a door, hammer out a crude hoe, or shoe a horse. The crafts were intimately related to the households of a farming people, and for the most part the articles made were simple in construction and utilitarian in purpose; ornament and display were secondary considerations.

If we wish to examine the products of the craftsman who demonstrated an outstanding talent in fashioning a given article embodying beauty as well as precision, we must turn

to the colonial cities—Boston, Newport, New York, Philadelphia, and Charles Town—or, as time passed, to Portsmouth, Salem, Providence, New Haven, Lancaster, Annapolis, and Norfolk. Only in the coastal commercial
centers were conditions favorable to the development and
specialization within crafts to be found: a large population,
sufficient wealth to purchase luxuries as well as necessaries,
and an ample supply of materials and superior tools required for the fabrication of every kind of goods. These
communities alone provided a labor reservoir from which
journeymen and apprentices might be drawn. Taken together, such factors made for what the economist calls a
division of labor.

Historians have been prone to emphasize the commercial
role of the colonial cities to the exclusion of their other
activities, but a closer examination shows that second only in
importance to their import and export traffic was their manufacturing. In a city of 40,000 people, like Philadelphia—
the second city of the British Empire in 1776—thousands
of artisans and craftsmen (masters, journeymen, apprentices) toiled daily to make the goods and provide the services
needed by town and country folk.

Probably the most important element in the development
of craftwork was population: its growth, its character, and
its concentration in the cities. In 1690 the combined inhabitants of the five leading towns numbered but 18,600, and
the total for the twelve colonies only slightly exceeded two
hundred thousand; by 1776 over 108,000 people lived in
the principal urban centers, and the total for the revolting
provinces was about two and one half millions. In terms of
arts and crafts, this unprecedented increase, which Europeans but dimly realized, meant a home market growing at
such a rate that imports from Great Britain could not satisfy
it. As a consequence, prospects for urban artisans looked
more promising each decade. With the widening of the
rural areas tributary to each city, made possible by immi-

gration and the extension of highways and colonial post, urban craftsmen were called upon to perform more and more services as well as to supply additional goods for the hinterland at the same time that their local custom increased.

It should not appear strange that many of the Old World's artisans, impressed by the stories of high wages, good markets, better prices, freedom from medieval gild restrictions, and by prospects of a more respectable place in society, ventured across the ocean to try their luck in America. Was not the colonial best known to Europe a craftsman —a printer?

As the century opened Huguenots, fleeing from religious persecution, supplied the towns with their first foreign labor element. A surprising number were silversmiths. Again in the years of peace after the fall of Quebec, French wig-makers and hairdressers arrived in the cities, frequently arousing the envy of English perukemakers like the one who inserted a spite advertisement in a Manhattan newspaper in pig French: "Me makee all in de Bon taste, Alamode de Paris; and me no chargee above three Hundred per Cent more than all de Workingman's in Town." [2]

Usually, however, when we speak of eighteenth-century immigration, we have in mind the droves of Scotch Irish and Germans who arrived in nearly every ship after 1720. Among those who came as indentured servants were many craftsmen, some of whom doubtless resumed their trades after serving their time, but the great majority went into the country, took up lands, and became husbandmen. There can be no question of the paramount part they played in household manufacturing. Concurrently, there was a small, though very important, self-induced, free movement of highly trained artisans from Europe to the cities of America. At Philadelphia, New York, and Charles Town, the metal and printing trades, among others, benefited from the immigration of Palatines. Dublin-trained clockmakers and watchmakers, silk dyers, and other craftsmen appeared in large numbers after 1760 to seek a better livelihood in the colonies.

But, above all, it was the Englishman who made the greatest contribution to the handicrafts of our earliest cities. This was the great age of British craftsmanship and enterprise, but to many journeymen the land seemed brighter to the westward, and they sailed away from London, Bristol, Manchester, and Hull to swell the number of skilled craftsmen in the colonial cities. To few people did America beckon more invitingly than the trained artisan.

The distribution of immigrant artisans among the several cities is illuminating. Boston drew its many craftsmen from its own population or that of Old England; only a few Irish came over in the sixties and seventies. Newport received almost none. Although the largest number settled in Philadelphia, that community also trained many of its own citizens in the several trades, but it was at New York, and especially at Charles Town, that native-born artisans were definitely in the minority in the last decades of the colonial period.

An eager welcome awaited the immigrants on these shores. A definite aura of superiority attached to European-trained artisans, and, recognizing its snob appeal, few of them failed to exploit this advantage in the colonial press. The lure of the imported was even greater then than in our own day. If the provincials could not have an outfit from London, the next best thing for the gentlemen of New York, for example, was to patronize "John Vogue, Taylor and Embroiderer from Paris," whose name we strongly suspect was assumed for the delectation of the colonial trade; while Charles Town ladies sought out Mariah Martin, "Hair-Dresser and Mantua-Maker from London and Paris," who passed as "a complete Mistress of those Arts" in South Carolina.[3]

This continual addition of new blood from the mother country and the Continent proved of incalculable value in

Figure 8. Combining fine workmanship with banking, silversmiths were the aristocrats of the crafts.

Figure 3. Many delicate operations were required in the making of a piece of pewter.

establishing an American craft tradition. Regular arrivals of skilled immigrant artisans ensured the transit of new modes, inventions, and techniques to America almost as soon as they developed abroad, and the competition they provided incited colonial craftsmen to improve their workmanship, if not to lower their prices. In the five cities, and later in other rising towns, immigrants taught native Americans their techniques and methods, and new skills and new crafts were steadily introduced along with new ideas, so that when freedom came the country was ready to embark on its own course of manufacturing. Tench Coxe acknowledged the debt in 1794 in his *View of the United States of America:* "A large proportion of the most successful manufacturers in the United States consists of persons, who were journeymen, and in a few instances were foremen in the work-shops and manufactories of Europe; who having been skilful, sober, frugal, and having thus saved a little money, have set up for themselves with great advantage in America." [4]

Now let us examine some of the industries of the colonial centers of population to discover how in the cities a larger market, a greater number of workmen, and more readily accessible supplies resulted in a subdivision of crafts, increased production and sale, and brought about a greater development of refinements and quality goods.

Anyone walking down High Street, Philadelphia, King Street, Boston, or Broad Street, Charles Town, in the eighteenth century could easily have distinguished townsmen from countryfolk by the striking differences in their clothing. City dwellers did not weave cloth for their suits and dresses, nor did they often fashion fabrics into wearing apparel at home. Dry goods were among the principal imports of colonial merchants, and the making of all kinds of clothing occupied the labors of more than a third of urban artisans. At any rate, in a day when ready-made clothes were virtually unknown, the services of tailors were in constant demand for the making of clothes, even more than for mending them.

Perhaps it was because they were so numerous in the city that Lord Bellomont complained in 1698 of the sheriffs who conducted New York elections as "the scum of the people, Taylors and other scandalous persons." Between 1701 and 1776 the Corporation of New York admitted 148 tailors to the freedom of the city, and many more undoubtedly worked there without the privilege (Figure 12). William Thorne claimed to turn out "all sorts of Gentlemens cloaths, and servants liveries, laced or plain, . . . by the best workmen that can be had in town. Likewise ladies riding habits and josephs." Six years later he had earned the reputation of a society tailor who charged fancy prices for suits—£8 to £10! We read with some surprise the announcement of Jacob Reed, Manhattan tailor, that "a choice Assortment of ready made Cloaths, both for Men and Boys, in full Suits or otherwise . . . of different Sizes, Colours, and Make, from a Superfine to a Bearskin," as good as any imported, could be had at his William Street shop.[5]

Bostonians were not all indifferent to the blandishments of a tailor from across the water. In 1763 Charles Dealy, from Dublin, claimed that he made beautiful clothes from "less Cloth and Trimmings than any other Taylor," and therefore deserved "encouragement from the Nobility and Gentry of the Town, and Country adjacent." Courtney and Son, London tailors, however, scorned the blarney approach and, when they announced their removal to a new shop opposite the State House in 1773, declared with some acerbity that their select clientele "renders a pompous Advertisement unnecessary." It is evident, too, from press announcements that the French and Indian War had placed heavy demands on the clothing trades in northern cities, for the advertisement of Samuel Blodgett at Boston sounded a martial note: "Ready-made Cloaths, Suitable for either

Officers or Soldiers who are engaged in the present Expedition against Canada." [6]

In Charles Town, on the other hand, good tailoring was not always available. In 1734 Mr. Commissary Von Reck and the Reverend Mr. Bolzius came up from Savannah to be measured for new clerical habits, but could find no one who understood how to do it. The problems of payment that I reported in the lecture on the rural South held true in its cities also, for we find Hugh Evans insisting in vain that all his accounts be paid within fourteen days. John Remington, who claimed a set of workmen "not inferior to any in America," solved the problem in 1756 by accepting either rice or indigo in payment for all accounts over £20. [7]

The tailor's craft achieved its greatest development at Philadelphia where, at the close of the period, at least 121 masters were actually at work and comprised fourteen per cent of the city's artisans. Many of them were prosperous enough to employ servants in addition to apprentices and journeymen. In 1771 over forty master tailors met at Carpenter's Hall to form the Taylor's Company of Philadelphia, an employers' organization designed to fix prices and limit wages paid to journeymen. [8]

A necessary adjunct of the clothing trades was the service of cleaning and dyeing, which was heavily patronized in every city. Most practitioners of this craft came over from England or the Continent, "having served a regular apprenticeship to that business," and made extreme claims that their "Cleaning was performed in as neat a manner as done in London" and their dyeing of fabrics done "to as good perfection, as those in Manchester." [9]

Other days, other ways. We tend to forget that our colonial forebears used leather clothing for everyday wear. In a land where so many cattle were butchered for salt meat and deer were slaughtered merely for their skins, leather was plentiful and cheap; its wearing qualities are obvious. Gentlemen regularly donned doeskin riding breeches, while all workingmen wore leather breeches and aprons, leather caps, and, in winter, leather leggings. Each city had its quota of leather-breeches makers who, on occasion, produced other leather apparel. When John Breese died at New York in 1744, his widow, Flora Breese, managed his wholesale and retail shop by herself for nearly a year, until John Brown, possibly her journeyman, married her and took over the business. At Charles Town in 1769, the *South Carolina Gazette* urged local workmen to purchase their breeches and gloves from Peter Girard, stockingmaker, because his goods were all of American or South Carolina make. "Philadelphia Leather-Breeches," like so many other Quaker City products, enjoyed more than a local popularity just before the Revolution.[10]

Since the New World was the chief source of the beaver fur needed in the European hat industry, it was but natural that colonials should also venture into the manufacture. When Parliament was told in 1732 that New York and Massachusetts made ten thousand hats annually, it hastened to protect English craftsmen with the "Hat Act," passed to throttle large-scale production by restricting American artisans to two apprentices, who were bound for seven years each, and by prohibiting exports of colonial hats. The general assumption has been that this statute ended a flourishing industry; actually there is evidence to prove that not only did Americans flout the law, but also that the manufacture of hats became a leading urban industry.

Rhode Island was, throughout the colonial era, a tiny commercial republic. As early as 1724 hatmaking was an important industry in her capital, for at that time William Pinniger distributed his Newport beavers all over New England "by Wholesale or Retail, at reasonable Prices." The Hat Act carried no more weight at Newport than the more notorious Molasses Act passed the following year. Artisans like Isaac Chapman imported New York beaver pelts and transformed them into hats in ever-larger numbers. Upon visiting the city in 1768, a Quebec merchant reported that "there is many hatters in this place, as they Carry on a good deal of Counterband Trade in that branch to the West Indies." [11]

A like development occurred in Boston. At the sign of the "Hatt and Helmet" in Newbury Street, Daniel Jones sold "the Best of Beaver Hatts of his own make, . . . warranted"; also English hats, and "Felt-Hatts, *the Manufacture of this Country*." Jones apparently acted as distributor for other hatters and regularly advertised that "Country Traders may be supplied with HATTS, . . . by Wholesale, for Cash, Treasurer's Notes or Credit." When he lost a stock worth £2,000 by fire in 1763, he announced that "by the Kindness of his Brethren of the same Occupation," such as Thomas Handasyd Peck and William Sowersby, "in inviting him to make use of their Shops and Tools," he would be able to supply town and country customers as usual. [12]

As one of the principal centers of the colonial fur trade, Charles Town naturally encouraged the hat industry. As early as 1746 the law was being defied in the southern metropolis where hatmaking was one of the very few crafts to succeed. Alexander Doyle went there from Philadelphia in 1755 to manufacture and "sell the best of Beaver Hats" in a Broad Street shop. Soon he found he had to compete with Motte and Snowden, local artisans, but all went well, at least as far as his business was concerned, for his troubles were of a personal nature—he was forced to announce in the public press that his wife, Hannah Doyle, had eloped from his bed and board, and the maddened hatter warned everyone not to give her any credit after August 11. In the seventies the partnership of Richard Harleston, from London, and Charles Roberts, from Philadelphia, became Charles Town's leading fabricators of beavers. [13]

Between 1743 and 1766, Manhattan, the other great center of the fur trade, granted freedoms to twenty-one hatters to practice their trade. Of these, Nesbit Deane, who emigrated from Dublin in 1765, was notable for his merchandising. He advertised regularly in Manhattan newspapers and, in 1771, boasted that his hats exceeded the imported article in "Fineness, Cut, Colour, and Cock, and also, by a Method peculiar to himself," turned rain and prevented "the Sweat of the Head damaging the Crown." At this time he commenced purchasing his beaver at the great Montreal fur market and established a branch at Albany to vend his hats.[14]

But in the manufacture of hats, as in so many other crafts, Philadelphia led all the cities. Its foremost hatter, Richard Swan, in 1767 received the dubious tribute of being mercilessly lampooned in the first native comic opera, *The Disappointment, or the Force of Credulity*. The 1774 tax assessment listed forty-three master hatters, thirteen of whom owned servants, giving point to General Gage's fear "that Foundations are laid in Philadelphia, that must create Jealousy in an Englishman." [15]

One of the most extensive occupations in every northern city was cordwaining or shoemaking, a craft that provided work for tanners, curriers, leather dressers, last makers, and heelmakers (Figure 3). Shoes were usually made to order and frequently in need of repair. At first, Boston was preeminent in the trade. John Shepard of Ann Street told the ladies in 1764 that he had "lately employed a Number of Hands from Europe, in their branch of Shoemaking, such as Silk, Stuff, or Leather," and since his shoes were Boston-made he hoped "they would favor him with their custom." Eventually, as we have seen, Lynn surpassed the capital in the manufacture of women's shoes. William Allen, cordwainer of Newport, mended shoes for four members of the Thurston family from 1758 to 1760 at a cost of £308 5s., which was a large sum even in inflated Rhode Island currency. Some idea of the size of this craft may be had from the facts that 271 cordwainers took out freedoms at New York, 1721-1776, and that the Philadelphia tax list for

1774 shows there were 334 master shoemakers, whose output was certainly not needed exclusively for the population of that city and its environs.[16]

One of the characteristics of urban craft development, pointed out earlier, was the subdivision of the crafts, made possible by growing markets and a steady labor supply. Woodworking provides an excellent example of this breaking down or specialization within a trade, for in the city it was divided and subdivided into rough carpentry, joinery, wood turning, carving, coffinmaking, cabinetmaking, looking-glass making, picture framing, wagon making, coachmaking, and a variety of other categories to meet the constantly widening demands of the colonial population.

In the eighteenth century, wood was used as a material in many articles that are today made of metal. The manufacture of bowls, dishes, carpenters' tools, many kinds of implements, and even buttons from wood gave employment to many artisans. In the city, too, coopering attained as great an importance as on the plantation or farm. Every household, for example, had its "caggs for butter," and several barrels for storing away salted fish and meats, wine casks, beer and rain-water barrels. The account books of Nehemiah Allen show that from 1697 to 1758 the repair of household containers for Philadelphians was a not unimportant part of his business, although, of course, it was the manufacture of casks and barrels in quantity for the export trade in flour, bread, and beef that made him and his sons wealthy.[17] Coopering, boxmaking, cratemaking, and like occupations, including the finishing of lumber, comprised the rough woodworking crafts.

The growth of colonial cities and towns stimulated the building trades, in which carpenters and housewrights joined with masons, bricklayers, plasterers, painters, and allied artisans in raising and decorating mansions for merchant aristocrats (Figure 1). Steady work, however, came from the erection of smaller houses for themselves and other craftsmen. Usually the master builders or carpenter-architects were drawn from among the carpenters, and it was they who provided the leadership for the building trades.

Furniture making, both for town and country, rapidly grew into one of the largest urban industries (Figure 10). Even at the opening of the century, the colonies imported no more than forty per cent of their furniture. The rest was made in American homes or shops, especially at Boston. In this connection figures on British exports of furniture to the colonies are revealing:

	Cabinetware	*Upholstery*	*Total*	*Per Cent*
1697-1704	£18,184	£47,441	£65,625	100
1720-1728	5,722	2,606	8,328	12
1740-1747	2,069	6,744	8,813	13
1760-1767	3,983	39,879	43,862	66

It is obvious that importations of furniture declined absolutely as well as relatively at the same time that population grew at a dizzy pace. In 1766 there were over a quarter of a million colonial families that had not bought a stick of imported furniture, and by the time of the Revolution another sixty thousand families had been added to their ranks. Rural inhabitants everywhere made what furniture they needed for themselves, but they seldom sold any of it except in the northern villages; American urban craftsmen had taken over the trade that had once offered the best market for English furniture makers.[18]

New England had, by 1731, begun to cut into this traffic, for she was furnishing the plantation country with "Scrutores, Chairs, and other Wooden Manufactures." Boston joiners shipped inexpensive chairs and tables in quantities to the Chesapeake, the Carolinas, and the West Indies throughout the century. As late as 1742 even Philadelphia homes were furnished with "Boston Chairs." In time Salem and also Portsmouth sought to rival them, but the enterprise of the woodworkers of Newport and Philadelphia eventually created real competition. The thirty-seven odd joiners who kept shop at Newport from 1700 to 1776 fabricated a surplus of tables, cabinets, desks, and chairs which Rhode Island captains disposed of at Antigua, Barbados, and other Caribbean ports of call. On November 16, 1764, Captain Peleg Bunker bought of John Townsend three desks and four tea tables valued at £482 to venture in the West Indies along with his usual cargo of "Rhode Island Chairs" that came from the shops of the nine master cabinetmakers of Newport. New York, Annapolis, and Charles Town also offered good markets for Rhode Island furniture. In 1769 the Rhode Island town exported 588 chairs, nine desks, and sixty-six tables.[19]

There is some evidence that the celebrated Windsor chair originated at Philadelphia, but, at any rate, before 1750 it was beginning to be widely used in taverns and public buildings because it was sturdy, comfortable, and cheap. Quaker City chairmakers ultimately beat the Yankees at their own game and sold quantities of Windsor chairs at Boston and Salem as well as to the southward. In 1769 they disposed of 768 Windsor chairs, in addition to other furniture, in other colonies. Success, as always, bred competition, and John Kelso and Adam Galer, who had served "A regular apprenticeship" at Philadelphia, introduced the manufacture of Windsor chairs at New York in 1774 where only a few months earlier John Ash had begun to make Windsor settees.[20]

Supreme among woodworkers was the craftsman who fashioned the "antiques," whose exquisite workmanship quite properly excites our admiration and thins our bank rolls today. In Georgian England, furniture making ordinarily included the activities of three separate craftsmen: the cabinetmaker, the joiner or chairmaker, and the upholsterer. The same categories ordinarily obtained in the colonies, although the cabinetmaker and the joiner were frequently indistinguishable. For purposes of clarity I will use the former artisan, always bearing in mind the opening sentences of Batty Langley's *Treasury of Designs:* "Cabinet-Makers, originally, were no more, than Spurious Indocile Chips; expelled by Joiners, for the Superfluity of their SAP. And who, by instilling stupid Notions, and Prejudice to Architecture, into the Minds of Youth educated under them; has been the Cause, that at this Time; 'tis a very great Difficulty to find one in Fifty of them; that can make a Book-Case."

Philadelphia's cabinetmakers brought their city to unquestioned leadership of the colonial furniture industry by producing expensive quality pieces as well as low-priced common householdware (Figure 10). From the early days many Quakers entered the woodworking trades: before 1720 at least seventy-eight are known to have found employment in the city. In the year 1774 fifty-six joiners, thirteen turners, ten chairmakers, eight carvers, and four upholsterers were listed for taxes—a total of ninety-one. These figures are for masters of trades only; their apprentices and journeymen are not taken into account, nor are looking-glass makers, japanners, lacquerers, and gilders included. Second Street, both above and below High, was the favorite location for the business, which before 1740 served principally the local market of a community whose unparalleled rate of expansion constantly called for quantities of balusters, mouldings, cornices, and carvings for new dwellings, and for chairs, chests, tables, and beds to furnish them.[21]

Using walnut, supplemented by "choice curl'd maple," cedar, and cherry woods, Philadelphia joiners from 1730 until about 1750 made furniture of the Queen Anne style, a mode lacking the elaborate carving, veneering, and gilding so fashionable in contemporary England. Cabinetwork and chairs were manufactured in imitation of imported pieces or after designs prepared by members of the gentry. No fixed patterns guided craftsmen at this stage, although they were thoroughly familiar with such classical elements as mouldings, beadings, columns, and capitols, as well as the egg-and-dart motive, by 1738. The cabriole leg appeared in 1742. Nine years before the publication of Chippendale's *Director*, Quaker City carvers produced ball-and-claw feet. During these years, too, artisans established a tradition of fashioning furniture of superior design and workmanship. It was, moreover, durable. Josiah Claypoole warranted his work for seven years, "the ill usage of careless Servants only excepted." By the mid-century, Philadelphia had a corps of artisans possessing all skills needed to produce fine cabinetwork and was ready for a major advance in the craft.[22]

This advance came with the publication at London in 1754 of *The Gentleman and Cabinet-maker's Director*, by Thomas Chippendale. Many of the plates in his de luxe catalogue were abstract designs rather than drawings of furniture. The truth is that he applied fresh and playful details from French rococo, neo-Gothic, and Chinese sources to pieces soundly designed and well constructed in the Queen Anne and early Georgian modes, which made a great appeal to carvers and joiners at Philadelphia where there were at least twenty-nine copies of his book before the Revolution. Chippendale's lavish use of mahogany also suited workmen who could procure it more easily than could Londoners. Before long Quaker craftsmen worked out from the abstractions of the *Director* a masterly "Philadelphia Chippendale" style that rivalled any mode produced in the mother country.

When Philadelphia Chippendale furniture is mentioned, one thinks immediately of Thomas Affleck, James Gillingham, Jonathan Gostelowe, Benjamin Randolph, William Savery, and Thomas Tuffts. From their shops issued finely conceived pieces in which rich carvings and sturdy construction were successfully blended—tall chests, chests-on-chests, secretary-bookcases, lowboys; card, sideboard, and Pembroke tables; splatback chairs. But especially interesting from our point of view is the influence of the sweet new style in providing openings for woodworkers who had served their apprenticeships in England, Scotland, or Ireland, and the specialization of crafts it made necessary. The highly competitive nature of cabinetmaking forced Pennsylvanians to a steady improvement in techniques of workmanship.

The adoption of the Chippendale style enabled wood carving and gilding to develop as separate trades, for few cabinetmakers were as skilled as the specialists whose services they hired. William Savery was principally a joiner or chairmaker and did not possess a single carving tool. From Belfast, by way of London, came youthful Hercules Courtenay with an extensive repertoire "in the newest taste," which immediately placed him at the head of his craft and brought him commissions from as far south as Baltimore, where he eventually joined the Ancient and Honorable Mechanical Company. Among other carvers who worked for cabinetmakers or joiners were Irish James Cornell, an associate of Courtenay, Richard Watson of London, and Edward Cutback, whose apprentice, William Rush, was to become America's first sculptor of note. Sofas were no longer made by the joiner but by the upholsterer. He performed the entire work himself by employing, in addition to journeymen upholsterers, journeymen joiners and chairmakers to construct the frames. In 1775 George Houghton, trained by the famous Trotter of London, made "new fashion'd French corner chairs, conversation stools, sofas, Venetian window blinds, and bedsteads of all sorts" at his upholstery shop in Second Street.[23]

Although at Philadelphia cabinetmaking became a fairly large-scale business permitting a genuine division of labor, some specialized artisans, tempted by competition, were willing to make any article a buyer requested. The bill William Savery rendered to Joseph Pemberton in 1774 included charges for mending a knife case, globe, and hobbyhorse; nailing a carpet on the stairs; and bottoming a

"Rocking Chair," besides making a mahogany clockcase and walnut coffin with silver handles; on his brother James's bill was an item of £1.0.0 for a "long ironing board with trussels." Similarly, David Evans seems to have made a specialty of Marlborough chairs, but frequently he turned out articles ranging from a piece of cornice for a house to a coffin or a "riding chair Carriage" at the same time that he was advertising in New York newspapers to sell fine cabinet-work with carvings by the noted James Reynolds. Sub-division of crafts and specialization by artisans in one branch were on their way, but the old method of working persisted. The new and the old would exist side by side, often in the same shop, for many years.[24]

The Philadelphia Chippendale School came of age in 1775 when "the ingenious John Folwell," Front Street cabinetmaker, announced that, with the co-operation of gentlemen at New York, Baltimore, Annapolis, and Charles Town, he planned to publish an American edition of *The Gentleman's and Cabinet-Maker's Assistant,* with new designs made in this country. His free rendering of Chippendale in the magnificent case he built for David Rittenhouse's orrery testifies to his competence as a designer, as does also his pulpit for Christ Church.[25] That the American edition of Chippendale was not published was one of the fortunes of war.

Significantly no gentlemen of Newport were listed as backing Folwell's undertaking (Figure 10). Where Philadelphia cabinetmakers achieved great success with current English modes, those of Newport, working in a community lacking contacts with the mother country either by direct trade or through immigrant artisans, produced a striking, native American style of cabinetwork. We have noted that joinery and other woodworking trades prospered on the Island of Rhode Island, where Quaker artisans also predominated. These same men produced superb quality furniture.

The flowering of cabinetmaking at Newport was due to the talents of one family—the Townsends. In all, there were fourteen Townsends and five Goddards, who were allied with them by apprenticeship and marriage, working at the trade prior to 1800, and it was they—Quakers all—who developed the famous Rhode Island block-front style of furniture. Christopher Townsend called himself a "shop joiner," and in April, 1738, he made a desk and bookcase which he shipped by Captain Pope to a friend of Abraham Redwood in Antigua; at the same time his brother Job made a desk and chair for Jahleel Brenton, customs collector at Newport. Job Townsend had five sons, Job, Jr., Edmund, Thomas, James, and Robert, all of whom became cabinet-makers. In 1746, in addition to other commissions, in which he was aided by his sons and apprentices, he completed an order valued at £94 10s., for a mahogany chest, dressing table, two dining tables, a tea table, a kitchen table, a maple tea table, and a maple stool for newly married Samuel Ward of Westerly, future governor of the colony.[26]

Job Townsend, Jr., learned joinery under his father and, upon completion of his service, set up shop for himself. From his Ledger we discover that he fashioned furniture of every sort, even unto a "wigg box," a checkerboard, a bird cage, and a "Wooden Horse." Wealthy Jewish families at Newport were among his best patrons; to J. R. Rivera he sold on one occasion a coffin for a Negro slave and "two Roller pins." Much of his pay from other craftsmen was taken out in trade, as in 1757 when he allowed Benjamin Dunham, the barber, to barter for three tables and a corner cupboard with "A Year's Shaven, a Cutt Wigg, a foretop to the Wigg," and twenty-four feet of mahogany. One wonders if the £17 "in cash" paid by Samuel Casey of Little Rest for a table desk and a mahogany bedstead was genuine, or of the erstwhile silversmith's own manufacture! A "Large Mahogany Desk," costing £230, that Job sold to Nicholas Andrese in 1767 was built with the assistance of

Brother Edmund, who made furniture for such important mercantile families as the Vernons. In sum, the Ledger shows the Townsends as a remarkable family, who co-operated one with another far beyond what might have been expected, even of Quakers.[27]

The evolution of the block- or "swell'd"-front style, surmounted by a shell, which has been appropriately termed "the most distinctively American product in woodwork," was begun by the elder Townsends, Christopher and Job. Christopher Townsend specialized in desks, as did his sons John and Jonathan. The last became very proficient in making shell blocked-front chests and desks. All workers employing this motive received their training in the shops of the elder Townsends or their sons.

One of them was a young Quaker, master of the sloop *Bathseda* out of Dartmouth in Massachusetts, who forsook the coasting trade about 1743 and apprenticed himself to Job Townsend. In 1746 he married the master's daughter Hannah, and within two years opened his own shop at Easton's Point in Newport. This was John Goddard. Mostly he manufactured inexpensive tables and chairs for export along the coast to Connecticut, and then to Virginia, the Carolinas, and the West Indies. In the sixties, however, he commenced making stately "sweld"-front secretaries and kneehole desks, which were "Costly as well as ornimental" and are regarded today as the supreme achievement of the colonial cabinetmaker's art.

In addition to Newport custom, Goddard and his three apprentices were swamped by the patronage of such prominent Providence Friends as Moses Brown, Jabez Bowen, and Governor Stephen Hopkins. Moses Brown scolded him with Quaker heat on October 3, 1763, for delaying delivery of a table and "Buro," for overcharging, and in general not acting "agreeably" to his promise. The customer is always right, thought the joiner, and meekly replied that he hoped "thou will think more Charitable of me, who have Endeavour'd to Serve thee and all my Imployers well according to the best of my Capasitye." John's brother James learned his trade from Edmund Townsend, and it is evident that family co-operation rather than the art of any one individual was the secret of Newport's achievement of a unique indigenous manner in cabinetmaking.[28]

So great was the need for metal articles in colonial cities and so expensive were imported English hardware and metal fittings that, notwithstanding the passage of the Iron Act, the finished-metal trades took a great spurt after 1750. Such progress was possible because, as we have seen, each year saw the production of more iron. To meet the wants of urban artisans, William Branson began to operate a steel furnace on High Street, Philadelphia, in 1730 or earlier. Stephen Paschall opened another in 1747, and fifteen years later Whitehead Humphrey placed a third in production on Seventh Street, where he made several improvements in the art of converting bar iron into steel and a new screw-cutting machine. About 1769 he went into partnership with John Zane, took over the Trenton Steel Works, and sold most of its output in Philadelphia. Erection of a plating mill at Byberry in 1746 and of Daniel Offley's anchor forge in the city completed the establishments supplying raw materials to the metal trades (Figure 17). Manhattan became in 1768 the only other urban center to have an ironworks within its limits when Sharp and Curtenius commenced casting stoves, boilers, plates, pots, and kettles at their "New York Air Furnace."[29]

Copper, an essential ingredient in brass alloys, existed in abundance, and mines at Cornwall, Connecticut, Bucks County, Pennsylvania, and one near the Potomac managed in 1766 by Herman Husband, future leader of Regulators and Whiskey Rebels, yielded ores of good quality. New Jersey produced the richest ore. At Colonel John Schuyler's mine on the Passaic near Belleville, from which 1,386 tons were exported in 1731, difficulty with water in the two-hundred-foot shaft led to the installation of the first steam engine in America. Joseph Hornblower of Staffordshire, whose father had been associated with Newcomen, arrived at New York in 1753 in the Moravians' ship *Irene* with engine parts in duplicate and triplicate because of the British law prohibiting the export of machines. Lacking skilled assistance, he took four years to set up the engine and had the pumps working in March, 1755. Until 1761 this ambitious Baptist managed the mines; then he joined John Stearndall in leasing them. Ore worth £700 sterling a year had been produced, but in 1762 the enginehouse burned down, destroying all the pumping equipment.[30]

Pressing demands from many crafts for iron, brass, copper, tin, and pewter fittings for their products provided as large a market for metalworkers as the public did for utensils and wares made to sell directly to them. Consequently after 1750 the metal trades developed a greater variety of auxiliary crafts than any other industry. In the cities the blacksmith's art was so split up that a country-bred Tubal-cain would hardly have recognized it. Philadelphia's fifty-two master "smiths" of 1774 comprised farriers, ornamental-iron workers, whitesmiths (who polished ironware), coopers' hoopmakers, ship's smiths, boatsmiths, axe and hoe makers, and ordinary blacksmiths. But there were also coppersmiths, gunsmiths, locksmiths, and tinsmiths; braziers, nail makers, pewterers, cutlers, even a pump maker and a razor grinder. In varying degrees the same divisions occurred at Boston, Newport, and New York, where, as we shall see, curious trades emerged that were unknown in the colonial metropolis.[31]

The bewildering variety of metal trades is, as the colonial press might have put it, too tedious to mention, but by a brief examination of several of the more unusual crafts we can gather an impression of the whole industry. The most intricate work in this category was performed by the math-

ematical-instrument maker, whose art represented a further
refinement of the precision required of the cutler and tool-
maker (Figure 14). William Williams of Boston made and
sold at his shop near the Long Wharf a large assortment of
Hadley's and Davis' quadrants, hanging and standing compasses of brass or wood, gauging and surveying instruments,
cases for instruments, large and small perspective glasses in
ivory, wood, and fishskin cases, plotting scales, protractors,
Gunter's scales, dividers, surveyors' chains, magnets, and
glasses measuring from a quarter of a minute to two hours,
and a lumber-measuring instrument "of a new construction." Anthony Lamb of Philadelphia and New York, and
Newport's Benjamin King, who on occasion made trips to
Charles Town, gained fame as makers of precision instruments for surveyors and navigators. But it was David
Rittenhouse who combined the craft with clockmaking when
he constructed his celebrated orrery, as a planetarium was
then called, inducing Thomas Jefferson to exclaim: "He has
not indeed made a world, but he has by imitation approached
nearer to its Maker than any man who has lived from the
creation to this day." Only the coming of the War of Independence prevented this ingenious craftsman-astronomer
from being appointed director of the first American observa-
tory, but Jefferson did remember him in afteryears and had
him appointed, like Newton, first superintendent of the
United States Mint.[32]

Perhaps the safest way to conserve one's wealth in the
colonial period was to turn it into silver plate. As a result
the services of silversmiths were always in demand, and
several, like Joseph Richardson of Philadelphia, actually
surpassed the work of English craftsmen (Figure 8). Although ownership of a pair of Richardson knives is the goal
of the modern collector, the equestrian feats of a Boston
silversmith have brought him more enduring fame. Few
Americans realize that Paul Revere was a first-rate silversmith and that the collection of his work in the Boston

Museum of Fine Arts is one of its treasured possessions. On the other hand, a distinguished American woman, whose childhood was spent in Paris, knew only of Revere because her family owned several of his finest pieces. Upon coming to Boston, she remarked in a puzzled tone, when she was shown the statue of Longfellow's hero, "I suppose it is proper to erect a monument to a silversmith, but why the horse?" The Bay Town led all colonial cities in silversmithing, and it is only fair to point out that Paul Revere's fame as a patriot should not obscure the merit of the master of them all, John Coney, or such superior workmanship as that of Jacob and Nathaniel Hurd, John Coburn, and other Yankee artists.[33]

Caspar Wistar, a German artisan, who settled at Philadelphia in 1717, was responsible for another phase of specialization in the metal trades. Simple, solid, orginal, and enterprising, this twenty-one-year-old Palatine introduced the manufacture of brass buttons (Figure 7). He affiliated with the Society of Friends in 1726 when he married Catherine Johnson of Germantown and soon became one of the leading colonial merchant-craftsmen when, as mentioned earlier, he ventured into the manufacture of glass. Wistar buttons were so superior to other American or imported articles that they won an intercolonial reputation as the "Famous Philadelphia Brass Buttons," and after his death in 1752 his son Richard continued to produce them.

Inevitably such success inspired inferior imitations. Perhaps, too, they initiated a familiar intercity rivalry when Henry Whiteman, who was trained under the Quaker City master, found it necessary after a ten years' residence at Manhattan to warn the public that, "as there are a great many of the Counterfeit Sort sold in this City, for Philadelphia Buttons, which, upon Trial, has been found to break very soon, and the Purchasers thereof considerably imposed upon," he has determined "to call those of his make New

York Buttons." But reputation tells, and within five years John Balthus Dash claimed to make the "best of French Horns, Philadelphia Buttons and Shoe Buckles." Richard Wistar met the competition of this Teutonic Gothamite in 1769 by the simple expedient of advertising in a New York paper that "he continues to make the Philadelphia Brass Buttons, well noted for their Strength, such as were made by his deceased Father, and are warranted for seven years." Fortunes garnered by father and son enabled a grandson to study medicine. The eminent Dr. Caspar Wistar, after whom the lovely Wistaria was named, inaugurated the famous Wistar Parties, so long a feature of Philadelphia society.[34]

Two Americans conducted another branch of the metal-worker's craft that attracts our attention because it was such a curious and yet a vitally necessary specialty. William Sheward probably sold more of his American-made needles than of his domestic fishhooks at his Philadelphia shop or through his New York agents, Murray and Watson, but Abraham Cornish, a fishhook maker from Exeter, England, whose manufactory was located in Boston's North End, was the outstanding artisan of this exclusive craft. "Cornish's New-England Cod-Fish Hooks" are fabricated from the best wire and "each hook prov'd before put up (which is not done in England)," read his trade notice. He further contended that several years of experience had demonstrated their superiority to the imported article. Cornish's course of marketing his entire output through the mercantile house of Lee and Jones and not in his shop was unique, and it was the distributors who advertised his product in the news-papers.[35]

From metalwork to technology was but a step, as the career of Christopher Colles nicely demonstrates. This youthful "Architect and Engineer" from Ireland came to Philadelphia in 1771 seeking employment as a designer of mills and hydraulic engines, but failing employment he conducted an evening school for mathematical and scientific subjects and gave a series of public lectures on pneumatics and mechanical philosophy at the hall of the American Philosophical Society to support himself. Meanwhile, at a distillery, he constructed a steam engine "for raising water" and requested the American Philosophical Society to judge its merits. David Rittenhouse, Owen Biddle, and Robert Proud reported to the members that they saw the engine "perform several strokes, tho' some of the materials not being sufficiently large and strong, owing to his attempting the execution of it at a very low expense, it did not continue in motion long; but . . . we are of the opinion that the undertaker is well acquainted with the principles of this particular branch of Mechanicks." There is, unfortunately, no record of who made the cylinders for this initial colonial attempt at steam power.[36]

Thus encouraged, Colles went to New York and persuaded the Corporation to carry out his plan to provide the city with water by means of a conduit system supplied from a reservoir with a steam-pumping plant. He was hired at £10 a month to superintend the construction. By good fortune he found workmen at Sharp and Curtenius' New York Air Furnace who could cast the cylinder for his engine, which local judges allowed to be "extremely well executed." When the engine was set up at the reservoir it developed power sufficient to raise two hundred gallons of water fifty-two feet per minute, and only the loss of the city to the British prevented the laying of the log pipes which would have given Manhattan the first large city water supply.[37]

One of the most spectacular symbols of colonial affluence and gentility was a gentleman's carriage, and as men grew richer in town and country the business of coachmaking prospered (Figure 13). It was a trade requiring the careful combining of talents of wood and metal workers, as well as the skills of other artisans; the blacksmith and the ornamental-iron worker assisted the joiner or coachmaker, the carver, the upholsterer, and the leatherworker in building a vehicle upon which the painter, japanner, and perhaps the heraldic-device limner placed the finishing touches. An elaborate industry such as this, moreover, demanded a large investment of capital, and not until after the middle of the century did American coaches begin to compete with carriages imported from London and Dublin.

Major Adino Paddock was the premier colonial coach manufacturer. A native of Boston, he began as a "Chaise-maker" in a shop near the Common in 1758, and the next year ran his first clearance sale by offering six second-hand chaises "under their value" to eliminate storage charges.[38] Approval by the best judges of his "newly-built Post Chariot, Hanging on Steel Springs," inspired Master Paddock in 1761 to undertake to finish any "Coach, Chariot, or other Carriage equal in Fashion and Goodness to the latest Models from England, at the prime Cost there, including one half the Freight." This bid for the Yankee carriage trade brought him many orders for "Travelling Chairs and Town Coaches" from all over New England and "Livery Lace" for servants as well. There are modern overtones in an advertisement of 1767 that he would "Take Old Chaises in part Pay for New," and that he had "horse nets" for sale. Paddock's business was extensive—he made carriages and sleighs of all kinds, he performed work for other Boston chaisemakers whose establishments were not large enough to undertake all operations, and he kept his sizable force of workmen busy building vehicles for sale up and down the New England coast. In 1774 this entrepreneur backed George Hamlin, who drove a hackney coach to any place in Boston for a shilling a person, and allowed him to stand for hire in his coach yard at Long Acre.[39]

Boston coachmakers manufactured chairs and chaises for export as early as the thirties. In 1743 John Lucas left to establish his business at Barbados; until 1747, at least, Cornelius Van Horne of New York sold "Boston riding chairs," while throughout the period Bay Town craftsmen shipped vehicles to Annapolis and Charles Town. The coachmakers of Newport made strong inroads in the Maryland trade of their neighbor in 1765 by shipping numbers of "Landaretts" and chaises with "Bellows Tops" to Henry Caton and other Annapolis merchants.[40]

Philadelphia and New York were excellent locations for the coachmaking trade even though they did not build for export beyond their respective provinces. Thomas Barton, David Swan, and William Tod made good livings supplying the needs of the Quaker City. Tod sold imported London chariots and phaetons, or made them, as the buyer required. In 1767 he advertised at Annapolis that he procured most of his materials from London where he had been "regularly bred to the Trade." Four master chaisemakers were serving Philadelphia at the close of the period. Manhattan likewise recruited most of its carriage workers from abroad. The first practitioner there seems to have been Nicholas Bailey who made and repaired "Shaes and Coaches" in 1740. The rise in prosperity occasioned by the French and Indian War caused a spurt in the trade as the number of carriages kept in town rose from four to seventy, ensuring five master artisans ample local custom. Of these Elkanah and William Deane from Dublin maintained the most elaborate establishment, making all kinds of wheeled vehicles, harness, and saddler's work, in addition to painting, japanning, and gilding. They guaranteed all coachwork to be performed in their own shop "at the prime cost of that imported," thereby eliminating insurance, freight, and assembling charges that always went with imported vehicles. Even so, it was a luxury craft; a plain coach cost £165 and a fancy one £200. So pleased was the Earl of Dunmore with the coach made for him that he persuaded Elkanah Deane to move to Williamsburg when he went there as governor in 1772.[41]

Perhaps the most complex mechanism that modern man has ever contrived is a battleship. At one and the same time it is a floating platform for the largest guns used in warfare; it is a hotel daily accommodating nearly 3,000 people; it is a school, a hospital, a laundry; it is a power plant capable of lighting a city the size of Seattle; and this is but a partial catalogue of its functions.

In the same fashion, but on a much-reduced scale, however, a three- or four-hundred-ton sailing vessel was the most elaborate undertaking of our colonial forefathers. The almost baffling complexity of building, launching, fitting, rigging, and finishing a great ship of the eighteenth century called forth the services of workers from nearly every craft in a colonial city. Shipbuilding is "one of the greatest Articles of our Trade and Manufacture," observed a Bostonian in 1749, "it imploys and maintains above 30 Denominations of Tradesmen and Artificers." [42] Thus, the construction of a large sailing ship represents, as does nothing else, the supreme achievement of early American craftsmanship.

From the Penobscot to the Savannah, in every colony, a certain amount of shipbuilding went on wherever timber grew near the water's edge. One could not go very far without hearing the ring of the shipwright's hammer or the rush of a vessel sliding down the ways. In the first part of the century, the cordage, sails, fixtures, and other gear needed to finish a vessel were brought over from England. However, the ancillary crafts grew rapidly in the great seaports after 1750. Since it proved more economical to bring timbers there, the industry tended to concentrate in or near Boston, Portsmouth, Salem, Newport, and Philadelphia. Thus it was that between 1769 and 1771 Massachusetts built thirty-five per cent of the entire colonial tonnage, New Hampshire seventeen per cent, and Rhode Island over eight per cent; or, in terms of topsail vessels, sloops, and schooners, 411 for Massachusetts, 179 for Rhode Island,

and 147 for New Hampshire. Nearly all of the shipyards on the Delaware were concentrated at Philadelphia or its northern and southern suburbs, Kensington and Southwark, at which in this period forty-seven large ships were constructed.[43]

Two general classes of vessels were built in colonial yards: "Topsail Ships" of various types and rigs, ranging from one hundred to over four hundred tons, for the transatlantic trade; sloops, the standard craft for fishermen and coastal traders, and schooners. Two of the latter were laid down for each topsail vessel.

Under ordinary conditions it took nearly a year to build a ship. Every operation on the hull, from laying the keel to decking the captain's cabin, demanded backbreaking labor by the shipwrights with whipsaw, broadaxe, adze, pod auger, plane, and chisel. Ships' timbers were framed much larger than for a modern vessel of comparable size, and in most cases, along with planking and ceiling, had to be carried on the workmen's shoulders. Because of the high price and scarcity of ships' hardware, little iron was used in Yankee vessels—cylindrical wooden pins known as treenails ("trunnels") held the timbers together. All necessary iron bolts and spikes were fashioned and all screw bolts were threaded on the spot. In contrast with the mighty U.S.S. *Missouri* whose designs consumed eighteen tons of blueprint paper, the colonial master shipwright used few or no plans. After erecting the stem and stern posts, he lined out each piece to fit in its designated place, and his men proceeded to prepare it and fit it into the frame beginning amidships and working toward each end.[44]

Constructing the hull and launching the vessel were but a small part of the shipbuilding process. Masts had to be stepped; spars, rigging, and running gear installed; sails fitted; and all the tasks called "Finishing" completed before the ship was ready to take on provisions and cargo for her trial run—which was not infrequently her first voyage as well. Here it was that the auxiliary industries came into play. So much cordage, "from a Spun-Yarn to a ten-inch Cable," was needed to rig a new ship that numerous rope-walks opened in each city (Figure 16). In a house near Beacon Hill where lines one hundred fathoms long could be walked, John Daniel managed Boston's largest rope manufacture in 1741. Outside there were a walk of one hundred and thirty fathoms and two smaller buildings where yarns and small stuff were made. There he and his workers produced every sort of cordage, white rope, tarred rope, and twine. Charles Town's leading ropemaker was Charles Reid, who lost his whole plant and eight tons of yarn ready for tarring when his establishment burned in 1771. Philadelphia had at least six ropewalks in 1774, and, like other colonial cities, all the crafts connected with shipbuilding were represented: three blockmakers, two riggers, five caulkers, two mastmen, five boatbuilders, and thirteen sailmakers who contributed to the completion of the vessels made by its forty-five shipwrights and joiners.[45]

Details about shipbuilding are hard to find, but among the papers of a leading Newport merchant, John Banister, is a set of accounts for the construction of the three-hundred-ton ship *Leathley* in 1740 that show convincingly how such an enterprise distributed profits widely and gave work to nearly everyone at Newport. Artificers represented twenty-three separate crafts, including shipwrights, joiners, carvers, cabinetmakers, blockmakers, and small-boat builders; ropemakers, riggers, sailmakers, smiths, founders, braziers, glaziers, painters, coopers, tanners, and bricklayers. Ten ship chandlers supplied the nails, bolts, hinges, anchors, naval stores, cordage, and other equipment for the *Leathley*; while bakers, brewers, butchers, and tallow chandlers, in addition to day laborers, white and black, and draymen also contributed to the enterprise. Captain Peter Harrison, who superintended construction of the ship he was to command, carried eighty-three different accounts for supplies and services on his books, one of the last of which was a charge of £10 for the compass, quadrant, and navigating gear made by Newport's famous Benjamin King. In a very real sense, the building of a large ship was a community enterprise.[46]

This lecture was designed to illustrate by means of selected examples the multiplication of trades and the rise of specialized craftsmen in colonial urban centers and to demonstrate the remarkable contrast between the practice of the arts and crafts in the cities and that in the countryside, north and south. Absolute measurement of the growing trades and industries of the larger American communities is obviously impossible, but two sets of statistics may be useful in bringing this part of the subject to a conclusion. New York developed slowly until 1750, yet 4,193 craftsmen were made free of the city from 1700 to 1776. They represented virtually every known craft and constituted forty-nine per cent of all who were granted freedoms.

Freedoms Granted at New York, 1700-1776 [47]

Craft	Number	Percentage of Total
Woodworkers	740	17.0
Leatherworkers	536	13.0
Metal trades	262	6.0
Millers and bakers	201	4.75
Shipbuilding trades	196	4.75
Building trades	155	3.5
All others	2,103	51.0

More informing is the tax assessor's list, made in 1774, for Philadelphia, Southwark, and the Northern Liberties. The total number of property owners out of a population of 40,000 was 3,432, of which 934 or thirty per cent were listed as craftsmen. These were artisans and heads of families, possessing property in the form of real estate, indentured servants, slaves, cattle, or horses, and do not by any means include even the entire class of master craftsmen, let alone their journeymen and apprentices. Even in these commercial centers, between one-third and one-half of the gainfully employed people were artisans.[48]

THE URBAN CRAFTSMAN
(2)

U RBAN GROWTH proceeded apace after 1750 as the colonial economy blossomed and matured with amazing
rapidity. Although commerce expanded and merchants increased their importations of European goods each year,
they never succeeded in satisfying the needs of a mounting
population, and, in spite of occasional gluts in the market,
colonials called for more and more of the products of city
craftsmanship. Furthermore, people simply were unable to
purchase what they desired from abroad, and this condition
provided an excellent opportunity for American artisans.
Many of them, in addition, profited from war orders that
British contractors paid for in pounds sterling during the
last French War.

Attempts by the King's ministers to reform the colonial
system after 1763 brought about American retaliation by
means of nonimportation agreements and patriotic drives to
attain self-sufficiency through manufacturing. It is usually
stated that these efforts to promote colonial industry failed.
The assumption is true if we examine only those hastily
projected cloth manufactories and public spinning contests
in the several cities, or the pious efforts to graft new crafts
on the rural South, which either waned or died out entirely
after 1770. But if we focus on the quietly normal rather
than the spectacularly abnormal course of the arts and crafts,
it is equally true that the lasting effect of the agitation of
the sixties was the speeding-up of a process that had begun
about 1700 and had been accelerating since the mid-century.

The rate of development of already established manufactures was quickened, as by a forced draught, and in 1770 industries were much further advanced than they would have been under ordinary conditions. Concerted political discontent had, indeed, promoted the arts and crafts.

In the two previous lectures I discussed the arts and crafts of the cities, small towns, and villages, and we have seen that the trades flourished as markets developed and communications improved. As the seaport towns achieved the status of cities, the crafts divided and subdivided allowing for specialization and refinement of skills. Now I want to examine the urban scene further and demonstrate that the growth of the cities and the accumulation of wealth and surpluses stimulated certain crafts, and that as other small towns grew they too acquired the trades and division of labor which we found to be contingent upon urban conditions.

The graphic arts embraced a group of crafts that could thrive only in an urban environment. Foremost among American artisans were the printers, who, by 1732, had established themselves in all the larger cities. Besides supplying his community with printed blanks, legal forms, business papers, and handbills of all sorts, the colonial printer usually acted as postmaster. He also printed pamphlets and books on a variety of subjects, often conducted a bindery, and, not infrequently, invested in the local paper mill. But his greatest contribution to his fellow tradesmen was the publication of a newspaper, which provided them with a much-needed advertising medium.[1]

By the third quarter of the century, every city had at least one newspaper, although the *Newport Mercury* was not founded by James Franklin until 1758. Throughout the period Boston was served by four newspapers, Philadelphia by two, and New York and Charles Town by one each. Philadelphians of 1776 could choose among seven papers. One came off the press every day but Wednesday and Sunday. German readers of town and country had Henrich Miller's *Pennsylvanische Staatsbote* sent to them every Tuesday, Thursday, and Saturday. The *Pennsylvania Mercury* of April 4, 1775, was the first paper to be printed with American types, which had been cast by Jacob Bay at Germantown.[2]

Closely allied with the printinghouses were engravers, whose art was in great demand the decade before the Revolution, chiefly for bookplates, letterheads, trade labels, and silverware. Joseph Garten, an itinerant engraver from the West Indies, worked in either gold or silver, engraved coats of arms, crests, and in addition performed "Bastard Carving" at Annapolis in 1753. Most of the immigrant engravers were attracted to Philadelphia. Henry Dawkins, Samuel Leach, John Poupard, James Turner, and Pierre Du Simitière were among the ablest of this craft. Unique as was the collection of "choicest tunes," engraved on copperplates, published by Jonathan Badger at Charles Town in 1752, the chef-d'oeuvre of colonial engraving was the first architectural book published in the colonies—the Philadelphia reprint of Abraham Swan's *British Architect*, containing sixty folio copperplates executed by John Norman, "Architect and Engraver," in 1775.[3]

Not a few engravers, upon receiving commissions to make copperplates for provincial currency, were, like Samuel Casey and Abel Buell, tempted to undertake a little similar work on their own. In 1751 Martin Binsky, upon promise of a pardon, turned over to the authorities eighty-one counterfeit South Carolina notes he had planned to smuggle into Philadelphia via Switzerland, and in 1776 Henry Dawkins, who had engraved the excellent plates of the first volume of the *Transactions of the American Philosophical Society*, was arrested on Long Island for fabricating Continental scrip. Massachusetts was agog in 1762 over the report in the *Boston Gazette* of June 28 that on "Wednesday last a Man pretending to belong to Windsor or Hart-

ford, in Connecticut, who took upon himself the name of
Giles Wolcott, Grandson to Governor Wolcott in that
Colony, made Application to some of the printers in Town
to purchase a Number of Printing Types, and afterwards to
an Engraver, to cut him a Plate in imitation of the Money
of that Colony, particularly 40s. Bills, but they immediately
gave Information to proper Authority, who after Examination committed him to Goal—He has since confessed his
name to be Stevenson, and that he belongs to Springfield."
Some brands of crime, at least, did not pay.[4]

Today painters would never be bracketed with artisans
and craftsmen, but even during the Renaissance the great
Leonardo da Vinci acknowledged in a treatise on painting
that in the cultural hierarchy the artist's rank was low—
inferior to that of the scientist or the mathematician or the
poet—and that he was commonly regarded as a "craftsman-
decorator."[5] In the English colonies the limner, or portrait
painter, rated even lower in the scale than the painters of
Urbino and Florence. John Singleton Copley complained
bitterly of the Boston attitude toward painting in 1767:
"The people generally regard it as no more than any other
useful trade, as they sometimes term it, like that of a Carpenter or shew maker, not as one of the most noble Arts in
the World."[6] Some master silversmiths and cabinetmakers
received as much acclaim as a good painter.

Often little or no distinction was made between the various kinds of painting. Gerardus Duycinck, Jr., of Manhattan, modestly announced in 1746 his intention to continue
the business of his late father: "Viz. Limning, Painting,
Varnishing, Japanning, Gilding, Glasing, and Silvering
Looking-Glasses, all done in the best Manner." A. Pooley
of Upper Marlborough in Maryland was another of these
utility painters who was willing to serve gentlemen with his
brush at anything that would bring in a shilling, "either in
the Limning Way, History, Altar Pieces for Churches,

Figure 10. Cabinetmakers at Newport and Philadelphia achieved both artistry and individuality of style in their work.

Figure 11. The whole family worked at the master's trade, as in this tinsmith's shop.

Landscapes, Views of their own Houses and Estates, Signs or any other Way of Painting, and also Gilding." [7]

Toward the close of the colonial period, however, wealthy and socially ambitious merchants and planters were willing to pay well for their portraits, as Copley himself would have been forced to testify, and, as his economic status rose, the portrait painter's place in society improved markedly. The Englishman, John Wollaston, who painted the "faces" of nearly three hundred members of the aristocracy from New York to Charles Town, must have made a handsome living by his brush. That he was not only socially acceptable but actually took some of the Maryland tobacco gentry by storm in 1753 is indicated by the following:

EXTEMPORE:

On seeing Mr. WOLLASTON's Pictures in Annapolis

By Dr. T. T.

Behold the wond'rous Power of Art!
That mocks devouring Time and Death,
Can Nature's ev'ry Charm impart;
And make the lifeless Canvass breathe.

The Lily blended with the Rose,
Blooms gaily on each fertile Cheek.
Their Eyes the sparkling Gems disclose,
And balmy Lips, too, seem to speak.

Nature and We, must bless the Hand,
That can such heav'nly Charms portray,
And save the Beauties of this Land
From envious Obscurity.

Whilst on each Piece we gaze,
In various Wonder, we are lost;
And know not justly which to praise,
Or Nature, or the Painter, most.

Young Francis Hopkinson's "Verses inscribed to Mr. Wollaston," published at Philadelphia in the *American Magazine*, were better but no more sincere.[8]

The transition of the painters from the category of ordinary artisans to the status of preferred craftsmen is admirably illustrated by the career of Charles Willson Peale. Son of a college-bred schoolmaster who had been transported for embezzlement, Peale learned saddlery as an apprentice to Nathan Walter at Annapolis, and in 1761 at the age of twenty rented a shop on Church Street where he practiced the saddlery and harness trades, supplementing them by upholstering and repairing carriages. "And as he is a Young Man, just setting-out in Business," read his notice, "he hopes to have the Employ of his Friends, who may depend upon being well and faithfully served." Three years later Peale announced that he "Makes, Cleans and Repairs Clocks, and Cleans and Mends Watches," in addition to "the Saddler's Business in all its Branches as heretofore." He also added sign painting to his repertoire, took a fling at silversmithing, and, he tells us, "once cast a set of stirrups in brass." But skill, versatility, and service do not always bring custom.[9]

Young Peale's talent for painting attracted the attention of some Maryland gentlemen, and they financed his journey to London in 1766 to study under Benjamin West, "the American Raphael." In 1768 and 1769 he successfully exhibited miniatures and oil portraits at the Royal Academy, but this natural democrat, never at home among the English aristocracy, returned to Annapolis in 1769. Nor did Marylanders' pretensions to gentility impress the former leatherworker. "If a certain E. V. does not immediately pay for his family picture, his name shall be published at full length in the next paper," read a personal, signed Charles Peale, in the *Maryland Gazette* of September 8, 1774. The next issue carried the following notice in Roman type: "Mr. Elie Valette Pay me for painting your family picture"; to which the following week came a reply: "Mr. Charles Wilson Peale; alias Charles Peale—Yes, you shall be paid, but not before you have learned to be less insolent." Curt treatment from this Clerk of the Prerogative Office meant nothing to the independent limner, who ran his notice weekly until November 3, at which time, we presume, he received his money.[10] Charles Willson Peale, greatest all-around colonial craftsman, soon moved to Philadelphia, where his success as a portrait painter brought him fame and linked his name with those of Robert Feke, Benjamin West, Matthew Pratt, and John Singleton Copley as the foremost native-born artists of colonial America.

A further indication of the growing complexity of the American urban economy was the appearance of craftsmen with new or unusual trades and the fact that there was a market for their wares. Wallpaper became fashionable in colonial cities after 1730, and, curiously, the business of paper hanging was taken over by upholsterers rather than house painters or plasterers. At Charles Town in 1756 "Booden, Upholsterer from London," advertises that he has "several sets of fine mock India paper, and others, for hanging of rooms, ceilings, staircases, etc., and puts them up in the best manner." He also sells and installs "Venetian window curtains," or blinds, which are popular everywhere. Benjamin Russell of Boston announces his readiness to ride out to neighboring towns to paper rooms for gentlemen who will pay his "travelling Charges." John Mason, Charles Town and Philadelphia upholsterer, charges twopence per square yard for "hanging paper" and insists that he will "engage the paper to stay up." By 1765, however, John Scully of New York, who had "served a regular apprenticeship" in London, entered upon the manufacture of wallpaper and borderings, which he hung himself. Wallpapers were made in Philadelphia as early as 1760, and "A new American Manufactory" was opened there in 1775 by Ryves and Fletcher, paper stainers, to "Make and Sell all kinds of Paper Hangings." At "heavy expence" they procured "proper hands" and materials from England to make their papers "excel in neatness of patterns and elegance of colour." Soon a cabinetmaker, Robert Moore, was selling their wallpapers at Baltimore. The next enterprise of Edward Ryves was to manufacture the first colonial playing cards in 1776.[11]

Many other novel crafts appeared in the large cities during these years, such as "Stucco Work, after the London taste," by James Clow, who made "ornaments for ceilings, consisting of foliage and festoons of fruits and flowers," at Philadelphia in 1763, and two years later at New York with a builder named Dobie. Then there were craftsmen who, by 1761, were making the newfangled "Umbrilloes, with Ivory or Bone Sockets and Sliders, and Mahogany Sticks," like Isaac Greenwood in the North End, Boston. Also there was Henry Wright of Annapolis who made his own whips, thereby avoiding "those Blunders which are the natural Consequence of the Ignorance of Children and Apprentices, and the Knavery of Careless Journeymen." He was not in business long. Gothamites were even vouchsafed a preview of Madison Avenue's future in the novelty trades when an ivory turner, Charles Shipman from Birmingham, made a specialty of toothpick cases, walking-stick heads, backgammon and chess men, billiard balls, and dice boxes.[12]

This bustling activity and multiplication of the arts and crafts received much of its stimulus from the continuing influx of immigrants, who came in even greater numbers after 1750. Into older, established trades they injected new vigor and a heightened sense of competition, and to the city dwellers of the Atlantic seaboard they also introduced most of the new crafts. The making of potash (potassium carbonate) from wood ashes was a rural process in which city artisans were vitally interested, because potash was an important ingredient in the making of soap and glass. In January, 1757, Thomas Stephens came over from London to place on sale his pamphlet, *The Method and Plain Process for making Pot-Ash, Equal if not Superior to the best Foreign Pot-Ash.* He then went to Charles Town and gave demonstrations of his method throughout the province of South Carolina. As his fame spread he planned to proceed northward by easy stages, stopping at Wilmington, Brunswick, Bath, Edenton, Norfolk, Hampton, and Williamsburg. The Virginia Assembly voted a sum of money to build a potash furnace at the capital to enable Mr. Stephens to "instruct any Persons who are willing to learn his Method," and William Gilliam guaranteed to buy all potash produced at eight pence a bushel. For some unexplained reason Stephens advertised his departure for England in May, but promised a speedy return.[13]

Although Thomas Stephens had successfully introduced the manufacture of potash in the South, in 1763 the Society for the Encouragement of Arts, Manufactures and Commerce at London sent James Stewart to New England "to propagate the making and manufacturing of alkaline Salts into Potash, Pearl-Ash, Cassop and Marktof-Ashes." He remained in the North instructing with such success that potash became a staple commodity of New York and New England and "a sure remittance" for European manufactured articles. Stewart arrived at Baltimore in 1771, eighteen months after the Society had ordered him there, and notified Marylanders that he would impart his knowledge and also undertake to erect air furnaces and other works to produce alkalines at half the usual cost to those who addressed a letter to him at the home of Henry James. The Society of Arts awarded a total of £894.15.6 in premiums in this unique effort to provide the colonies with a cash return.[14]

So far I have mentioned only the craft activities of one half of the city population. What of the urban woman; was her place always in the home? For the overwhelming majority the answer is yes. Many an artisan's wife, assisted not infrequently by his daughters, tended his shop and kept his accounts while he and the journeymen worked at their trades. But there were only a few occupations that a woman might enter by the apprentice route, such as millinery work, dress and mantua making, hairdressing, embroidery, and making artificial flowers. Mrs. E. Atkinson, "lately come from London," combined most of these crafts when she notified Bostonians that she "designs the making of Mantos, and riding Dresses, after the newest Fashion, the taking in all sorts of Millinary Work, teaching Young Ladies all sorts of Works, and dressing of Heads and cutting of Hair." At her house in Devonshire Street, Boston, Anne Ducray, also from London, made "Head Flowers, which for Beauty and Color surpass any imported." Mary Wallace and Clementia Ferguson of Ireland earned a living in New York making mantuas and dresses after London patterns, and at Charles Town, Mariah Martin, "from London and Paris, a complete Mistress of those Arts," included hairdressing and dressmaking, while her husband, Sebastian, worked as a painter and gilder.[15]

Occasionally we encounter a woman working in an occupation where she would be least expected. Anna Maria Hoyland informed the public at Charles Town in 1751 that at the house of her late mother, Elizabeth Sandwell, she performed "any kind of braziery, and tin work as her mother used to do," and, lest time should hang heavily on her hands, she also took in lodgers and conducted a sewing school for white children. Just as surprising is an advertisement in the *Boston Post Boy* by Elizabeth Shaw, "Shoemaker from London, . . . that she undertakes to make and mend Men's Leather Shoes, in the Neatest Manner—likewise makes all Sorts of Women's Silk, Callimanco, Russett, and Leather Shoes. . . . Her highest Ambition will be to gain the Esteem of her Employers." Let us hope that Saint Crispin watched over the future of this female cobbler! Mesdames Patience Wright and Rachel Wells, sisters from

Bordentown, New Jersey, monopolized a unique craft by opening a waxworks at New York. Their representations of George Whitefield, the murder of Abel by Cain, and the treachery of Delilah inspired an enthusiast to paraphrase Addison's tribute to Sir Godfrey Kneller:

> By Heav'n and Nature, not a Master taught,
> They give to Statues, Passion, Life and Thought.

Mrs. Wright eventually went on to London and European fame as a spy for the patriot cause as well as the talented predecessor of Madame Tussaud, while her son Joseph became a leading American painter.[16]

Many colonial widows carried on crafts formerly practiced by their husbands. In particular was this true of printing. When Anne Franklin, relict of Benjamin's older brother James, died in 1763, the *Newport Mercury* observed that "she was a widow about 29 years, and tho' she had little to depend upon for a living, yet by her Oeconomy and Industry in carrying on the Printing Business, supported herself and Family, and brought up her Children in a genteel Manner: all of whom she bury'd sometime before her death." Elizabeth Timothy took over her deceased husband's paper, the *South Carolina Gazette*, in 1739; Jonas Green's widow, Anne Catherine, conducted the *Maryland Gazette* from 1767 to 1776; and, after the death of her husband in 1773, Clementina Rind ran the *Virginia Gazette* for a time. On two occasions William Goddard turned over newspapers to his womenfolk: the *Providence Gazette* to his mother Sarah Goddard in 1765; and the *Maryland Journal* of Baltimore to his sister Mary Katharine in 1775.[17]

In general, the arts and crafts, like so many other avenues to a comfortable living, were closed to the women of the colonies. Many of them were driven more by "necessity" into the world's oldest profession than by "the badness of their hearts," as prosperous, virtuous women charged, asserted "Eliza" in the *South Carolina Gazette*. Viewing their opinion with scorn, she pointed out that millinery work and staymaking, trades suitable for women, were all in the hands of men. This is the real cause for prostitution, protested Eliza. "Were there a probability of women of small fortunes and genteel education to gain a subsistence, . . . we would not see one tenth part of those poor wretches, who are constantly parading this populous town." [18]

One of the most significant and interesting aspects of the maturing of colonial society was the emergence of secondary towns to serve hinterland areas distant from the large cities. With one exception, these communities, several of which grew into small cities before the Revolution, were seaports, and their histories parallel those of the urban centers I have been discussing. Most of them were situated in the North, especially in New England where agricultural opportunities were few and overpopulation had first developed. New Haven with a population of over eight thousand was the largest, but Portsmouth, Marblehead, Salem, Providence, and New London each contained about five thousand people at the outbreak of the Revolution. Rumors circulated at Newport that Salem was a very rich town, with more than £100,000 out at interest.[19] To the southward Norfolk and Baltimore were growing and faced a prosperous future as Maryland and Virginia turned more and more to the grain trade with the West Indies. An investigation of the rise of three of these small cities will serve to illustrate the general trend.

Portsmouth, with its excellent landlocked harbor near the mouth of the Piscataqua River, was the entrepôt for all New Hampshire, as well as its capital. Early in the eighteenth century it became the principal port from which masts and spars for the Royal Navy were annually exported in the great mast fleet and also the lumber mart of New England. Besides, the Pepperells, Frosts, and Atkinsons maintained a large fishing fleet to supply bank cod for a lucrative trade to

Spain, Portugal, and the Caribbean. Shipbuilding naturally developed into a major industry along the Piscataqua, and between 1765 and 1773 the small city enjoyed a veritable boom. Sixteen topsail vessels and twenty-nine sloops or schooners slid down the ways in 1769; in 1771, fifteen and forty of each. At this time the Portsmouth area produced a total of 147 vessels with a tonnage of 9,614, or seventeen per cent of the entire colonial output of ships. This was an achievement exceeded only by the great province of Massachusetts Bay.[20]

Portsmouth's foremost shipbuilder was Colonel George Boyd whose yard was at the North Mill Pond. According to his experience, it took an entire year to construct a staunch ship, the timber for which had to be cut in the fall if the vessel were to be built the following summer. On July 5, 1773, he had seven ships on the stocks at once, and on the average he produced ten new ones each year. Although he frequently failed "to get to windward" of his correspondents, he did succeed in sending off nine ships between November 1, 1773, and March 4, 1774. A self-made man, known as the "Portsmouth Croesus," Boyd rose from the foremanship of Myrick's ropewalk to be master of "White Village" and its lovely gardens—the show place of the city. The *New Hampshire Gazette*'s account of the colonel, printed as he sailed for England in 1774, described him as the builder of more vessels than any other man in the province—"no less than 12 Ships and 2 Brigs within a Year past. It may be said . . . that he is the most lucky Genius of the present Day in the mercantile Way." I wonder what Captain Archibald MacPhaedris, Sir William Pepperell, John Langdon, and other Piscataqua shipbuilders thought of this "profile"! [21]

The demands of shipbuilding, the lumber and mast traffic, and the town's foreign commerce produced an increase of population, which numbered 4,590 by 1744. Many people engaged in trades ancillary to shipbuilding. Elisha

Holbrook moved his sail loft from Kittery to Portsmouth where he purchased a quarter of an acre of land containing a dwelling, a small barn, and sail loft. William Hopkins was but one of several blockmakers in town. Portsmouth supported numerous ropewalks, such as John Clapham's well-equipped establishment at the North End, operated with a Negro slave, Colonel Boyd's walk, and those of John Langdon and Richard Winter (Figure 16). From Samuel Dennett's blacksmithing forge at Kittery came winding anchors, chain plates, ring bolts, caulking irons, gimbals, tackle hooks, and "rudder irons" for new ships. Before the Revolution, despite the rapid growth of crafts in the town and nearby villages, New Hampshire artisans were unable to produce the quantities of hemp, cordage, iron, and canvas needed at the shipyards, and most ship chandlery had to be imported at very high prices from English firms such as Cruger and Mallard of Bristol, or Lane, Son, and Fraser of London whose wares proved far superior in quality to domestic work.[22]

Other craftsmen opened shops to meet the requirements of the growing community. The majority of them were local or country-bred folk, although a number of journeymen who had learned their trades in Boston, and occasionally in Europe, began to advertise in the *New Hampshire Gazette* founded in 1756 by Daniel Fowle, who was himself from the Bay Town. A second paper, the *Portsmouth Mercury*, had a brief career from 1765 to 1767. An extensive furniture industry grew up at Portsmouth; in 1771 its cabinetmakers shipped out to the West Indies 562 chairs, 103 desks, thirty-five tables, and nine cases of drawers. These 709 pieces were fifty per cent more than the exports of Philadelphia, its nearest competitor. The clothing trades seem also to have prospered. In the seventies three hatters, William Douglas from Boston, James Gronard, and James Beck, were busy making the "Bever, Beveritt, Castor and Felt Hats" they sold along with those imported. Several fulling and dyeing establishments sprang up to process the large quantities of woolen and linen cloth woven by the Scotch-Irish workers of the New Hampshire countryside. John Hickey guaranteed in 1771 to "Dye and Press Homespun Cloth" as cheaply as it was done at Kittery or Stratham. Edward Griffiths, "Tailor and Habitmaker from London," charged £1 8s. for a suit, but a native, Christopher Faxon, would make one for sixteen shillings in cash or country pay (Figure 12). Portsmouth gentledames had no cause to shop in Boston when William Warden fashioned stays of the latest London mode, "either turn'd, plain, back thread, or French Hips," at Griffiths' King Street tailoring shop.[23]

Artisans in the metal trades soon competed for a market hitherto supplied from abroad via Boston. Near the Mill Dam, Richard Cotter, cutler, ground razors, made or mended locks, and advertised to do "various other small Jobbs in the Iron Way," and Thomas Conner performed tinner's and brazier's work. Although very little pewter was made in the colonies, John Gooch produced plates, basins, porringers, and exchanged new pewter for old "at the Halves" (Figure 9). The growing prosperity of the New Hampshire capital was attested by the presence of two watchmakers and three silversmiths.[24]

Any community ruled by such a wealthy oligarchy as that formed by the Atkinsons, Jaffreys, and Meserves, and headed by genteel John Wentworth, would patronize luxury crafts. These families supported peruke makers and hairdressers, like substantial Isaac Williams, who kept two apprentices, paid nearby farmers fancy prices for "good live Horse Hair," and was not in the least disturbed by the competition offered when William Knight left the Thames for the Piscataqua in 1773. Erection at this time of many of the elegant mansions for which the town is famous provided constant employment for such painters and gilders as George Doig from London and Thomas Warren, late of

Boston. Each drew coats of arms also, and the latter painted carpets and floors in imitation of carpets. By the outbreak of the War for Independence, although its craftsmen could not supply every article needed, Portsmouth had made a good beginning in many trades and was on the verge of training native artisans to supply the back country.[25]

The rise of Providence from a tiny country village to a city of over four thousand people in 1774 was in large measure the achievement of the driving energies of the Brown family. Beginning about 1720, James Brown and his brother Obadiah embarked on the career that was to make them and their descendants the outstanding business family in American history. The key to their success was commerce, but they also established certain crafts that enabled them to freight their vessels with local cargoes. A rum distillery to furnish his captains with currency for the African traffic was operated by Nicholas Brown. As early as 1736 Thomas Harding, Providence blacksmith, forged "35 pare of hand coofs" for John Brown's sloop *Mary*, bound on a slaving voyage to the Guinea coast. In 1765 the brothers opened the Hope furnace, and within three years Nicholas Brown and Company was sending pots, kettles, and ashpans to Nantucket, Norwich, and New York, as well as to Dominica and Surinam.[26]

The Browns and other Providence merchants entered upon whaling, and in 1753 Obadiah Brown established a spermaceti candleworks at Tockwotton, near Providence, under the management of Benjamin Crabb. When he proved unsatisfactory, Brown, working out the process for himself, produced 300 barrels for the first year. In addition to the head matter brought in by Narragansett Bay whalers, the Browns purchased large quantities from Joseph and William Rotch of Nantucket and New Bedford. Providence candles were famous up and down the coast, and were sold in large quantities at New York, Philadelphia, Charles

Town, and the ports of the West Indies, because of their superior quality.

In 1761 Obadiah Brown and Company and in 1763 Nicholas Brown and Company were the leading firms in the "United Company of Spermaceti Candlers," an organization of the principal candle manufacturers of Boston, Newport, Providence, New York, and Philadelphia. It allocated set proportions of the annual supply of head matter to each firm and fixed the price at which the members would purchase it from the whalers. The importance of the Browns in this arrangement is indicated by their allotment of twenty out of each one hundred barrels. So well kept were the secrets of candlemaking that they were not known on Nantucket until 1772! [27]

The Powers, Tillinghast, Hopkins, and other families followed the mercantile lead of the Browns by sending out ships to traffic with rum from their own distilleries, put up in casks made in their own cooperages. Shipbuilding naturally developed in a community so near the supply of timber and so devoted to the sea that by 1764 it kept forty vessels running to the West Indies and fourteen coasters in service. Many of the first ships owned by the Browns were built at Roger Kinnicutt's yard, and in 1740 John Banister of Newport had Benjamin Darling build a three-hundred-ton ship for the London trade.[28]

Sensing that the location of Providence at the head of Narragansett Bay, with ready access to the back country of Rhode Island and southern Massachusetts by way of the Blackstone Valley, held out a promising future, many journeymen moved up from Newport to try their luck as master craftsmen. Elias Callender opened a goldsmith's business; Benjamin Bagnall, Jr., and John Easton entered into clock and watch making, advising the townspeople that it would no longer be necessary to send their timepieces away for cleaning or repairing. Local gunsmiths began to manufacture excellent firearms for which there was soon to be great demand. Cornelius Cooper, brushmaker, on the west side of the Great Bridge, paid ready money for hogs' bristles and also was the first New Englander to make "Spit Blacking Balls for Shoes and Boots." [29]

Providence craftsmen soon competed with Newport in the carriage export trade, although they never excelled, if they equalled, the quality work of the Townsends and Goddards (Figure 13). New York was the best outlet for vehicles made by George Whipple. In 1764 he shipped five chaises and chairs to Manhattan, and the next year he dispatched to Anne Devisme three riding chairs and two desks at the same time that he billed Nicholas Carmer for seventeen maple desks and three vehicles—"to 1 Riding Cheear which you Sold to a man that Run away which you have not credited my Account with." In 1757 Gershom Carpenter, Grindall Rawson, Benjamin Hunt, John Power, Phillip Potter, and Joseph Sweeting, all joiners, drew up standard prices for their cabinetwork—for a case of lock drawers, £33; for a plain desk, £45; for a desk with two tiers of drawers, £55; for a maple or walnut highboy, £70; for a bedstead with high posts, £12; for a mahogany highboy, £100; for a highboy with crown and claw feet, £150— all in inflated Rhode Island currency and considerably lower than those prevailing at Newport. [30]

On the other hand, the leading Rhode Island pewterer, Joseph Belcher, as well as many other Newport craftsmen, advertised in the *Providence Gazette* that not only were his wares cheaper than those procured at Boston, but that he also carried on the brazier's and founder's business at his Thames Street shop (Figure 9). Indeed, the growth of Providence threatened Newport's very existence and started a prolonged economic struggle in which the eventual victory of Providence was clearly portended in 1770 when the Browns succeeded in having the newly established Rhode Island College moved there from Warren. The progress of Providence, "which was the other day but a straggling vil-

lage, [yet] does now bid fair to rival this town in great-
ness," impressed even Bostonians.[31]

On what was Pennsylvania's eighteenth-century frontier,
there occurred a phenomenon entirely different from that
observable in the appearance of secondary seaports—this
was the rise of the first large inland city in America. Lancaster, located on the unnavigable Conestoga Creek, sixty-
three miles inland from Philadelphia, owed its remarkable
expansion not to seaborne commerce, but to the steady improvement of inland transportation, to the westward-
retreating beaver, and to the unceasing immigration of the
period. The surrounding country, rich with iron ore and
limestone deposits, attracted German newcomers, many of
whom were imaginative and highly skilled artisans. Here
the metal trades centered to supply the companies of Shippen and Lawrence, Levy and Franks, and Wharton, Bayn-
ton, and Morgan with articles needed in the Indian trade.
Scotch-Irish and Palatine settlers streaming through the
town on their way southwestward to the Valley of Virginia
or the Carolina Piedmont created a new and more permanent market for potters, furniture makers, weavers, saddlers, and allied craftsmen.

Founded in 1730, by the close of the era Lancaster had
600 houses and a population of between four and five thousand, mostly Swiss and German artisans, whose destinies and
cultural life, as one might expect, were directed by a few
native Pennsylvania and Scotch-Irish families headed by
Edward Shippen and the Reverend Thomas Barton.

"Lancaster is a growing town and making money," declared Thomas Pownall during a visit in 1754. "A manufactory here of saddles and pack saddles, also of guns."
Each of these industries drew its support from the fur trade,
at least until the end of the French and Indian War.
Leatherworkers were kept busy fashioning saddles for the
pack horses that carried the traders' goods over the moun-
tains to the Ohio country, and when the beaver trade

slackened they made saddles, shoes, and harness for the pioneers. The leather trades employed more artisans than any other; in 1773 thirty shoemakers, ten tanners, seven saddlers, five skinners, two saddletree makers, and one boot-maker were on the Lancaster tax list—a total of fifty-five master craftsmen, who doubtless had many journeymen and apprentices working for them.[32]

From the earliest days the German residents of Lancaster wove quantities of cloth from the wool and flax raised in the country. Weaving, of course, was a rural household activity, but contrary to what one might expect, as the community became more urbanized, the industry grew rapidly, so great was the need of emigrating settlers for clothing to take to the back country. Nearly every kind of domestic textile was produced in the town—stockings, shirts, sheeting, blankets, and even curtains.

The coinciding of three factors produced a boom in the cloth trades: the marked improvement of county highways that made Lancaster a great trading center after 1764; the westward movement; and the intercolonial effort to encourage domestic manufactures. "Such a spirit of Industry prevails among the inhabitants of the Town of Lancaster," stated New York and Philadelphia papers of June, 1770, "that upwards of 27,739 Yards of Linens, Stuff, etc., have been manufactured" during the past year, and stuffs for 8,000 more are in the looms. Fear of taxation, moreover, prevented all the output from being reported. Of one Lancaster dame it was said that "although she has the care of one of the genteelest and best accommodated public houses in the boro, yet above 600 yards are to her credit." Notwithstanding the fact that in 1770 one-third of the households in town were engaged in making linens and woolens, this form of manufacture was rapidly being displaced by regular weavers. The industry also gave rise to auxiliary crafts. Fifteen master weavers and nine master stocking weavers, employing numerous journeymen and

Figure 12. A fashionable city tailor's establishment.

Figure 13. Coachmaking was an urban luxury craft.

apprentices, presided over the textile trades of the locality and were aided by wool combers, fullers, and blue dyers, as well as reedmakers and joiners who constructed their looms.[33]

We are often told that in the colonies the arts and crafts deteriorated because of the corrosive effect of the wilderness upon the skilled worker. In many cases this was true, especially in the rural areas. We have also observed that in the cities craftsmen produced articles which, both in design and utility, equalled those of their contemporaries in Europe. It now remains to point out that the Swiss and German residents of Lancaster and its environs, located on the hither edge of civilization, evolved from inferior imported articles two pieces of intricate craftsmanship representing not a recession from Old World standards of quality and beauty, but a marked improvement upon them in all respects. I doubt whether, with the exceptions of the pioneer axe and hoe, which were also shaped to new American conditions, the settlement of this continent could have been achieved successfully without the Pennsylvania rifle and the Conestoga wagon.

The Pennsylvania rifle (popularly known as the Kentucky rifle because it proved so valuable in the Dark and Bloody Ground) evolved out of necessity. European rifles brought over in the eighteenth century failed under pioneer conditions. Clumsily constructed with bad sights and a very large bore, they also took too long to load. The American solution of the problem was worked out in eastern Pennsylvania, perhaps at Lancaster, but at all events the demand for firearms at this fur-trading depot attracted such expert gunsmiths as the Roessers, Leman, Feree, Stenzel, Allbright, Folecht, and Le Fevre. Swiss Peter Leman made improved rifles at his forge a few miles out of town in 1721, and by 1730 the Lancaster industry was well known in the Middle Colonies. There alone were the market and a ready supply of excellent bar iron and choice gunstock timber.

Engaged in repairing imported pieces in their "Log Cabin Shops," gunsmiths soon recognized the necessity for a new type of rifle that would be better balanced and more economical of powder and ball. From the experiments of numerous artisans, who also incorporated suggestions made by experienced riflemen, there gradually emerged the superb Pennsylvania rifle. They lengthened the barrel to improve its accuracy; for economy they reduced the bore by one-third; they made the trigger guard sturdier; they improved the balance; they designed better sights. Strong, graceful, accurate, functional, this new weapon was in a class by itself—it was a Pennsylvania, a Lancaster, product. The greatest single improvement was the making of the ball slightly smaller than the bore and encasing it with a greased patch which, fitting easily into the lands of the rifle, imparted the spin to the bullet. Now the piece could be loaded rapidly without requiring much effort in ramming home the ball. Nor was it necessary to clean the rifle as frequently as before the introduction of the greased patch.

Lancaster was pre-eminently the center of the manufacture of the Pennsylvania rifle, and before 1776 the province monopolized the industry. Wherever the pioneer went he took a rifle with him; it had arrived in the upcountry of South Carolina by 1750. Between 1775 and 1780 at least seventeen master gunsmiths worked in the town. Matthew Roesser, the finest of the Teutonic artisans, opened his gunshop before 1744. Moreover, he trained native-born, Scotch-Irish William Henry, who came out of his indentures in 1750 to become the most celebrated firearms maker before Samuel Colt. Soon after he set up as a master, Henry was made armorer to General Braddock and ordered to Virginia. Following the defeat he returned and resumed manufacture of weapons for the frontier trade. It was not long before he began retailing hardware and traders' supplies, eventually becoming a merchant in partnership with Joseph Simon until 1759. Like his friend David Rittenhouse,

Henry was an ingenious mechanic, inventing a "Sentinel Register" for heating a house, and between 1776 and 1778 giving serious consideration to the problem of navigation by steam power. His gun manufactory was the largest in the colonies, and with his son William Henry, Jr., of Lititz, he opened at Nazareth a building to make gunstocks. During the War for Independence, Henry executed many government contracts for thousands of stands of arms.[34]

Until the late colonial period, Lancaster was the western terminus of the wagon traffic, and it is not surprising to learn that along the banks of the creek upon which it was situated German artisans evolved the sturdy, useful, and picturesque Conestoga wagon which, again, is better known to our times as the prairie schooner. Modifications of the short, wide, and dumpy English covered wagon were gradually made in Chester County early in the century, but the German wagonmakers of the Conestoga Valley built vehicles of such excellence that they acquired a reputation throughout the province. By 1750 a favorite stopping place of teamsters in Philadelphia was at the sign of "the Connestoga Waggon" on Market Street above Fourth. These huge "ships of inland commerce," so-called because of their long, deep beds, with a lengthwise and crosswise sag in the middle to make the load shift toward the center rather than against the end gates on hills, was as unlike its English ancestor as the Lancaster rifle was unlike the German Jäger rifle. Drawn by sturdy Conestoga-bred six-horse teams with bells, and driven by a driver seated on an outboard or astride the off horse, this giant vehicle, with canvas top sloping outward on bows following the line of the ends of the body, was a familiar sight along the highroads between Philadelphia and Lancaster and on the "Great Philadelphia Wagon Road" south to the Yadkin as well.[35]

The manufacture of either a rifle or a wagon was complicated, calling forth the highest order of craftsmanship. Besides the skills of the ironworker, a rifle stock required those of the turner and joiner. Similarly, some of the most beautiful and intricate hardware produced at Lancaster was used on the Conestoga wagon, and, of course, its wheels had great iron tires. Thus the thirteen blacksmiths, five wheelwrights, twenty joiners, seven turners, and other artisans of Lancaster were kept very busy. Additional trades sprang up in the town which teemed in 1770 with the activity of 264 master craftsmen—sixty-six per cent of its taxpayers. Among them I may mention twenty-two masons, fifteen coopers, nineteen tailors, seven hatters, three clockmakers, and three silversmiths. Well might Crèvecoeur say that to the mechanical knowledge of those German artisans Pennsylvania owed much of its unrivalled prosperity.[36]

Evidence has been offered in these two lectures to support my contention that the colonial craftsman attained his greatest development both as a fabricator of needed articles and as an artist with his hands in an urban environment. There is, however, one further matter to consider. In my discussion of distinguished colonial artisans, I have not mentioned one who lived in Annapolis, Williamsburg, Norfolk, Wilmington, Savannah, or even Charles Town. These southern communities are definite exceptions to any generalization about the favorable influence of urban conditions on the growth of native craftsmanship. The factors mentioned in the first lectures as militating against the arts and crafts in the rural South for the most part also frustrated a full flowering in the villages and towns of the region. Artisans of the urban South suffered from an absence of patronage. Poor communications and a widely dispersed population further restricted the emergence of a vigorous and original native craftsmanship. Tobacco, rice, and indigo called the tune.

Such conditions forced artisans to confine their activities principally to the retailing of imported goods and the making of repairs. For example, James Geddy, Williamsburg gunsmith, who kept a shop on the Palace Green, featured in his advertisement "neat Fowling Pieces and Large Guns fit for killing Wild Fowl in Rivers," newly imported from London, rather than firearms of his own design and make. Later, he turned to the importation of silverware with which he did fairly well, although his own skill in that craft seems to have been restricted to the production of spoons. Only three pieces of silver made in colonial Virginia have ever been found, and no native furniture forms, characterized by a local style as in northern towns, were ever worked out by Virginia joiners. The sole trades to enjoy any permanency and success at Williamsburg were printing, introduced by one of the best of colonial printers, William Parks, in 1730, and the paper mill on Archer's Hope Creek that he erected with the financial support of Benjamin Franklin in 1744.[37]

Much the same situation prevailed at Norfolk, the only urban center in the Old Dominion, which by 1776 had a population of nearly 6,000, and at Wilmington and Savannah, the principal towns of North Carolina and Georgia. A persistent refrain, echoing from each of these localities, emphasized the scarcity of trained labor; and yet, had there been an ample supply, they still offered no future prospects for the independent craftsman.

A fair measure of the obstacles confronting artisans in southern towns is their difficulty in collecting debts owed to them. The small craftsman's meager resources did not enable him to give the extended credit proffered by London merchants or local factors and planters. The number of artisans in Annapolis who resorted to tavern keeping to supplement their incomes is really amazing. John Anderson performed "all sorts of cabinet work . . . in the neatest manner," prior to 1754 when he moved his shop to Macubbins' on the Parade and opened a tavern. As a further side line he sold candles and bacon until his death four years later, when his tools and supply of mahogany were put up for sale. Among those who at one time or another combined

the tavern business with their regular trades were a block-
maker, a peruke maker, a shoemaker, a shipwright, a hat-
maker, and Elizabeth Ferguson, staymaker.

When it came to doubling in liquors, lo, the silversmiths
led all the rest. James Chalmers moved his shop in 1754
into the "Great Brick House" near the Church, where
formerly George Neilson and Philip Syng, also of that
trade, not only made silver tankards and mugs but dispensed
the contents to thirsty customers. He left off tavern keeping in 1758 but was back at the same old stand two years
later with the announcement that mine host of the Golden
Ball has commodious rooms, good beds, the best of liquors,
fine stables, and that he continues to perform the silversmith's trade "as usual." One of Maryland's finest craftsmen went Chalmers one better, for, in addition to providing
"good Entertainment for Man and Horse" and practicing
his own craft, James Inch had an indentured servant from
London repairing clocks and watches, a good cooper making
tobacco hogsheads and barrels, and at the dock "a good
Boat and Hands to carry Passengers, Carriages, and Horses
across the Bay." [38]

Charles Town, metropolis of the South, has been mentioned frequently in these lectures, yet it is a matter for
special comment that this city of twelve thousand people did
not nourish an outstanding craft or produce a single eminent
workman before the Revolution. Recently the Charleston
Museum has published data on fifty-two silversmiths working in the colonial city, but the little that remains of their
work is not notable. Such an able London-trained jeweler
as John Paul Grimke soon had to abandon the manufacture
of silver and jewelry and focus his advertisements on a fine
stock of imported English baubles and his chasing, engraving, and repair services. Refitting ships of the London rice
fleet seems to have been the only work of the city's several
shipyards, outside of the construction of a few small craft
for inland waters, although there were many shipwrights

resident there and the finest live oak timber was right at hand. A beginning was made with the industry in 1763, but not until five years later did local shipyards commence to build large ocean-going vessels.[39]

For a few years, 1760-1766, Benjamin Hawes and Company engaged in the business of coachmaking until the competition of English coach builders seems to have been too much for them and the enthusiasm for home manufactures died out. Laughton and Bookless met the same fate in 1771. Only one positively identified piece of prerevolutionary Charles Town cabinetwork survives although numerous joiners, chairmakers, carvers, gilders, and upholsterers advertised their services in the three newspapers. Of these Thomas Elfe was one of the most capable, but his work never measured up to the standard set by the cabinetmakers of Newport and Philadelphia. Notwithstanding a provincial law of 1741 denying a liquor license to any person "bred to the trade of a carpenter, joiner, brick layer, plaisterer, shipwright, wheel-wright, smith, shoemaker, taylor, tanner, cabinet-maker, or cooper," expert and creative artisans seldom found the South Carolina city a congenial place in which to practice their trades.[40]

Colonial craftsmanship came into full bloom in the seaboard cities where a very large proportion of the population was composed of artisans daily engaged in making or repairing goods. Although in the rural villages of the northern colonies the crafts also developed, it was in the urban centers that specialized trades prospered. The presence of many establishments devoted to the same trade supplied the competition necessary to stimulate advances in the arts and crafts. Colonial society had grown to such an extent by 1750 that a number of secondary urban centers sprang up to fill new demands for the services of merchants and artisans. In every colonial city, craftsmen forged to the front as an important element in the economic and political scheme of things; everywhere, too, except Charles Town and her sister communities of the South, they were making articles, especially in the two foremost crafts of the age—silversmithing and cabinetmaking—of a perfection rivalling work done in France and England and unmatched by the rest of Europe. In an urban environment the arts and crafts of the American colonies attained a high level of development, and it is fitting and proper that we should recognize today that this achievement was truly remarkable.[41]

THE CRAFTSMAN AT WORK

WALK WITH ME in fancy along the north side of Market (High) Street in the Philadelphia of 1772 at about eight o'clock on a bright morning in June. On our right the countryfolk have been astir in the market stalls and the tradesmen have been hard at work in their shops since before six and will remain there till darkness brings a close to their labors. Crossing Third Street with the eastern sun directly in our eyes, we come to the door of Townsend Speakman's "Chymical Shop" and almost collide with Madam Deborah Franklin who is just stepping out with some Turlington's Balsam and Queen's Pearl Washball. A few doors along at the New Printing Office, formerly kept by Mrs. Franklin's husband, now representing the province in England, we discover Mr. David Hall standing at a case and instructing a new apprentice in the correct handling of the compositor's stick, while in the rear room his partner, William Sellers, and two journeymen pressmen are rapidly printing up the few remaining copies of the *Pennsylvania Gazette* which is due out today.

Proceeding from this busy scene to the corner of Second Street, we now turn north into the woodworking district, noting the signs of James Gillingham and William Savery. Walking up as far as Vine, we enter the pewterer's shop of William Will, which is both wholesale and retail. His wife and daughter take down from the shelves for our inspection several pewter basins, flagons, mugs, tankards, and plates, either imported from London or made by the proprietor. Next we go into a small building to the rear of the shop to watch the men at work (Figure 9). Mr. Will is seated before a bench assembling the several parts of a tankard; an apprentice wearily cranks the great wheel that turns the lathe at which one of the master's sons is polishing a napkin ring; another apprentice is rolling a plate mould as he pours in the hot metal; and over by the forge a journeyman is carefully pouring pewter into a small mould, a task requiring all his skill.

Leaving this place and strolling east on Vine Street, then south on Front, we pause momentarily before a tinner's shop, at the Sign of the Funnel (Figure 11). The day is so warm that the entire front of the establishment has been opened by removing the windows, thus affording a full view of the interior. This too is a family business; there at the right are the mother and daughter industriously shining tinware by hand as the father and two boys cut, hammer, and file sheet metal for funnels and tinplates. Farther down the street between Arch and Market opposite Combe's Alley, we walk into the exclusive tailoring establishment of Paton and Letts, formerly of London (Figure 12). On a great table by the window, four needleworkers are sitting "tailor fashion" sewing garments; over at the fireplace a lad is heating irons; at a small table Mr. Paton is cutting out a pair of silk knee breeches, while Mr. Michael Hillegas, elegant proprietor of the nearby music store, is standing before a mirror somewhat self-consciously as Mr. Letts measures him for a handsome new waistcoat.

Thus we see that, but for a few noteworthy exceptions, colonial arts and crafts belonged in the economic category known today as small business. The basic industrial unit was the family, and success or failure in a given trade depended entirely upon its head, the master craftsman that conducted the business. He it was who opened and operated the shop, who purchased tools and raw materials, designed the product, instructed the apprentices, supervised journeymen, procured commissions for work, and who sold ready-made goods over the counter. The quality of the workmanship and the materials, every step in the manufacturing process, and all dealings outside the shop were his responsibility. Charged with the proper conduct of his trade in all its phases, the master was responsible also for the education, housing, feeding, and clothing of his apprentices, and customarily for the boarding and lodging of journeymen, as well as for the health, comfort, and moral welfare of his entire household. It is no wonder then that, despite the small scale of the average undertaking, nearly as many artisans proved inadequate to the task as succeeded in it.

Because the crafts were organized around the family, there were comparatively few differences among establishments in the country, the village, or the city. Such as existed were more in degree than in kind. In rural or village communities, the artisan was usually something of a farmer; in consequence, he owned his house rather than rented it, and it was apt to be much larger than that of the urban worker. Space being no great consideration, he frequently maintained his shop in a separate small building to one side or in the rear of his residence. In the larger towns and cities, on the other hand, the craftsman lived in a small house, ordinarily of two stories, with his shop occupying the first floor and his family in the cellar kitchen and rooms on the second floor. Nicholas Roosevelt was better housed than most New York tradesmen in a roomy two-story dwelling on Thames Street "with seven fireplaces, a large yard, in which is a pump and cistern, and a garden and grass plot. Likewise a silver smith's shop." A typical artisan's house near the Dutch Church on Nassau Street was advertised in 1757. It had three stories, two rooms to a floor with fireplaces in each, and a kitchen and cellar in the basement. In a spacious village like Williamsburg, Virginia, the tinsmithing business of Mary Stith was divided between the "Forge" operated in a small building on the back of her lot and the

"Shop" conducted in a tiny story-and-a-half brick structure fronting on Duke of Gloucester Street. There were living quarters on the second floor, and Negro Jenny lived "below stairs." [1] Shipbuilding, of course, and other crafts like the metal trades had to be located away from the crowded trading areas.

An artisan just starting out for himself did not need to make a large investment; tools and materials were not costly. Of the hundreds of occupations practiced at London in 1747 it was estimated that eight required £5 "to set up a master"; ten needed £10; twenty-five needed £20; ninety needed £50; and seventy-five required £100. In present-day values this means that $150 to $2,500 would be sufficient capital for a man to enter a trade, purchase tools and stock, and maintain himself until he completed his work for sale.[2] The amounts would have been about the same in the colonies.

After the Great Fire of 1760 gutted a large part of Boston, the inhabitants submitted inventories of their fire losses in the hope of receiving assistance from the authorities. These afford a rare glimpse into the homes of craftsmen and are worth examining in some detail because they reveal not only the wealth of the master but list the tools and materials he owned. Isaiah Audebert, a prosperous cabinetmaker, valued his stock of mahogany and black walnut lumber at £169.12.0, three "Marlborough Chairs" and seven mahogany chairs at £69, and his work benches and tools at £25.10.0. The itemized list of tools and other articles lost by Daniel Ballard is one of the most detailed and complete records of the equipment of a substantial joiner's shop that I have ever seen— "rubbit plains," "Oge plains," "Squairs," "Gimblets," "bivils," "fluting tules," "hinges," "Cumperseses," "Crucked Tules," "Mallits," and many more items worth £466.12.6. At the boatbuilding yard of Ebenezer Cushing and Son, the flames destroyed "Axess," "Adsess," "wipsores," "Orgers," "Corcking irons," "ouers and Bothucks," "molders," and a "Conew" totalling £100, besides "12 fad em of 3 Inch Rope" and other "artickels." One can still sense the poignancy of this public tragedy in the laconic claim of Moses Collier, another boatbuilder: "a Count of what I Lost in the line of Bots and tules and Stuf as near as I Can Cercorlate, was the hole was tenn Pound thirteen and eight pence." And I can report with confidence to posterity that the imaginative workmanship of these tradesmen far surpassed their inventiveness in orthography, which they acquired in the days before Noah Webster forced us all to spell alike.[3]

Most colonial crafts remained small undertakings. One or two apprentices, often the master's sons, comprised the labor force, and occasionally his wife and daughters waited on customers in the shop. Journeymen, scarce and highly paid, were found only in the more pretentious establishments, and, if Philadelphia is typical, only the distillers, tailors, cordwainers, hatters, shipwrights, and blacksmiths kept any appreciable number of servants.[4]

There was always something pressing to be done every working hour the master had. When the finest of the colonial silversmiths died at Boston in 1712, the Reverend Mr. Foxcroft, preaching the funeral sermon, said of John Coney what was equally applicable to many a worthy artisan: "He was a rare Example of Industry, a great Redeemer of his Time, taking care to spend not only his Days, but his Hours well, and giving Diligence in his Business; yet this (as he sometimes modestly professed) not from a selfish worldly Principle, but from a sense of the Worth of Time, and Conscience of Duty; to serve his Generation, and employ Talents. . . . He was excellently talented for the Employment assigned and Took a peculiar Delight therein. . . . He managed his Affairs with Discretion, . . . He was a Humble Man."[5] For the colonial craftsman's trade was his calling as well as a means of livelihood; it was a way of life.

Traditionally the skills of a given art or mystery were

transmitted from father to son. It was pretty much, as I have suggested, a family matter. But, more often than not, artisans were trained by the apprentice system. Promising boys were bound out by their parents to some craftsman from four to seven years, or until they were twenty-one, during which period they were to live with the master's family, be fed, clothed, and taught the secrets of his trade. Samuel Sparepoint was apprenticed at New York to John Yerworth and his wife Martha for seven years from December 28, 1719. During this term the master agreed "by the best means or Method that he can, [to] teach or Cause the said Apprentice to be Taught the Art or Mystery of a Shipwright, . . . finding and allowing unto his said Apprentice, Meat, Drink, Washing, Lodging, Apparell and all Other Things Necessary and Convenient for his . . . Apprentice." At the expiration of his term, Young Sparepoint was to be provided with "a sufficient New Suit or Apparell, four shirts, and two Necletts." [6]

Usually the contract, or indenture, specified instruction in reading, writing, and cyphering to the rule of three and often, in some cities, stipulated additionally that the apprentice should be sent to night school at either his parent's or master's expense. Thus Charles Le Roux, noted Manhattan goldsmith, agreed "to suffer" Jacob Ten Eyck, aged fifteen, "to go to the winter Evening School at the Charge of his Father," and Nicholas Anthony, cordwainer, merely contracted "to learne the said apprentice to read and write three Months Each winter," but John Goelet, feltmaker, agreed to allow Abraham Cannon "Every Winter to go in the Evening School" at the master's charge during his seven years' term. [7]

During the period the apprentice, so runs the indenture form, "shall his said Master _____ faithfully serve, his secrets keep, his lawfull Commands gladly every where Obey; he shall do no damage to his said Master, nor see to be done by Others without letting or giving Notice to his said

Master; he shall not waste his said Master's Goods, nor lend them unlawfully to any; he shall not Committ fornication nor Contract Matrimony within the said Term. At Cards, Dice, or any Other unlawfull Game he shall not play, whereby his said Master may have Damage; with his Own Goods or the Goods of those during the said Term without Lycence from his said Master he shall neither buy nor sell. He shall not absent himself Day or Night from his Master's service without his leave, nor haunt Alehouses or Playhouses, but in all things as a faithful apprentice he shall behave himself toward his said Master, and all during the said Term." [8]

There were in the colonies, as in England, two kinds of apprenticeship. That just described was entered into by "voluntary" agreement of the apprentice, with the consent of his parents. The other was "compulsory." Every colony kept bastards and orphans off the poor rates by binding them out as apprentices to "inure them to useful labor." Under this second dispensation, naturally, indentures did not provide for much schooling or for elaborate freedom clothes. At the expiration of his period under a wheelwright of Perquimans County, North Carolina, an orphan boy was promised a year-old heifer and his sister, a cow and a calf, "besides the Custome of Country" in apparel. [9]

Perhaps the most rigid, yet kindly and effective, application of the apprentice system was that of the Pennsylvania Moravians at Nazareth. A vocational school opened in 1757 wherein sixteen Bethlehem youths were "automatically and dogmatically" assigned to learn various trades, as shoemakers, tailors, farmers, and "writers." They also received elementary instruction in reading, writing, arithmetic, and music; their writing books were inspected once a week. Later additions to the curriculum of this, probably America's first, trade school consisted of blacksmithing, gunsmithing, locksmithing, weaving, carpentry, and masonry. [10]

Under any but an indulgent master, literal observance of

the apprentice's indenture portended a strict regime that virtually denied a normal boy any outlet for his bursting energy save that of hard work and frustrated every youthful impulse. Harsh masters, of course, were not uncommon. I can think of no adequate punishment for the Boston ropemaker who permitted a poor apprentice from the Isle of Jersey to freeze to death out on his walk on a bitter January day. The courts endeavored to support the claims of abused apprentices. At New York justices released James Jamison from his contract with Henry Broughton in 1718 when they learned that he had been "Grievously disfigured in his face and was in danger of Losing his Eyes" from "very immoderate Correction." As in all times growing boys needed a reasonable amount of discipline and had to be jacked up at their work, but apparently the system served its purpose reasonably well, and the lot of the ordinary apprentice was not an unhappy one.[11]

Although the apprentice provided a partial solution to the master's labor problem, only too often he proved a sore trial. Who has not seen Hogarth's masterly delineation of the Idle and Industrious Apprentice? The system seldom took aptitude into account, for colonial artisans were as yet innocent of that modern institution called vocational guidance. Prospective apprentices were never made to play with blocks or given I.Q. tests. Likely lads being hard to find, masters had to advertise for them, and, as those of us familiar with the servant problem are well aware, there was no point in being particular. The newspapers of every community were full of notices of apprentices wanted. In Albany in 1769 James Fairchild merely announced that he needed "an Apprentice Boy" about fifteen years old for his blacksmith's shop; and the same year a Bostonian advertised indiscriminately for "Apprentices. Half a Dozen Boys is wanted, about 14 Years of Age, to learn the Art of Hackling Flax and Weaving Linnen." A Boston japanner sought an "ingenious Lad," and a recently arrived peruke maker naïvely stated that "none need apply but those [parents] who have a lad of sober and promising genious, and are willing to give a Premium." This English custom never gained acceptance in America where masters needed apprentices more than the boys wanted work.[12]

Boys would be boys—even in the eighteenth century. It would have been mighty strange had colonial apprentices not dared to slip out at nights to go wenching, gambling, drinking, or all three. The breezy *New England Courant* shocked many Bostonians in 1722 with an account of a house, not one hundred doors from Old South Meeting, "said to be kept by a very remarkable British Woman, who in the Summer Season sometimes makes her publick Appearance in a handsome Jacket, edg'd with a fashionable Gold Lace, wearing a monstrous hoop'd Petticoat and a Black Hat with a Gold Edging. This little Prude of Pleasure" dazzled the males and had many "Nocturnal Gallants," including "Sea Officers, Journeymen, Gentlemen, Merchants, Apprentices and the like," who danced "Naked . . . with young Girls," even during the time of divine services. Wild apprentices, it appears, contributed heavily to the secularization of the Puritan capital. Sometimes, too, they paid the piper, like the New York lad who broke his arm while out on "one of those disorderly riotous Frolicks, that are most unreasonably practised annually" at the New Year. Down at Charles Town, William Dicks took an orphan, Robert Fisher, as an apprentice, but the boy drank so heavily his master could not control him, and the craftsman persuaded the wardens of St. Philip's to take him back. The miserable youth was then sent to sea.[18]

Whether it was resentment of discipline, hard work, and correction, or because they were misfits, or merely the result of itchy feet, many apprentices ran away. Benjamin Franklin is but the most famous of them, and, as he later admitted, Brother James had not treated him unfairly. Printer Parks advertised in his *Virginia Gazette* of June

13, 1728, for the return of a truant apprentice who "makes Locks, and is dextrous in picking them." A few years later, a New York printer described a runaway as "pretty much pitted with the Small Pox, wears his own hair, and is much bloated by drinking, to which he is most uncommonly addicted." Three boys under indenture lit out from King William Court House in Virginia in 1767 for Bedford or North Carolina, it was thought by their master, Francis Smith, who thereby lost a bricklayer and two carpenters much valued for their knowledge of the crafts.[14]

So acute was the need for trained workmen in the New World that it proved well-nigh impossible to maintain the standards set by the Elizabethan Statute of Artificers, especially the seven years' indenture requirement. Four-year contracts were not at all uncommon, and expediency forced a shortening of the term to three years in a few places. However, the Common Council of New York decided in 1711 that apprentices with only four years of training were "seldom masters of their trades" and insisted upon the full period of service in all local indentures, but this practice fell into disuse by 1731. With less success, the same effort was made in Rhode Island, Virginia, and South Carolina. In the latter colony, too, the law required an apprentice to serve out a full term even after attaining his majority.[15]

When an apprentice had completed his period of service and had learned his trade, he became a journeyman, or at least he was free to offer his labor to any master craftsman who would hire him, and when he had saved a large enough sum he could set himself up as a master craftsman. With high wages and a labor shortage, ambitious young journeymen were soon able to go into business for themselves. Throughout the century wages were much higher in the colonies than in the British Isles, and, although living costs were also greater, all observers agreed that the colonial artisan experienced a constantly rising standard of living. On the eve of Independence, for example, the "lower classes" of New Jersey, "such as servants and labourers, artizans and mechanics in the villages," were described as "very well cloathed and fed; better than the same people in Britain. Tea, coffee, and chocolate, among the lowest ranks, are almost as common as tea in England." When the prospect of opening one's own shop or farming one's own acres was contrasted with working, even at high wages, for someone else, there should be no surprise that the journeymen usually chose one of the former alternatives.[16]

The temptation to seek lands to the westward was great. Governor Henry Moore of New York told the Board of Trade in 1767 that artisans were naturally drawn into agriculture, and indentured servants with trades, when they were freed, took up small tracts on which they preferred to live patiently in poverty, because they owned them, rather than to work at good wages in the trades to which they had been bred. "The Master of a Glass-House; which was set up a few years ago, now a Bankrupt, assured me that his ruin was owing to no other cause than being deserted in this manner by his servants, which he had Imported at great expence, and that many others had suffered and been reduced as he was." The case of James Hartlove, barber and peruke maker of Annapolis, was typical of the trend in the South and not unlike the situation in many northern towns as well. He announced in 1770 that he "returns his sincere and hearty Thanks to his good Customers for the Encouragement he has met with in this City, but having heard of Something more advantageous in the Country he is determined to leave Town."[17]

Craftsmen who needed a "good Journeyman" kept the advertising columns of the provincial press well filled. The demand was greatest in those regions where the trades were undeveloped and efforts were being made to promote them. Such was the case at New York in the fifties and at Hartford in the seventies; it was always so in the South.[18] From January, 1772, to December, 1773, Purdie and Dixon's

Virginia Gazette carried numerous attractive offers for journeymen of every sort—saddlers, bricklayers, cabinetmakers, plasterers, tailors, weavers, sawyers, barbers, chairmakers, shoemakers—and no takers appeared. Charles Town craftsmen played into the same bad luck, and one marvels at the optimism of a tailor advertising in 1758 that he wanted, immediately, two journeymen "who must be good workmen," when all he offered were "the wages commonly given." [19]

Robert Pringle of South Carolina crossed to London in 1746 carrying a "memorandum" to inquire "For a Printer for Charles Town, for a Watch Maker or two, for Ship Carpenters and Caulkers, for Midwives, for Blacksmiths and Braziers, for Sailmakers and Ropemakers, [and] for a Silver Smith." There is no evidence of his success, but he did try to tap the proper source, for it was from the ranks of English journeymen, who saw no opportunity to become masters at home, that the higher wages and better prospects of America drew recruits for the highly specialized or newly developed crafts. Over a hundred weavers from Spitalfields and other places were said to have emigrated to New York and Boston in one week late in February, 1767, and the next month a South Carolina newspaper quoted a London report that "Numbers of our manufacturers are shipping themselves off for the regions of America." Hard times, the introduction of labor-saving machinery, the Wilkes agitation, and the abnormal demand for craftsmen generated by the "Buy American" campaign of the late sixties merely swelled an emigration already long under way. [20]

At no time in the eighteenth century were there ever enough journeymen, even though Philadelphia and Boston eventually turned out more than the local labor market absorbed. The situation of the expanding printing trades was often distressing, for good compositors and pressmen were highly skilled and took a long time to train. Peter Timothy of the *South Carolina Gazette* wrote despairingly to Benjamin Franklin in 1754: "You may judge of my Hurry, when I tell you I am (and have been these 4 months) the sole inhabitant of my Printing office, (excepting a Negro Boy, whom I'm Teaching to serve me at the Press.) I discharged my villanous Apprentice, . . . A Lad very capable of the Business and might have been of vast Service but for 3 years has always pulled the contrary way; owing to an unhappy affection for Drink, Play and Scandalous Company." The only solution was to hire a journeyman printer, and we find the Charlestonian advertising regularly for one. James Davis ran into the same impasse at New Bern, but John Johnson of Savannah's *Georgia Gazette* apparently had the greatest difficulty. From August to September, 1762, he steadily sought an apprentice and then for five months a journeyman, and all in vain; again from 1767 to 1770 he repeatedly advertised for journeymen printers whom he never seems to have located. In 1772, Alexander and James Robertson attempted without success to attract two journeymen compositors to the shop of their *Albany Gazette*.[21]

When journeymen were available, as often as not they were men of poor character, drunkards, and drifters, for the ablest and most ambitious men forged ahead on their own. Journeymen were a well-named lot, however, because, regardless of their trades, they seem to have been constantly on the move. So badly were they needed that they could usually find new jobs if they did not like those they had. Sometimes they had to change localities from sheer necessity. James Gordon, journeyman goldsmith of Philadelphia, tiring of his wife, set out in 1774 for New Haven where he got work in the famous Abel Buell's shop. There he espoused "one Nancy Thompson, (so-called)" on the marriage certificate issued by the very respectable Reverend Chauncy Whittlesey. Ere long he ventured up to James Tiley's silversmithing shop at Hartford and was living happily with Nancy when the alarming news reached him that his lawful wife, with a prior-dated certificate signed by the equally respectable Reverend Mr. Sproat of Philadelphia, had taken the road in pursuit of him. James and Nancy left precipitously, and no trace of them could be found when Mary and her infant reached Hartford in dire need. Her pathetic appeal for news of her husband, who was thought to be in Rhode Island, promised him "full employment" at Master Tiley's if only he would return to his wife and child—minus Nancy, "so-called." [22]

Many journeymen proved willing but were badly trained or incompetent. This was the case in northern New Jersey where, in the fifties, complaints arose that artisans were not required to serve as apprentices for more than three years. The graphic comment of one embittered writer denounced them as being "Rather Jobbers and Coblers than Workmen," and it is "almost incredible to think what a Number of such Insects infest this Country." Apprentices ought to be made by law to serve seven years. [23]

We must refrain, however, from placing all the blame for the failure of the supply of craftsmen on the apprentice and journeyman. Hours of labor were inordinately long. The colonial worker never experienced the joys of the forty-hour week; twelve to sixteen hours a day—from sunrise to sunset—were commonly his lot. Then, too, some masters were hard to work for, and many of those who failed, and their numbers were large, frequently did so without paying off their help. Throughout the southern colonies, moreover, he constantly faced ruinous competition from slave labor that nearly drove him out of his trade.

The Negro artisan, unless he were free, in effect occupied the place of the journeyman. On the plantation he usually learned his trade from a white master craftsman and then practiced it without remuneration; in the towns his master either used him as a journeyman at his own shop or hired him out for stated periods. The former practice naturally obtained in Virginia where town life was undeveloped. Slaves were widely used in plantation trades as sawyers, carpenters, coopers, and blacksmiths. "Though for the most Part they be none of the aptest or nicest," observed the Reverend Hugh Jones in 1724, "yet they are by Nature cut out for hard Labour and Fatigue; and will perform tolerably well." Despite his belief that they did not work as well as Indians in some trades, many slaves actually became excellent craftsmen. Richard Chapman wrote to England for tools in 1739: "I have a couple of Young Slaves, who are carpenters and Coopers, who are just beginning to be of Great use to me." Toward the end of the period the trustees of Philip Johnson's estate in King William County regularly rented out his two Virginia-born Negro carpenters and "several good spinners." [24]

On the Carolina plantations even more Negroes worked at crafts. In 1751 Governor Glen placed a high value on the native-born slaves of his province who had been trained as "useful Mechanicks, as Coopers, Carpenters, Masons, Smiths, Wheelwrights, and other Trades. . . . I know a Gentleman who refuses five Hundred Guineas for three of his Slaves." [25] There can be no doubt of the vital role played by the Negro artisan in the progress of plantation manufactures in the late colonial period.

A few free Negroes, many of whom were mulattoes, were bound out by the Virginia County courts. David James's free Negro was bound to James Todel, "who is to teach him to read the bible distinctly, also the Trade of a gun Smith," reads a Princess Anne record of 1729. Likewise, Ned Anderson was bound out to a tanner and to be taught to read. At Spotsylvania in 1774, Stephen Jackson, a free mulatto, voluntarily apprenticed himself to a hatter. [26]

"The laborious business here is chiefly done by black slaves of which there are great multitudes," wrote Peletiah Webster when he visited Charles Town in 1765. In every common craft and many specialized ones, Negro artisans were found at work. "To be Let, to work in Charles Town, at five shillings a Day each, Four able Negro Men, who

have been used to labour for Brick layers," a typical advertisement stated. If one needed a cooper, a carpenter, a cabinetmaker, a shoemaker, a plasterer, he had but to turn to
the newspapers to find their services advertised by their
masters. Prior to the Revolution at least three Negroes,
Limus (valued by Andrew Dupuy's estate at £300 in 1740),
Abraham (who sold in 1768 for £810), and Joe (a mustee
who ran away when John Paul Grimke hired him out to
James Oliphant), were silversmiths.[27]

White journeymen found themselves unable to compete
in some trades with Negro artisans, whose services were
rented at a low rate. In 1742 a grand jury presented as a
grievance the prevalent custom of hiring out Negro tradesmen, but to no avail. Conditions in the shipyards grew so
intolerable that Andrew Ruck and eighteen other ship carpenters in a petition to the Grand Council invited attention
to "the Great Number of Negroe men chiefly employed in
mending, repairing, and caulking of Ships, Vessels and
boats" at Charles Town, stating that the petitioners were
white men who, having "served their times to the trade,"
now found themselves with almost no work and forced to
consider leaving the province. Before entertaining the
grievances of the workmen, the Council called in the owners
of the shipyards, who stoutly maintained that they employed only their own slaves and in no wise glutted the
labor market. They contended that the complainants were
"wanting in nothing but Industry, and a more frugal Way
of Life," even citing instances when Ruck refused to work
for "Extravagant wages," and "that many times they have
Refused to work at all." The Committee of the Assembly
sympathized with the white artisans and recommended a bill
to set fair wages for both whites and blacks, but pressure
from the yard owners seems to have forestalled its passage.[28]

So many Negro craftsmen had entered the trades by 1751
that the Assembly prohibited any inhabitant of Charles
Town from keeping more than two slaves "to work out for

Hire, as Porters, Labourers, Fishermen, or Handicrafts-
men," and four years later it forbade any master to allow
his slaves "to carry on any handicraft trade in a shop by
himself, in town, on pain of forfeiting five pounds every
day. Nor to put any Negro or slave apprentice to any
mechanic trade or other in town in forfeit of one hundred
pounds." A loophole was inserted, however, by the provision that, so long as any master employed one white apprentice or journeyman for every two Negroes, he might teach
his trade to his own slaves. But this conflict between white
and black labor was not resolved in colonial days, and the
plight of the journeyman was a legacy to another age.[29]

The South was not the only region in which white workers felt the pressure of cheap slave competition. Philadelphia workingmen complained to authorities as early as 1708
that their wages had been forced down by the hiring of
Negro laborers, and Governor Clarke reported to the New
York Assembly in 1737 that artisans were protesting, with
reason, of the "pernicious custom of breeding slaves to
trades whereby the honest and industrious tradesmen are
reduced to poverty for want of employ, and many of them
forced to leave us to seek their living in other countries."
Yet the practice continued, at least at Manhattan. Even in
New England, where the proportion of Negroes was very
small, there were native-born slave artisans like Exeter, a
cooper who ran away from his master at Merrimac in 1768;
Caesar, who built the handsome interiors of the Hart house
at Portsmouth; and his friend "Prime" Fowle, pressman
for his master's *New Hampshire Gazette*.[30]

Since most craft enterprises were one-man businesses, I
must get on with the masters and their activities. It should
be clear from what has gone before that Philadelphia
was the great center of craftsmanship. In 1775 Patrick
M'Robert was much impressed by the activity of Quaker
City artisans: "They have made great advances in most of

the British manufactures here, such as making most kinds of hardware, clocks, watches, locks, guns, flints, glass, stoneware, nails, paper, cordage, cloth, etc. etc." There more crafts thrived and more goods were manufactured than in any other American city. From there, also, many well-trained journeymen went out to begin as masters in other communities, particularly at Annapolis and Charles Town and after 1768 at the rising port of Baltimore.

Philadelphia trained craftsmen for nearly every trade. Southern communities drew on her for many of them but particularly for silversmiths. Arriving at Annapolis about 1715, Caesar Ghiselin was only the first of many who went down to Maryland. Philip Syng and Thomas Sparrow followed him, and John Carman, David Evans, and Robert Mullam located at Baltimore. In fact, the people of Calvert's province so valued Philadelphia silverwork that Charles Dutens of the Ring and Dove on Arch Street thought it worth while to advertise in the *Maryland Gazette* that he could handle orders sent by the post.[31]

Quaker City watch and clock makers likewise went south to Maryland. William Faris, Thomas Sinnott, and Thomas Martin were of the group that settled in Annapolis, and Thomas Morgan, with the assistance of two journeymen watchmakers from London, opened a shop on Gay Street, Baltimore, promising to follow Philadelphia prices. John Sprogell, who had formerly "worked with general Satisfaction for several Maryland Gentlemen," remained in Philadelphia but advertised safe and quick service for those who would leave their watches at the Annapolis Post Office for the rider to carry up to Philadelphia.[32]

Many workers in the furniture trades found their way to Charles Town even though Charles Warham, the first important American cabinetmaker to settle there, came from Boston in 1734. Josiah Claypoole went down from Pennsylvania six years later to make "Desks and Book Cases, with Arch'd Pediments and O. G. Heads" in addition to "Coffin

Furniture." John Biggard, turner, introduced local manufacture of Windsor chairs "as cheap as any imported" in 1767, but the Philadelphia gilders Bernard and Jugiez shrewdly kept their busy Front Street shop, content to use the columns of the *South Carolina Gazette and Country Journal* to notify Charlestonians of their fine line of looking glasses and reasonably priced "Paper Mashie Cieling." Gerard Hopkins was but one of the Philadelphia-trained journeyman joiners to rise to affluence as a master of his trade at Baltimore. At least two Carolina artisans, Edward Weyman and John Mason, reversed the normal trend by moving up to Philadelphia in search of a better market.[33]

Colonial craftsmanship came into full flower in the seaboard cities, where a very large proportion of the population was composed of artisans busily engaged in making and repairing goods. In the city a man's relation to his fellows exerted a more profound influence on the formation of his character than his relation to nature. His success at his calling depended on his ability to match his capacities against those of others, upon quick-wittedness, and detachment. The presence of many small establishments in the same trade provided the competition necessary for advances in both the design and utility of the article. Improvement made at one shop in a given community rapidly became the common property of the craft, resulting often in the gradual evolution of a definite local style, as in the cases of the Quaker cabinetmakers of Newport and Philadelphia and the silversmiths of Boston.

Early in the century, not realizing that competition was the life of trade or that American conditions were much different from those of the Old World, both New York and Philadelphia, being incorporated cities, clung to the medieval custom of requiring those who desired to conduct a trade or craft within their limits to pay a fee and take out a "freedom." Concern over the arrival of "strangers" at Boston and Newport was more lest they become a burden on the poor rates than an attempt to restrict the labor supply. Charles Town, having no local government at all, never regulated newcomers. Actually colonial cities felt no real need to protect their artisans against interlopers as had medieval towns; rather did they want to attract and encourage them, so loud was the cry for their services. By 1740 regulation was on the decline everywhere; even at Manhattan, where it persisted longest, after 1751 freedom fees were light and wages high. Moreover, an increasing number of craftsmen worked at their trades unmolested without bothering to take out freedoms.[34]

Among many of the master craftsmen who worked in close proximity with their fellows daily, there emerged an incipient professional spirit that fused with the age-old desire for exclusiveness (or monopoly), impelling them to form various organizations for mutual benefit. When the century opened there were no trade gilds with medieval practices and concepts to be engrafted on modern bodies designed to answer New World needs. The final effort to set up craft gilds came at Philadelphia in 1718 when the Mayor and Common Council resolved that "such of the Trades or Manufactors . . . as desire to be . . . Incorporated" might do so. Only the cordwainers and tailors availed themselves of the privilege, and their organizations seem to have promptly died out.[35]

Such ideas about association as did not spring from discussions among local artisans were introduced by masters and journeymen newly arrived from the mother country and could be adapted to suit American conditions. The first and most sustained expression of the professional spirit appeared in 1724 with the founding of the Carpenter's Company of the City and County of Philadelphia by James Porteus, Samuel Powel, Ebenezer Thompson, John Harris, and six other master housewrights. One of its earliest acts was to draw up a uniform scale of prices for employees and workmen. At Boston in the same year "thirty-two principal Barbers" met at the Golden Ball, attended by a trumpeter, and concerted to "raise their Shaving from 8 to 10s. per Quarter," as well as to "advance 5s. in the Price of making common Wiggs, and 10s. on their Tye ones." With less fanfare Bay Town booksellers convened to establish "a company and raise the Price of their Goods." In 1741 the caulkers united to refuse payments made "in notes on Shops for goods, or for money," and in 1747 the tanners sought to prevent a rise in the price of hides.[36]

Artisans in the New York building trades combined to protest against New Jersey interlopers, who paid no local taxes, with as much vehemence as the cigarette dealers of our own day but received short shrift from the City Recorder, who termed the complainants "obscure people altotogether unknown to us in person and name." Ship carpenters seeking employment in Manhattan in 1758 found themselves unable to bargain for wages because the owners of the yards had agreed to fix eight shillings a day as the standard price.[37]

A lull in organizational activities seems to have occurred that lasted until the sixties when more societies appeared. The Carpenter's Company was the only one of the earlier bodies to survive. Its restriction of membership to masters alone caused the rise of a rival company, which it absorbed in 1752. A schism took place in 1769 over the differences about increasing the membership fee and especially about methods of measuring and valuing carpenters' work, resulting in the founding of the Friendship Carpenter's Company with the low entrance fee of five shillings instead of £4. "The Society of House Carpenters," active in New York in 1771, maintained a headquarters at the house of David Philips, where the members could be reached by prospective clients. Over at the Quaker City the thirty-nine masters in the Cordwainer's Fire Company, formed in 1760 and dissolved in 1773, were as much interested in schemes for recovering runaway servants and apprentices as in extinguishing fires. The Taylor's Company of Philadelphia, established in 1771, pledged its forty-odd members not to sell under prices set by their body and not to pay journeymen more than four shillings per diem or fifteen shillings a week in addition to board and lodgings.[38] That Newport, an active craft center in an age when all manner of associations were being made, never resorted to any kind of organization may be ascribed in part to the absence of immigrant artisans and other "interlopers."

It is very easy for us moderns to assume that because an article was handmade it was therefore of superior design and quality. Sometimes it was; often it was not. I think a good case can be made for the statement that modern laws regulating the quality and materials of many kinds of modern manufactures and those requiring labels bearing an approximation to the truth provide us with a surer guarantee against fraud than the colonial consumer enjoyed. For inferior goods were made and sold in those days, and not infrequently. Casks of false sizes, made of green staves, were often worked off on unsuspecting purchasers, as were bad flour, poorly tanned leather, and unsatisfactory repair work. Boston officials viewed 70,000 shingles shipped from Weymouth on August 21, 1725, and ordered 61,000 of them burned, "they not being according to law." [39]

Government regulation of trade was not only accepted but expected in the eighteenth century, and both colonial assemblies and municipal bodies spent much time framing laws and ordinances to ensure the consumer good quality and honest weight or measure when he made a purchase of locally produced goods. In each community a corps of official viewers, surveyors, and measurers existed to reduce cheating and misrepresentation to a minimum. Proud and jealous of their reputations, honest craftsmen often took measures of their own against fraudulent work. When Caleb Bull advertised to sell beaver hats made by Jonathan Roberts, "a noted Workman," for twenty-seven shillings at his Hartford store when they cost thirty at the hatter's shop, the master countered with a notice that he had made the hats to order for Bull, who supplied the fur, and that these hats contained seven instead of eight ounces, "the Common Rule, notwithstanding the Fur was bad, and I advised said Bull to mix a great Part of the Fur with Rakoon, as not fit for Beaver Hats—This I am obliged to inform the Public of, to save my Credit." Bull's lame attempt to shift the blame to the craftsman in his next advertisement is not convincing. Although there was far more wit than truth in the second William Byrd's oft-quoted remark that none could slip through a penal statute like the saints of New England, enough sharp practices existed to arouse the concern of honest Yankees. In 1750 the *Boston News Letter* printed a set of "Rules proper to be observed in TRADE," enjoining all tradesmen to "Lay a good foundation in regard to principle," and to "Be sure not willfully to overreach, or deceive your neighbor; but: . . . Strive to maintain a fair character in the world." [40]

Besides fabricating goods in his shop, the colonial craftsman had to market them. Most articles that artisans made were what were known as "spoken" or "bespoke goods"; that is, made to order for a customer. Thus suits of clothes, cloaks, dresses, and shoes were nearly all produced from special measurements; and silverware, fine furniture, and carriages were made on individual order. In rural villages nearly every craftsman restricted his work to spoken goods, but in the cities and larger towns where the market was greater many artisans made up and kept on display various modes and styles of jewelry, buttons, hats, cloth of several weaves, and many kinds of ironware for the shopper who happened in to select what he or she wanted. The hardware and cooperage trades were such that the output was about equally divided between the two.

In the large urban centers, where competition was keen,

merchandising became a real problem. I have pointed out earlier that, in the case of the production of large amounts of furniture, merchants bought up quantities from a number of chairmakers or joiners and shipped them off to distant markets. This was also true of other products, for we read in a *Virginia Gazette* of 1737 about the arrival in the York River of the sloop *Swallow* from New England with a cargo of "Cheese, Dishes, Chairs, Iron Potts, Tables, Cyder, Wooden Ware, Axes, Cranberries, Salt, Cod-Fish, Rum and Molasses," or of the arrival of a vessel at Charles Town in 1741 with rum, salt fish, window frames, sashes, chairs, axes, and whale oil. Joseph Pease Palmer was the Boston agent in 1744 for consignments of Philadelphia flour, bar iron, and leather breeches gathered from several sources and shipped north.[41]

Most craftsmen preferred to handle their own sales and even avoided the widely heralded auction system so much used at Boston by booksellers and others. Perhaps it was because of the questionable practices of auctioneers like Martin Bicker of Boston, who had "a Person at his door to invite Gentlemen and others to his public Sales" and gave "Dissatisfaction to some Gentlemen shopkeepers in particular." William Linthwaite of Charles Town agreed to supply Indian traders and storekeepers with his brass, copper, and tinwares at wholesale, "tho' they take as small a quantity as they please." Enterprising Daniel King, a Philadelphia founder, occasionally notified Marylanders of his intention to be at Annapolis to sell his brass firedogs, fenders, shovels, tongs, and chimney backs, but more often Quaker City artisans depended on the newspapers in other towns, the postrider or stage wagon, and peddlers to dispose of their wares.[42]

In the columns of their newspapers, which circulated and were read widely in town and country, colonial printers provided their fellow craftsmen with an advertising medium of which they made instant and effective use. Many of the

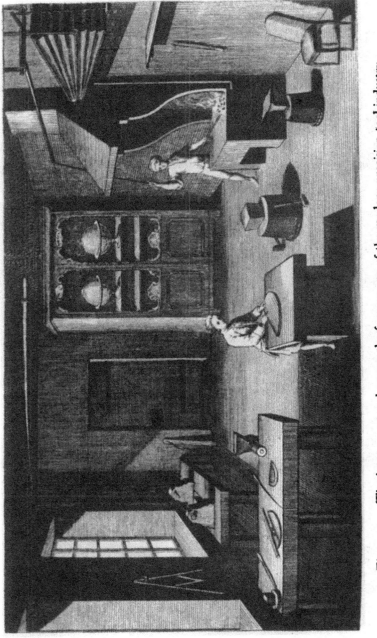

Figure 14. The instrument maker was the forerunner of the modern precision-tool industry.

Figure 15. Urban artisans fashioned instruments for those who "sang and fiddled at midnight."

obnoxious devices we think ultramodern in their absence of integrity appeared in embryo in eighteenth-century gazettes: the misrepresentation, the overstatement, the fake claim, the threat, the testimonial, the snob appeal. Even the presently popular "surprise technique" was in use in 1775 at Wethersfield, when William Beadle suddenly closed a spirited description of his offerings of whale bone, sewing silk, and nails with the query: "I wonder if this ADVERTISE-MENT will do any GOOD." Then as now, of course, truth was not infrequently resorted to as an advertising dodge.[43]

Colonial Americans, like most of their eighteenth-century contemporaries, spoke frankly, often bluntly, when they had a mind to do so. Polite treatment of rivals was rather rare, and plain speaking even found its way into the advertising columns of the local press. To forestall competition from untrained Charles Willson Peale at Annapolis in 1768, William Knapp announced that he had just acquired a completely new apparatus for use in his trade of watchmaking and repairing. "It is with Concern," says his advertisement, "he finds himself reduced to the disagreeable Necessity of cautioning the Public against the continued Butcheries practised by many Pretenders to the Business, whose Inabilities are too frequently experienced by the Employer, as heavy Charges inevitably follow, to rectify the Errors of those Tinkering Performers, and the Mechanism of the Piece is often destroyed, beyond the Power of Art to repair." This sort of wholesale reflection without proof upon the merits of your business rivals and their products has a very familiar ring when we recall such gems of distortion as the wearisome falsehoods in cigarette advertising.[44]

The American career of John Simnet, "Watch Finisher and Manufacturer of London and Dublin," furnishes a most instructive commentary upon the nature of competition in the crafts and of the clash of personalities frequently engendered. Simnet opened his shop opposite Mr. Staver's Tavern in Portsmouth, New Hampshire, and on January 6, 1769, advertised in the local gazette that he was recently come from London where he had had twenty-five years' experience in the craft. All was apparently quiet along the Piscataqua until the *New Hampshire Gazette* for March 17, 1769, carried a notice that Nathaniel Sheaff Griffith, clock and watch maker at the Sign of the Clock, near the Parade, not only undertook to make and repair clocks of all kinds, but would mend and clean all watches brought to him by the western and eastern postriders as well and cheaper than anyone in the country. Now Griffith was a local boy and evidently made inroads on Simnet's trade.[45]

One week later Simnet released his first communiqué, giving his considered and expert opinion of Nathan'ls merits as a repairer of watches: "A Tinker or Smith, near where I dwell, intending to fleece the Ignorant, and diminish the Repute of his Neighbours, has resolved to shew himself void of Grace and Shame, by publishing some egregious Falsehoods,—first by writing himself a Watch Maker—next that he mends and cleans Watches in as neat a Manner as any One in Town or Country, and much cheaper; notwithstanding 'tis well known to the Trade and others, that 'tis scarce in any Man's Power, either in Town or Country, to restore them after he has mended, that is mangled them. Any Person who employs this Watch Butcher, are desired to cause him to write a Bill, of every Particular, and the Price, and by applying to me may have the Work examined, to see if any Damage is done it, as more London Watches carefully executed at Home, are destroyed by People practising on them, than by the effect of Time." After this analysis, Simnet challenged Griffith to produce a watch of his own making "at Mr. Staver's Tavern, in Portsmouth, where some Judges will assemble. If he do not he will be deemed a disgrace to the Art, and an Impostor to the Public." [46]

Unlike Wilhelm Meister, Griffith did not appear with

his masterpiece at Mr. Staver's Tavern, but he continued to compete so successfully that Simnet deemed it necessary to begin a further exchange of amenities by enlightening the good folk of the province in the *Gazette* of April 14: "The entire Satisfaction I have given the Public, employed on numbers of imperfect Watches, after ev'ry other Workman hath either practised on them in vain, or given them up, gives me occasion to intimate to Gentlemen, that 'tis much easier to me to repair a Watch before, than after another has with mistaken Judgment, operated upon it, *and they save the first Expence.*—If I do not my Watch perfect, I charge nothing, and engage to put in order the very best, and the very worst Watches. My Price for mending and cleaning, from as low as a Pistareen. Small repairs gratis." [47]

In the next issue of the newspaper this foray drew an adroit rebuttal emphasizing the native note: "As the said Griffith is well known in this Province, Gentlemen may with Safety leave their Watches in his Custody to mend, and depend upon their being seasonally returned, which Circumstance alone is well worthy the Attention of the Owner, least by a Bait, in mending for the low Price of a Pistareen, he may endanger the Loss of his whole Watch; Every Itenerant, or Walking-Watch Manufacturer, especially those who carries their whole stock upon their Backs, should bring Credentials of their Honesty, before they can be Trusted with Brass, much more than Silver and Gold Watches. Some Men may have Watches to sell, which for want of being known, may admit of a Doubt, whether they came honestly by them." [48]

In the words of Ring Lardner, Simnet "didn't have no answer." The best he could do was to advertise in July that he would clean watches in thirty minutes and repair them in six hours, the owner to be at no second charge to him, John Simnet, "regular Citizen of London, Finisher to Mr. Gray and Mr. Elliott, Watch-Makers to his late and present Majesty:—Also, Finisher and Manufacturer to all

of Note, of the Trade in England and Ireland." In August
he complained that he was well known to be the best of the
craft in town, yet here is a lad, who with others "gets well
paid for what they don't and can't do." Griffith may claim
he can do work best and cheapest, but Simnet will contract
to perform the same in half the time at half the price. In
September Nathan'l said he would repair watches at half
of Simnet's price: "Let him mend as cheap as he will. I am
not a Finisher to all the best original Workmen in the Old
Country; but if I don't do my Work well, I charge nothing." What price watch repairing![49]

And so it went on into the next year. On May 8, 1770,
Simnet in some desperation announced that all watches recently brought to him for repairs have previously been in
the hands of the "best Performers" but are in very bad condition. "N. B. All who please to apply, may depend on
being faithfully and punctually served, with such Watches
as Mr. Nathaniel Sheaff Griffith can make, and mending in
general as perform'd by that Genius, without any Charge,
and Welcome."[50]

On June 29, 1770, the "furriner" (for surely they called
him that in Portsmouth) made a last ditch stand in

A Squib—To the Tune of Miss Dawson's Hornpipe

In yonder *Hutt* is to be seen,
A Hungry GIANT *lank and lean*,
With well patch'd threadbare Coat of Green;
To cover Round Shoulders;
With unfleg'd Chin, and foolish Face,
A Greasy Hat, with worsted Lace,
Poor NAT (tho' in a wretched Case)
Makes sport, for his beholders.

Poor NAT?—Poor Johnnie, rather. For while Simnet won
at repartee, Griffith got the business. With this verse Simnet
bowed out of Portsmouth and headed southward, mumbling
to himself and perhaps evolving in his fertile brain the im-

mortal phrase—Damn Yankee. Between June and August 23, 1770, he had set up shop at Manhattan, as the "original maker from London." A flash of the old fire was evident in his card of December, 1771, stating: "This Advertiser will continue, (far as it may be put in his power) to prevent you being imposed on by apperance, inability, or covetousness will labour to save his employers expence, and gain to himself, and the real makers in England, desires not to charge twice for mending the same watch, having dwelt in this city near four years . . . [actually 17 months!] [51]

While Simnet struggled along at Gotham, what of Nathaniel Sheaff Griffith? He prospered; perhaps having eliminated his rival, he was able to raise prices. At any rate he took on a line of silver shoe buckles, hired himself a fine London (mark me, London!) workman to clean and repair his watches, and when the curtain fell on the colonial period in April of seventy-five Nathan'l was the leading clock and watch maker north of Boston.[52]

Less exhilarating, but of more interest to the craftsman, was the matter of payments and credit relations. From such account books as survive, it is evident that very little cash changed hands in his shop. Money, particularly small change, was always scarce, and, as I have had occasion to point out during these lectures, goods or services usually took the place of cash payments. Caleb Bull was willing to sell those seven-ounce beaver hats for twenty-seven shillings in cash or thirty shillings "Country Produce in Hand." [53] Advertisements of artisans willing to accept "Country Pay" are legion.

Credit accounts ran on almost endlessly, it seems, and it is certain that purchasers who paid in cash were rare. The ledger of Dr. Benjamin Morris, who had among his Philadelphia patients tradesmen of thirty-four different occupations, indicates that he took many of his fees in services or goods, and the cabinetmaker David Evans sold 98.8 per cent of his goods on credit in 1774. In times of stringency

the small artisan, who was usually in debt to a local merchant either for financing purchases of raw materials or for
other necessaries, found himself unable to extend credit to
his customers and at the same time stay solvent. Many
could not meet their engagements and went under. The
situation was doubly bad when it was so hard to get in payments. A Philadelphian purchased £1.2.9 worth of sta-
tionery from Robert Aitken in 1772 and did not pay for it
until sixteen years later! Jonathan Prosser, a Williamsburg
tailor, thanked his customers for past favors in 1772 but at
the same time warned that, because of "Many bad Payments" and the expense of suits for collection, he could in
the future work only for cash. Less punctilious was the
refusal of Thomas Gates at Charles Town to sell for anything but real money, "without which the Game is up, etc.
I Play no more. I am weary." [54]
Credit rather than cash payment was the rule everywhere.
A long chain of credit stretched from the London magnates
to the colonial urban merchants and from them through the
craftsmen to the consumers, who were often themselves
artisans. Collections were slow and credit had to be long
term. Many debts proved bad; in the case of one Philadelphia watchmaker, they amounted to thirty-seven per cent
of his sales. From an economic point of view the use of
credit was indispensable because of the shortage of a circulat-
ing medium and it undeniably encouraged productive activity. But the fact that many craftsmen found themselves in
the status of chronic debtors brought on grave social and
political repercussions. [55]

THE CRAFTSMAN AS
A CITIZEN

A NY ACCOUNT of the craftsman as a citizen must perforce begin with his social position. Historians have recently been discovering that class arrangements—by which I mean the accepted ranking of groups in a community—played a determining part in the history of the eighteenth century. To men of that age, status seems to have bulked larger than economics and, in large measure, to have governed the course of political events. In the American colonies, society was more fluid than in the British Isles; whether they were aware of it or not, the colonists were witnessing the fascinating spectacle of timeworn European concepts of class relationships undergoing a transformation or relaxation—sometimes gradual, sometimes rapid, but always inevitable—which would eventually spell the end of monarchy and terminate rule by aristocrats.

Contemporary Englishmen defined the mechanic arts "as such Arts wherein the Hand and Body are more concerned than the Mind." Furthermore, they used the terms *mechanick* and *mechanical* to connote something "mean, base, pitiful," because the "mechanick Arts or Handicrafts are more mean and inferior than the Liberal Sciences." There were gentlemen on these shores also who viewed the crafts with contempt. In 1744 in New Jersey, Dr. Alexander Hamilton was told by Dr. Thomas Cadwalader that "the House of Assembly here . . . was chiefly composed of mechanicks and ignorant wretches; obstinate to the last degree."[1] During the agitation preceding the separation from

England, Tories and timid conservatives usually ascribed every riot and scene of mob violence to the machinations of "the Mechanicks," as though they were indeed mean, base, and pitiful men. Who, then, were these "mechanicks"?

The colonial social structure resembled a truncated pyramid, for no king and nobles occupied the choice positions at the top. The customary separation of men into "the better, middling, and inferior sorts" was reasonably accurate. Where in this scale did the colonial craftsman belong? We must know whereof we speak. Surveying the years from 1750 to 1776 I find that he will not fit into the Procrustean bed of Marxian analysis which makes him exclusively a proletarian. The fact is that craftsmen could be found in every rank from that of the privileged urban gentry all the way down to that of the white indentured servants and Negro slaves. They constituted a vertical, not a horizontal, section of colonial population.

Let us take a look into the record. In rural areas north of Maryland the village artisan occupied the same place in society as the yeoman farmer. He was independent, self-sufficient, respected; and, in New England, he enjoyed the local franchise, participated in town meetings, and was elected to such town offices as sealer of leather, inspector of casks, or culler of staves. Less favored politically in the Middle Colonies, he nevertheless was looked upon as an important adjunct to the community, while his prosperity brought him ample recognition from his farming neighbors. The few independent artisans of the rural South stood on a plane of equality with the small farmer, for, like the Virginia Jarratts, they were generally farmers themselves. Everywhere the country artisan definitely belonged to the "middling sort" to whom the application of the label "mechanick" in its derogatory sense is a misnomer. Of lower class craftsmen, there were next to none in the rural society of the North because there were so few journeymen wage earners, but in the southern colonies Negro slave workers on the plantations did indeed constitute a large group.

It is in the cities that we find craftsmen in every walk, every rank, of colonial society. The numbers in each of the three classes varied widely in different sections of the country. Admission to select circles was always possible for persons of great wealth; an approved marriage, intellectual eminence, and collegiate training were other effective means of entry, and membership in the modish religious denominations of a community was always an important catalyst. Probably more craftsmen achieved social distinction at Philadelphia than in any other community, for there the crafts reached their highest development and prosperity, and more artisans amassed wealth. Friends virtually monopolized some crafts, as I have pointed out earlier. Peter Kalm noted in 1748 "that the more well-to-do employ only Quaker artisans if they can be found." [2] The predominance of the Society of Friends, with its recognition of the dignity of handwork, permitted the acceptance of many as Quaker grandees.

This was especially true in the more skilled trades of the house carpenter, the silversmith, and the cabinetmaker. On the rolls of the Carpenter's Company are such Quaker names as the two Samuel Powels, William Coleman, Samuel Rhoads, Edward Warner, Isaac Zane, and James Bringhurst—the cream of the Front Street aristocracy. Anglican Philip Syng, masterworker in silver, became junior warden of the Masons and served on the vestry of fashionable Christ Church before he was elected the first Treasurer of the American Philosophical Society. Mechanical genius and scientific achievement raised David Rittenhouse; Charles Willson Peale owed his elevation solely to artistic talent. As the name suggests, Owen Biddle, maker of clocks, watches, and mathematical instruments, ironmaster, merchant, inventor, stood high in the esteem of those who placed social prestige above spiritual qualities in Philadelphia's Quaker gentry.[3] Among the Friends of Newport, the same situation prevailed.

As at Philadelphia and Newport, many a prospering Boston artisan turned merchant and then entered the upper class by the normal route of success in business. But a craftsman who acquired a fortune in trade and no longer clung to leather-apron ways and appearances usually found himself welcome in select circles and eligible for many of their privileges and honors. The progress of John Singleton Copley from the rather humble station of a son of an immigrant tobacconist to the apex of Boston's aristocracy nicely illustrates what could be accomplished by a judicious combination of wealth and fame with a brilliant marriage. The will to perfect himself in his craft by "severe study" and application gave him "resolution enough to live a batchelor" to the age of thirty-one. By 1769 his brush was earning him three hundred guineas annually, which, as he informed Benjamin West, was "a pretty living in America." It also enabled him to marry the beautiful and dignified Susannah Farnum Clarke, a union placing him on terms of equality with the Winslows and others of the forward echelon of the Massachusetts gentry, and to build for her an imposing mansion with the first "Peazer" on Beacon Hill.[4]

Less successful and less dazzling but more instructive was the career of the carriage maker, Adino Paddock, as he shrewdly made his way to the threshold of Massachusetts society. Born into a solid yeoman family of Harwich, he came up to Boston with his widowed mother about 1736 and was bound out as an apprentice to learn the trade of chaisemaking. In 1758 he opened a shop of his own near the Common. Already a member of St. John's Masonic Grand Lodge, he became junior warden in 1758 and senior warden the following year. He rose to the same positions in the Master's Lodge in 1760 and 1761. He had made enough of an impression by 1759 to be chosen a sealer of leather by the Town Meeting, an office to which he was reelected annually until 1764, when the inhabitants promoted him to the important and responsible position of fireward.[5]

This advancement must have proceeded in part from Master Paddock's emerging military reputation. Entering the militia, as was required of every young man in the province, he soon displayed those talents for leadership and good fellowship so necessary for advancement in rank. Before 1764 he had become a captain in that impressive colonial military outfit, the Ancient and Honorable Artillery Company. Profiting by instruction from the British officers at Castle William, he became an excellent drillmaster and disciplinarian, whose company was noted for its efficiency. In 1771 he was a major, and by 1775 he was Colonel Paddock in charge of the colony's train of artillery. He claimed later that he had refused an offer to command the patriot artillery, the position afterwards given to Henry Knox.

The location of his coach shop on "Common Street" led Paddock to take a deep interest in Boston Common where, in 1762, he transplanted a number of English elms. He made the protection of the trees bordering the Common his special concern, offering rewards for the detection of vandals and persuading the Selectmen to set up a row of posts to guard the elms near the burying place from passing vehicles. He enjoyed the privilege of keeping his cow on the Common, and there he erected and maintained the Artillery Company's "gun house." On training days he had only to step across the street to the place where he "exercised" his command at their guns and put on his spectacular sham battles "in a Manner that did Honour to the Officers and Privates." [6]

Always a willing and tireless worker for the community, Adino Paddock was chosen fireward annually for ten years. In 1769 he was placed with such local worthies as John Scollay, John Rowe, John Hancock, Samuel Adams, Thomas Dawes, and William Cooper on the important Boston Committee on the State of Public Affairs. In 1772 he served as Warden of the Poor and with those superintending the erection of an overflow workhouse on the Common, and the following year on the committee to procure the first public street lights used in Boston. One of the highest honors the town could confer came in 1773 when the craftsman was selected as a member of the committee to inspect the schools of Boston. Referred to in the records as "Captain" or "Major," by 1772 Paddock was supporting the title of "Esquire." [7]

The very nature of his craft, which called for the employment of a number of journeymen painters, gilders, joiners, and smiths, in effect made Adino Paddock a "big business" man of that time and brought him constantly in contact with a rich and wellborn clientele. That this self-made man should have held conservative views was only natural, and Paddock, shrinking from association with his more radical fellow tradesmen, was not chosen a fireward in 1775. Soon he was stigmatized as a Tory, and when he departed with General Howe for Halifax his property, which he valued at £3,151, was confiscated. Arriving in every sense of the word, Adino Paddock was an outstanding citizen of Boston, and, had it not been for the Revolution, it seems almost certain that he or his children would shortly have entered the upper class.

Two conspicuous instances of craftsmen who climbed the ladder of social success occurred in New York. In 1724 a youthful mathematical-instrument maker named Anthony Lamb was standing in the gallows at Tyburn awaiting execution as an accomplice of the notorious Jack Sheppard, when his sentence was commuted to transportation to Virginia for seven years, because this was his first offense. Completing his term, he went to Philadelphia where he prospered as an instrument maker and proprietor of a private school for technical subjects. Moving on to New York he married a Miss Ham and soon acquired a solid and respectable place in the community of tradesmen. His son,

John, learned and practiced his father's trade for a time before he branched out and became wealthy as a wine and sugar merchant. He married Catharine Jardine, of Huguenot lineage, and gradually began to move with the gentry of Manhattan. As leader of the New York Sons of Liberty, Lamb's career as one of the great, sincere, but irrepressible, agitators of the revolutionary era and his war services are well known. Especial significance attaches to his story since it so well demonstrates the fact that a man's parents proved no bar to gentility, even for an artisan, provided he had the other qualifications.[8]

With the exception of William Bradford, who was born into the Philadelphia Quaker gentry, probably the only colonial printer to win admittance to the upper class was James Rivington of New York. After dissipating a small fortune in London, he crossed over to America in 1760. As a bookseller, he failed again in 1766, but marriage to Elizabeth Van Horne, a gentlewoman of good sense and excellent connections, forced him to settle down at New York as a bookseller and printer. *Rivington's New York Gazetteer* appeared in 1773 and immediately rated a high place among colonial newspapers; while its proprietor, noted for polite manners, real talents, and excellent taste in dress, won a position as a favorite among the Tory mercantile aristocracy of Gotham, whom he loyally defended in his columns until the "mechanicks," led by "King" Sears, raided his shop on November 27, 1775, broke up his press, and scattered the types over the street.[9]

Because the way to wealth was, for the most part, closed to southern artisans, few of them were ever able to improve their status. Consequently, the English country gentleman's tendency to look down a well-bred nose at tradesmen was more pronounced in the southern planting provinces. In 1772 when Robert Du Val needed carpenters, joiners, sawyers, and bricklayers, he concluded his advertisement with the statement: "Any discreet Tradesman (especially a Carpenter) content if he can make a genteel Provision for himself and Family, by an honest Industry, and not ambitious to rank as a Gentleman, simply in these Qualifications, Extortion, Insolence, and Laziness, may expect Encouragement by settling at Richmond Town." Stung by this gratuitous sneer, "the Mechanicks in the lower Parts of Virginia" countered with the charge that Du Val and his ilk were not only themselves "Adepts" at extortion, insolence, and laziness but also at "Pride, Envy, and Malice." [10]

Although some craftsmen managed to consort with the upper class, the overwhelming majority of master artisans took their station with the "middling sort," who embraced most of the population in colonial cities. Where a tradesman was ranged in this large group depended somewhat upon the particular trade he practiced—whether it stood high or low in the accepted ranking of crafts; but principally it hinged upon the master's worldly success. Well-established tradesmen who owned their shops, the land upon which these stood, other tangible property, and who possessed an education beyond the mere capacity to read and write were known as "respectable" or "reputable tradesmen" and, in northern communities, were looked upon from above with aristocratic approval. When some "substantial mechanics" founded New North Church at Boston in 1712, it was reported that they did so "without the assistance of the more wealthy part of the community excepting what they derive from their prayers and good wishes." These men made up the "small business" group of the eighteenth century. Such a person was Nathaniel Balch, whose ready wit and ability at mimicry were so well known that both Josiah Quincy and John Adams made note of him in their journals.[11]

Less skilled craftsmen and those engaged in the rougher trades of a water-front society were usually spoken of, when they had to be, as "the inferior mechanicks." The only accessions the lowest class received from the ranks of arts and crafts were indentured servants, whose status was transitory,

Negro slaves, and the not very numerous group of journeymen. Apprentices were minors and, with the exception of
those bound out by public authority, can be regarded as be-
longing, like their parents, to "the middling sort."

Southern gentry, particularly the lawyers and merchants
of Charles Town, lumped all craftsmen together as "the
profanum vulgus," a species of mankind to be respected only
because it was "humani generis." "I see no reason why I
should allow my opinion to be controlled by them," declared William Henry Drayton. Men of liberal education
should not mingle with those "who were never in a way to
study, or to advise upon any points, but rules how to cut
up a beast in the market to best advantage, to cobble an
old shoe in the neatest manner, or to build a necessary
house." That this attitude reflected more than mere haughty
superciliousness was borne out by the more democratic
Josiah Quincy, Jr., when in 1773 he deplored the absence
of any political concern for South Carolina artisans, although he observed at the same time that "the middling
order in the Capital are odious characters." [12]

Whatever the status of a colonial craftsman came to be,
however, it is certain that such American conditions as freedom from gild restraints, higher wages, and the greater
dignity of labor guaranteed the artisan a better social position than he ever enjoyed in Old England. And it is equally
certain that tradesmen were to be found at every level of
colonial society; so if we persist in using the term "mechanick," with its disparaging overtones, we must be unusually careful to use it correctly.

In the eighteenth century clothes did not necessarily make
the man, but dress was, without doubt, the badge of class.
This becomes evident from a comparison of several portraits
by John Singleton Copley. His grandees of the New England mercantile aristocracy, such as John Bours of Newport,
Nathaniel Sparhawk of Kittery and Portsmouth, or Thomas
Hancock and William Brattle of Boston, are studies in the

richest finery as well as of character. When we turn to his likenesses of Peter Pelham and Samuel Adams, we discover the "go-to-meetin'" clothes of the engraver and former brewer were far more sober in color and severe in cut, resembling the everyday habits of the gentry. A very clear impression of the dress of the craftsman may be gained from the two paintings of the bachelor silversmith, Nathaniel Hurd: the first shows him with a black turban and a mole-colored jacket or banyan, lined with pink and open at the neck, and a dark blue-green waistcoat; in the second, intended to portray the sitter in working costume, he wears a green turban and a shirt with the sleeves cut off just below the shoulder, revealing his bare arms. In Copley's justly famous portrait of Paul Revere, the silversmith has on a blue waistcoat over an open shirt, his hair is unpowdered, and he holds a teapot of his own making, while his tools lie on the table before him.[13]

The only garments missing in these craftsmen's portraits are the leather apron and leather breeches, which were universally worn as workingmen's apparel. One readily recalls Poor Richard's circle of artisans called the Leather Apron Club. In 1764 a Boston newspaper ran the announcement that "a great number of the respectable tradesmen" of the town had met and resolved to wear only leather "for their Working Habits," and those of local manufacture, because of the necessity for retrenchment in expenses consequent upon the postwar depression and the anticipated effects of the Stamp Act.[14]

Craftsmen and their families led a quiet existence, consisting largely of long hours and hard work. Generally serious, sober, and highly moral, they were regular churchgoers whatever their denomination. Nearly all rural artisans and most of those in the cities belonged to some church; the Congregationalists in New England and the Presbyterians in the Middle Colonies embraced the largest number, although at New York, Philadelphia, and Charles Town

Figure 16. Ropewalks for the manufacture of cordage could be found in every American seaport.

Figure 17. In the cities the blacksmith's craft was subdivided into many metal trades, such as anchor forging.

many prominent craftsmen communed with the Anglicans. What opponents called "enthusiasm" in religion attracted urban tradesmen, and they helped to form the enormous audiences that flocked to hear the great George Whitefield preach between 1739 and 1770. At Philadelphia they even succeeded in putting pressure on Anglicans and Quakers: "I suppose as Whitefield has preached among the Church of England, presbyterian, Dutch, Baptist and Swedes Congregations," remarked George Roberts with some apprehension in 1763, " 'twill not be long before he begs permission to mount our Quaker Gallery." [15]

If I were to single out any quality of urban craftsmen for particular comment, it would be their driving desire to get ahead in the world. They were men of ambition; they were consciously on the make. To raise themselves and their families above their present level, to get into the "white-collar class," so to speak, was their goal; and this irresistible aspiration provided the force to repeal the "Great Law of Subordination," eventually bringing about the democratization of American society. This attribute worked more ferment among city artisans than in any other element of colonial population, or at least it concentrated there and motivated their activities—social and political, as well as economic.

Notwithstanding long hours of work, recreation was eagerly indulged in by tradesmen in the cities, where nearly as many varieties were open to them as to the aristocrats. Clubs formed in taverns and pothouses frequented by artisans just as they did where gentlemen convened; discussions of every kind took place. Everywhere among the "substantial artisans" freemasonry was popular, and their parades excited much admiration—and envy. Numerous tavern shows, like the performances of "Punch's Opera" at Philadelphia and New York in 1747, the Manhattan slack-wire exhibitions of "the celebrated Anthony Duggee," or a view of "The Microcosm, or the World in Miniature," which was shown all over the continent and earned its owner a fortune and easy retirement, attracted many a stray shilling from the artisan's pocket. The sport of kings has, ironically, always been one of the most leveling diversions, and especially at Charles Town, Philadelphia, and New York craftsmen attended and bet on races with the gentry in much the same fashion as all England does at Ascot today.[16]

No more striking evidence of the determination of middle-class artisans to rise in the social scale can be adduced than in the blossoming pride and aspirations of the younger members of their families. One gentleman condemned as "an evil" to be suppressed "the universal affectation of dress which prevails among the sons and daughters of inferior mechanicks, and which exposes them to the laughter and ridicule of the world." Often did they divert their betters at Manhattan as they strutted "in the Park of a Sunday," the latter insisting, sometimes unfairly, that awkwardness always showed beneath the finery.[17]

Another place to see and be seen, as well as to be entertained, was at the theater. Despite objections on moral grounds by religious groups, stage plays gained a permanent foothold in all the cities from New York south. Journeymen found the lure of the footlights irresistible and spent their wages freely for three-shilling balcony seats, where their conduct proved far from restrained. David Douglass offered a pistole reward at New York on May 10, 1762, to anyone who should "discover the Person who was so rude as to throw Eggs from the Gallery upon the Stage last Monday, by which the Cloaths of some Ladies and Gentlemen in the Boxes were spoiled and the Performance in some Measure interrupted." At both Philadelphia and Annapolis, gentlemen complained of the "Sons of Liberty" who mounted the stairs and became "Gallery Ruffians." [18]

Middle-class tradesmen came to resent the theater as much or more for its ostentatious upper-class gentility and expense as on moral grounds; in fact, by the 1760's opposition had become thoroughly secularized. A Manhattan "Multitude" tried to stop the giving of plays in 1766 because such amusements proved too extravagant for hard times. The next year an artisan bewailed the effect of the "Temple of Satan" on his wife and five children. Playhouses are indeed bad for such "a common tradesman, as I am," but, "Sir, I cannot help thinking, that Tho' we Tradesmen are thus inferior to the gentlefolks, yet they ought not entirely to overlook what concerns us." Cash is very scarce but first his fourteen-year-old daughter begs to attend the play, then her mother determines to go, and he has to give in and accompany them. They cannot be content with gallery seats and he ends up by taking a twenty-four-shilling box and has to "shell out" two shillings more "for oranges and sugar plumbs." But the family are so pleased that they now read only plays and prate endlessly of nothing else. "I guess I am not the only man who has reason to make this complaint; many find it hard work to keep their Children from the Play House," which is the plaything of the rich and wellborn. O tempora, o mores![19]

Middle-class faith in education as the surest route to success came over from England as a part of the intellectual pattern of the colonists. New World conditions forced them to re-examine the usefulness of the old classical curriculum, handed down from the Renaissance, and the efficacy of ecclesiastical control. Here the craftsman exerted a potent influence toward replacing Latin and Greek by practical and vocational subjects taught under secular auspices. In rural areas and villages, of course, children attended whatever school there was, but because in the cities public institutions clung to the old familiar course of study we have the anomaly of patronage of private schools by artisans of the middle class.

The rise of the private evening school in America came as a direct result of the apprentice system. As we have seen, most indentures required the master or the parents to pro-

vide the apprentice with elementary instruction, often "at
the night School." The first of these of which I have found
record was at New York in 1690, but they became a regular
addition to the accepted system of schooling in all towns
and cities in the next century. Numerous private masters
opened schools at Manhattan for the growing artisan population. One teacher ran the gamut of courses in 1746 when
he advertised instruction in "Reading, Writing, Arithmetick,
vulgar and decimal, Merchant's Accompts, Mensurations
of Superficials and Solids, and all Manner of Artificer's
Work, Geometry, Trigonometry, Surveying, Guaging,
Dialling, Gunnery, Navigation." Six years later, Robert
Leech departed from the "immemorial" New York custom
of keeping a night school in the winter only by staying open
from six in the morning to eight at night "the Year
Round." [20]

Special private schools, day and night, catered to the
needs of the tradesmen in other cities. Isaac Greenwood,
A.M., who drank his way out of the Hollis Professorship
of Mathematics at Harvard, for several years after 1738
kept a private school where Boston apprentices and artificers
could learn applied mathematics, and Richard Pateshall held
an evening school for the same subjects in 1758. Down at
Newport in 1763 Thomas Howland conducted "a good
night School" for apprentice lads, and James P. Halpin,
limner, living appropriately at Mrs. Feke's, gave evening
classes in his craft. One of Philadelphia's many teachers of
vocational subjects was Anthony Lamb, instrument maker,
who successfully taught practical mathematics, surveying,
and navigation for twenty-six years. There in 1767 eleven
night schools combined to set standard hours and fees for
instruction. Isaac Greenwood showed up at Charles Town
in 1744, conducting a night school from three to eight P.M.
daily at the Surveyor's Office. Here also Joseph Hancock
taught classes in the "art and Mystery of Ship Building, on
Moderate Terms," and Francis Nicholson qualified youths

as "Tradesmen, . . . very accurately," in 1769 and later years.[21]

Master craftsmen displayed a great eagerness in several communities for what we call adult education. They made up a considerable proportion of the audiences for the many lecture courses in natural philosophy and the new electricity given from Boston to Charles Town by Dr. Adam Spencer, William Claggett, Lewis Evans, Ebenezer Kinnersley, and William Johnson. At Philadelphia they were active among the working members of the American Philosophical Society, and at Baltimore forty-nine members from all crafts united in 1763 as the Mechanical Company of Baltimore to further their interests in several ways.

Nearly all craftsmen were literate, and many were avid readers of local newspapers, pamphlets, and books that would add to their practical knowledge. Everywhere bookstores sold them copies of treatises on building, ironwork, cabinetmaking, surveying, and the useful arts. The fine collection at the Loganian Library in Philadelphia was composed of subjects "out of the reach of the generality of People," but its few readers were nearly all "obscure mechanicks who have a turn for mathematics." Twenty-six Quaker City artificers organized the Union Library in 1746, and eleven years later two other subscription libraries with strong artisan representation were formed. No other city showed as much interest in promoting libraries, but, in all, evidence that tradesmen were given to consulting books is forthcoming.[22] Reading for instruction was just one more aspect of the craftsman's consuming ambition.

As colonial opposition to imperial authority gathered headway after 1763, artisans and craftsmen, commonly termed the "Mechanicks," sprang into the public ken almost overnight and, thenceforth, took a more and more decisive part in urban politics—especially of the extracurricular variety. This sudden appearance of the craftsmen as a political force frightened many upper-class conservatives at the time and since has puzzled observers who have been at a loss to understand its meaning. To describe the movement for middle-class participation in government as merely the manipulation of the mob by self-seeking or disgruntled leaders from above provides but a partial and inadequate explanation, for we have just seen that the urban tradesman had a long train of grievances of an economic and social nature. Now we must look into his political status to see what opportunities he had to redress inequalities by due process of law.

The American colonies were ruled internally by a series of thirteen aristocratic cliques in their own interest, and as the colonial era neared its close possession of the franchise, long denied by the gentry, became a matter of pressing importance to the craftsman. In the countryside, he generally owned enough land to satisfy real-property requirements for voting, and in the villages of New England he could freely enter into town affairs. Such was not the case in the cities where the majority of artisans lacked sufficient personal property or did not pay taxes high enough to enable them to share in either local or provincial government.[28]

An examination of the requirements for the exercise of the franchise in the seaboard cities clearly reveals the situation. New England communities like Portsmouth, Salem, Boston, Providence, Newport, and Norwich were governed by town meetings in which it may be said in general that every householder who was the head of a family was entitled to participate in local affairs, both as a voter and as an officeholder. Anyone who held a freedom from the Corporation was accorded the franchise at New York, and, although it cost £5, perhaps eight per cent of the population voted. Philadelphia was ruled through a close corporation by a little oligarchy, which even many merchants resented. To vote in provincial elections, where alone the artisans stood a chance of making their desires felt, one had to have been a resident for two years and possess either fifty acres of land or personal property valued at £50. In three city wards, only thirteen per cent of those taxed in 1754 were assessed for £50 or more; twenty years later, but one taxable in ten, or, to put it somewhat differently, only one resident out of fifty, was eligible to vote. Pennsylvania's election laws obviously prevented the voice of the "mechanick" from being heard in the land. At Charles Town, all members of the Church of England might vote for vestrymen and parish officers, but the southern metropolis, having no centralized local government, was ruled directly by an Assembly elected on the basis of real-property ownership. Under such a dispensation, of course, the artisan vote was all but eliminated.[24]

In short, an ambitious, thriving, capable group of people in each town found their aspirations thwarted by the refusal of the merchant aristocracy to accord them recognition—economic, social, political—commensurate with their achievements. Resentment of those who did not have the wisdom and foresight to read the signs of the times and share their power with the artisans, who sincerely believed they had earned it, welled up everywhere, and, save at Boston and Newport, this bitterness eventually transcended that against the unfortunate new policies of the mother country.

The close of the French and Indian War ushered in the usual period of deflation and rapid economic readjustment, but it was made more stringent in the colonies by Parliamentary prohibition of the issuance of more paper currency and stipulations that the new revenue duties and taxes must be paid in specie. Rigorous enough at any time, these regulations occurred just as the flow of gold from war orders and British Army purchases dried up and as the full force of a postwar depression struck the colonies. In the cities many shipyards and ropewalks were idle; journeymen were unemployed; and in the absence of business for these trades, as we have seen, a host of subsidiary crafts were immediately

affected. The Sugar Act of 1764, with its three-penny duty
on foreign molasses, not only closed down distilleries at
Boston, Newport, New York, and Philadelphia, but injured
the merchant class as well. About this time, John Adams
was told that nearly a thousand New England families were
dependent upon John Hancock and his commercial activities
for a livelihood, and of these a substantial portion were
Boston artisans.[25]

Hard times bore heavily on the average craftsman. A
money shortage commonly calls for an extension of credit
and easier terms for debtors, but these the tradesman could
not afford to give; nor could he secure the credit he needed
from his merchant. The bankruptcies of the large mercantile houses of Wheelwright at Boston and Richardson in
Newport attracted public attention, but the failures of many
craftsmen in each seaport passed virtually unnoticed. They
were, however, acutely felt. Small businesses of artisans collapsed by the dozen in each city, and many formerly prosperous masters were thrown into debtors' prisons by
merchant creditors. The number of craftsmen imprisoned
for debt at New York, for example, increased steadily down
to the outbreak of the Revolution, and after 1769 their
plight was so desperate that friends took up collections of
food for them. At Philadelphia in the winter of 1766 "the
wretched condition of the debtors now in gaol, without food
or Raiment in this rigorous season," aroused the compassion
of their fellows, who were beginning to perceive that this
practice was a social as much as an economic problem. They
agitated for its abolition after 1770. Other cities also had
their quotas of confined debtor artisans. Imprisonment for
debt thus became a subject mentioned by artificers only with
great bitterness, as the antiaristocratic sentiments of these
men kept pace with their anti-British feelings.[26]

What, then, did the middle-class craftsmen want? Did
they have a program? Did they understand the issues of the
time? Or were they simply men of brawn and muscle, un-

thinking persons, the leather aprons, directed in all their doings by the shrewd manipulations of such renegade gentlemen as Samuel Adams, Samuel Vernon, "King" Sears, Charles Thompson, and Christopher Gadsden?

My answer is that in all probability they had a clearer notion of what they wanted and how to get it than the so-called "better sort." Certainly the "mechanicks" displayed greater unity than the gentry, who split on nearly every fundamental issue.

First and foremost, the craftsmen wanted to have their say about internal politics. They wanted to vote. Administration from above having failed, they wanted to share in making the laws. I do not mean to imply that they insisted upon, or even desired, representatives drawn from their own ranks, as did the Jacksonians. Actually, they were still most willing to have gentlemen with their superior talents, superior education, superior knowledge of the world, their superior oratorical powers, to represent them; but they did insist upon the right to choose among gentlemen, and upon gentlemen realizing whence came much of their support. To this end they did not propose to hand over the franchise to the riffraff; they did intend that every taxpayer should be allowed to vote. They sought enfranchisement of their own class that they might be in a position to forestall aristocratic class legislation, to protect their own during hard times from imprisonment for debt, to enforce wholesome laws for the encouragement of virtue and prevention of vice and immorality, to establish schools with masters paid by the public "to instruct youth at low prices," to provide a measure of rotation in office. By such means, they said, the danger of perpetuating "an inconvenient aristocracy will be effectively prevented." [27]

Having formulated these views about domestic liberties, what of their attitude toward Great Britain? Here their colleagues of the press, lawyers like the "Pennsylvania Farmer," and the clergy of the Congregational and Presbyterian churches supplied them through newspaper, pamphlet, and pulpit with the same arguments everyone else received. Many of those artisans who had been born in the British Isles and were recent arrivals had less love for the mother country than American-born craftsmen, who knew of it only remotely. Enforcement of the Sugar Act and tightening of the customs service brought genuine distress to northern centers, and when the Stamp Act passed tradesmen of all towns realized the significance of the threat to their liberties as printer after printer drove it home in his newspaper. The use of the troops at Boston in 1768 was followed the next year by the employment of force against the Wilkites in London. What happened there might easily happen at New York, Philadelphia, or Charles Town, and against us, reasoned politically alert "mechanicks." [28]

When the time came for concerted action, the craftsmen had at hand numerous familiar agencies which could be readily transformed into protest bodies merely by "working the political engine." In the train bands, as the militia was then called, craftsmen filled nearly all the positions of noncommissioned officers and acquired experience in handling groups of men. Often too, especially in New England, they were elected lieutenants and captains. Everywhere the more prosperous tradesmen participated prominently in the deliberations of the fire companies when they actively promoted the cause of American manufactures during the sixties. Through the Carpenter's and Taylor's companies of Philadelphia artisan sentiment was easily mobilized. "It being Cucumber Times with many of the Taylors in Town," reported the *Boston Gazette* in 1765, "they beg the Prayers of all good People that the Stamp Act may be repealed, as most of their Customers have declared they will have no new Cloaths made, until such time." The Mechanical Company of Baltimore not only lent its rooms for the organization of the Sons of Liberty in 1766, but thirty-six of its members joined up, and this tradesman's organization came gradually to shape the rebellious policy of the city toward the "rule of Governor Eden and the British Lion." [29]

At taverns like the Green Dragon, next door to the printing office of Edes and Gill at Boston, where craftsmen congregated, means of liaison between craftsmen and representatives of the more radical merchants were constantly being worked out. At the opposite end of the social scale, in the shipyards and ropewalks of each port, word could be passed out to journeymen and apprentices with certainty that it would circulate like smoke among the "inferior sort" along the water front. And, of course, the use which "the Loyall Nine" (two distillers, two braziers, a minor merchant, a jeweler, a painter, a printer, and a master mariner) and Samuel Adams made of the Boston Town Meeting needs no further comment, save that identical procedures were followed in town meetings at Newport, Providence, and the several large towns of eastern Connecticut, where, as the Customs Commissioners reported in 1768, "the lowest Mechanicks discuss upon the most important points of government, with the utmost freedom." [30]

Certain agencies existed by which the "mechanicks" of one community could get in touch with those of another. Many craftsmen belonged to the Freemasons and communicated with their brethren at a distance on political as well as fraternal matters. The American Philosophical Society served as a clearinghouse for ideas and a means for promoting domestic manufactures. Most potent of all were the newspapers, which circulated throughout the colonies and whose policies remained always in the hands of "patriot printers." Finally, as the conflict sharpened, the "Sons of Liberty," a congeries of organizations that sprang up simultaneously and apparently spontaneously in every colony, were loosely joined by maintaining a correspondence, centering at New York. Because of the very nature of their trades and activities, artisans generally regarded local issues as more pressing than those of continental and imperial import, and they never succeeded in effecting intercolonial organization to the extent that the merchants did. Yet the beginnings made were not without significance.[31]

The "mechanicks" had leadership as well as organization. From their ranks they produced a number of clear-thinking and bold captains, who crystallized their discontents, formulated plans, and joined with other groups in precipitating the revolutionary movement. Many of these men were printers: Benjamin Edes and John Gill of Boston; Solomon Southwick of Newport; John Holt of New York; William Bradford of Philadelphia; and Peter Timothy of Charles Town, to mention a few. Their little newspapers were priceless weapons for propaganda and agitation. The most adroit handler of mobs was Captain Ebenezer Macintosh, whom even Tory opponents admitted was clever, "sensible and manly." This former soldier, who had served with Abercrombie at Ticonderoga, was of small stature, dressed genteelly, and was a great reader of poetry—doubtless he knew Thompson's "Ode on Liberty" by heart. He was a cordwainer by trade and served Boston as a sealer of leather before he took over as "First Captain General of the Liberty Tree" and gave everyone proof of his superb qualities for leadership by parading his one hundred and fifty well-disciplined bully boys through the streets to the terror of the Tories. Later he was a giver of tea parties. That he named his son, born in 1769, after Pasquale Paoli, whose patriotic fight for freedom of Corsica so electrified England, is sufficient proof that this artisan was fully abreast of the times and alert to the meaning of liberty. A wealthy Charles Town blacksmith, named William Johnson, joined with Joseph Veree and John Fullerton, house carpenters, Nathaniel Libby, boatbuilder, George Flagg and Benjamin Hawes, glaziers and painters, and Edward Weyman, upholsterer, to head the "mechanicks" of that city in opening the revolution in South Carolina.[32]

It is not my intention to trace the role played by urban

craftsmen in each incident leading to the War for Independence, although, I might add, it very much needs chronicling. But I do wish to point out briefly the methods the artisans used to achieve their goals. You will bear constantly in mind that normal political channels were closed to them.

That they resorted to violence and destruction of property, or merely threatened to do so, to coerce both the royal authorities, as at Boston and New York, and the upper classes, as in Newport and Charles Town, is well known to readers of our history. Rioting was an old story in colonial cities. It had become more or less traditional since 1700, and there is a most familiar note in the piece published in the *Boston News Letter* of February 20, 1766:

T 'other Ev'ning sitting in my [tavern] Stall I read in the Ev'ning Post, a pompous Account of the warm Disposition of certain Artisans to serve the Sons of Liberty, whenever their Service was required. Very Well. I am at their Service too, and have been indefatigable therein whenever any Thing happened in my Way.

Jack Cobbler

Covert allusions to what might happen, such as this, were not infrequently coupled with such direct remarks during times of stringency, as that "it would be a tremendous service to all concerned if wealthy men would pay their tradesmen's bills. Tho the sums seem trifling to them, they are vital to the poor Mechanic and Tradesman, . . . so slender are his means and credit." [33]

Where political agencies were not available, new devices came into use. One was the extralegal public meeting at which a vote was taken on an important pending question after a full round of oratory had been listened to. At Charles Town on October 1, 1768, for instance, "a number of the principal Mechanics . . . , assembled under some Trees, in a field adjacent to the rope walks," to choose six gentlemen to represent the people of the city in the Commons House of Assembly. The Liberty Tree was consecrated after the meeting, and that night the "mechanicks" paraded on Broad and King Streets. An annual observance of the repeal of the Stamp Act was regarded as necessary to remind the people that their liberties had been endangered and might be again. On such occasions apprentices and journeymen were much in evidence. The 1766 Hartford celebration ended in a tragedy when a gunpowder explosion in the Brick School House killed a blacksmith's apprentice and badly injured the sons of a hatter, a joiner, and two other apprentices. Craftsmen also organized to support the nonimportation movement, as when those of Boston, in 1770, "unanimously resolv'd not to have any Trade or commercial intercourse whatsoev'r, with the Merchants of New Hampshire, while they are counteracting the laudable exertions of the other colonies, for the common good, by continuing their importation of European goods." [34]

Perhaps the most enduring and constructive effort of the artisans and craftsmen was their part in the movement for American manufactures to supplant English importations, which had been inaugurated by the merchants. Into this first "Buy American" campaign they eagerly entered by refusing to purchase imported goods and by measurably increasing the collective output of their shops. Caleb Bull of Hartford carried Lynn shoes, local sole leather, and Hartford nails, while another shopkeeper sold "New Haven distilled Rum." A large store opened at Philadelphia to sell nothing but Pennsylvania manufactures; Boston had a similar emporium; and both of these aroused envy in Connecticut where provincial clothiers were summoned to Hartford by James Taylor to exchange information useful to their trade. In far-off Charles Town Thomas Shute's store specialized in "All American Manufactures" brought in from northern cities. [35]

Every occupation, as I pointed out earlier, received encouragement from this movement for self-sufficiency, and the production of local goods mounted. In this manner American craftsmen stood to profit by the political situation, and their self-interest naturally buttressed their patriotism. Encouraged by attempts to cut off competition from abroad, artisans began to look with favor on what came later to be known as protection of infant industries. When wealthy young Samuel Powel was about to sail home from London in 1765, after a grand tour of Europe, to occupy his new Philadelphia mansion, his uncle, Samuel Morris, wrote him that "Household goods may be had here as cheap and as well made from English patterns" as any imported and pointedly warned that Quaker City folk were strongly opposed to the bringing in of English goods: "I have heard the joiners here object this against Dr. [John] Morgan and others who brought their furniture with them." [36] Thus did political conditions favor the emergence of the Philadelphia Chippendale style.

At Charles Town, where local craftsmanship had long been eclipsed because of the rage for things English, artisans gladly seized the opportunity to strengthen their trades by supporting all anti-British measures and energetically promoting home manufactures. Governor William Bull blamed their conduct during the Stamp Act on the artifices of those who imbibed the principles of Rhode Island and Boston. It is possible, however, that the chance to improve the economic status of their crafts supplied more of a driving force to the activities of South Carolina craftsmen than any other single factor. Merchants who imported quantities of English goods at lower prices than American articles were their chief competitors and as such were heartily resented. The rice and indigo planters sided with the "mechanicks" in this provincial contest for power. The only way to encourage local industry, wrote one of them, is to patronize nonimporters exclusively. "You cannot expect the merchants will begin this matter themselves," he insisted. "Oblige them to it, by declaring you will deal with none that do import extra articles." Action of this kind will certainly bring about "a happy coalition of our Interests and that of the Merchants into one immediate self-interest." That in the long run Charles Town workingmen did not gain greatly was not their fault nor that of their leaders, but stemmed from conditions far beyond their control.[37]

When the War for Independence came, the craftsmen as a class gave it their wholehearted support. Those who did not labor on the home front producing weapons and supplies for the Continental Army and the various militia bodies entered the ranks and contributed their skills to the military or served in other public capacities. Benjamin Franklin, printer, Roger Sherman, cordwainer, and George Walton, carpenter, signed the Declaration of Independence. John Lamb became a brigadier general of artillery, and Colonel William Bradford was wounded in battle. For a time Charles Willson Peale commanded a company, and, when a lull occurred, either cobbled his men's shoes or painted portraits of patriot officers. Possessing qualities of leadership, many craftsmen had army experiences like that of Jonathan Gostelowe, the Philadelphia cabinetmaker, who served first as a commissary of military stores and then as a major of artillery. By far the largest number served in the ranks and, when the war was over, returned quietly to their shops again, hoping that it had all been worth while.

Did they win what they had fought for? To this question I can give only a qualified answer. Pennsylvania's Constitution of 1776 was the sole instrument of the Revolutionary era to translate the hopes and aspirations of the craftsmen into fundamental law, for it was in that state alone that the old ruling class was completely divested of power. This document was drawn up by Benjamin Franklin, David Cannon, George Bryan, David Rittenhouse, and Dr. Thomas Young—representatives of the middle class, who fully understood what the craftsmen and their farmer allies wanted. Elsewhere the artisans made fewer gains, but their faith in the future continued. Henceforth democracy was on the march. The American Revolution was only the entering wedge, and it was not until Jeffersonian gains were capped by the emergence of the common man in the time of Andrew Jackson that the urban tradesman would see his political and social status brought into line with his economic achievements.

This, then, is the story of the craftsman who gave colonial society many things of use and beauty; it is the tale of men and boys who wrought with their hands and tools, as well as with their minds, in the building of an American society; it is the chronicle of our first manufacturers and of our first laboring men.

NOTES

Notes to Chapter I

1. *An addition to the Present Melancholy Circumstances of the Province Considered* (Boston: S. Kneeland, 1719), 7.

2. Louis B. Wright, ed., Robert Beverley, *History and Present State of Virginia* (Chapel Hill: University of North Carolina Press, 1946), 295.

3. Nathaniel B. Shurtleff, ed., *Records of the Governor and Company of Massachusetts Bay in New England* (Boston: William White, 1853-54), II, 249-50. For urban crafts in the seventeenth century, see Carl Bridenbaugh, *Cities in the Wilderness: The First Century of Urban Life in America, 1625-1742* (New York: Ronald Press Company, 1938), 35-38, 42-44, 47-49.

4. Hunter D. Farish, ed., Henry Hartwell, James Blair, and Edward Chilton, *The Present State of Virginia and the College* (Williamsburg: Colonial Williamsburg, Inc., 1940), 9-10.

5. Hugh Jones, *Present State of Virginia* (London: 1724, reprinted for J. Sabin, New York, 1865), 38; Alfred J. Morrison, ed., Johann D. Schoepf, *Travels in the Confederation* (Philadelphia: William J. Campbell, 1911), I, 33.

6. Harry J. Carman, ed., *American Husbandry* (New York: Columbia University Press, 1939), 343.

7. *Virginia Magazine of History and Biography*, XVI (1908), 83; *South Carolina Gazette*, Charles Town, January 31, 1774; C.O. 5: 1327, p. 127, Library of Congress Transcripts.

8. *Virginia Gazette*, Williamsburg, March 5, April 17, 1752; *Virginia Gazette* (Rind), April 6, 1769; *William and Mary College Quarterly*, 1st ser., XI (1903), 236; *South Carolina Gazette*, March 5, 1741; Public Records of South Carolina, IV, 78-81, Historical Commission of South Carolina, Columbia.

9. *South Carolina Gazette*, February 9, 1733/4; January 4, 1734/5; March 8, 1770; Rosamond R. Beirne, "William Buckland, Architect of

Virginia and Maryland," *Maryland Historical Magazine*, XLI (1946), 199-218; Alonzo T. Dill, "Tryon's Palace," *North Carolina Historical Review*, XIX (1942), 119-67.

10. *American Husbandry*, 182, 308.

11. *Maryland Gazette*, Annapolis, May 16, 1765; July 11, 1771; *South Carolina Gazette*, March 18, 1756; February 17, 1757, Supp.; *Cape Fear Mercury*, Wilmington, November 24, 1769.

12. Louis Morton, *Robert Carter of Nomini Hall* (Williamsburg: Colonial Williamsburg, Inc., 1941), 96, 114; *South Carolina Gazette*, January 29, 1756, Supp.; August 4, November 17, 1758; *Cape Fear Mercury*, November 24, 1769; *North Carolina Gazette*, New Bern, May 5, 1775; William Tatham, *Essay on the Culture and Commerce of Tobacco* (London: Vernoe and Hood, 1800), 53.

13. *South Carolina Gazette*, September 16, 1756, Supp.; *Maryland Gazette*, February 14, 1750; May 16, 1765; June 1, 1769; July 16, 1772.

14. *William and Mary College Quarterly*, 1st ser., V (1896), 110; XI (1903), 154; Rev. Robert Rose, Diary, September 25, 1749, Colonial Williamsburg, Inc.; *Virginia Gazette* (Dixon and Hunter), January 7, 14, 21, November 18, 1775; *Virginia Gazette* (Purdie and Dixon), January 30, 1772; *Norfolk Intelligencer*, August 4, 1774; *South Carolina Gazette*, October 31, 1765.

15. *Cape Fear Mercury*, November 24, 1769; January 13, 1773; August 7, 1775; *South Carolina Gazette*, January 29, 1756, Supp.; February 7, 1757; Yates Snowden, "Labor Organizations in South Carolina, 1742-1861," University of South Carolina, *Bulletin*, No. 38 (1914), 7.

16. Henry Whitely, "The Principio Company," *Pennsylvania Magazine of History and Biography*, XI (1887-88), 289; *William and Mary College Quarterly*, 1st ser., V (1896), 20-22; Frances N. Mason, *John Norton & Sons: Merchants of London and Virginia* (Richmond: Dietz Press, 1937), 28, 120, 152, 156-57; Schoepf, *Travels*, I, 65.

17. John S. Bassett, ed., *Writings of Colonel William Byrd of Westover* (New York: Doubleday, Page and Company, 1901), 345-86; Lester J. Cappon, ed., *Iron Works at Tuball* (Charlottesville: Tracey W. McGregor Library, 1945).

18. Whitely, "The Principio Company," 193-96; Morton, *Robert Carter*, 166; "Journal of a French Traveller in the Colonies, 1765," *American Historical Review*, XXVII (1921), 73; *Maryland Gazette*,

December 28, 1733; July 19, 1745; June 10, 1746; February 21, 1765; May 28, July 30, 1767; Lester J. Cappon, "Iron-Making—A Forgotten Industry of North Carolina," *North Carolina Historical Review*, IX (1932), 332.

19. *Maryland Gazette*, June 4, 1767; *Virginia Gazette* (Rind), November 24, 1768; November 30, 1769; October 4, 11, 1770.

20. Whitely, "The Principio Company," 289; *William and Mary College Quarterly*, 1st ser., V (1896), 20-22; Mason, *John Norton & Sons*, 28, 120, 152, 156-57; Schoepf, *Travels*, I, 65.

21. Walter A. Bean, "War and the Colonial Farmer," *Pacific Historical Review*, XI (1942), 442n., 443n.

22. *Maryland Gazette*, March 2, 1751; September 23, 1761; October 8, 1767; May 26, 1768.

23. *Maryland Gazette*, February 2, 1769; *Virginia Gazette* (Rind), July 26, 1770; *William and Mary College Quarterly*, 1st ser., XI (1903), 245; *Virginia Gazette* (Purdie and Dixon), January 30, June 25, 1772; *Virginia Gazette* (Dixon and Hunter), February 21, 1777.

24. This is made clear by a study of the Spotsylvania County Records in which craftsmen are conspicuous by their absence. William A. Crozier, ed., *Virginia County Records: Spotsylvania County* (New York: Fox, Duffield and Company, 1905), I; Robert A. Brock, ed., *Official Records of Governor Dinwiddie* (Virginia Historical Society, *Collections*, new series, III-IV, Richmond, 1883-84), I, 30; *Virginia Gazette* (Rind), July 23, 1767.

25. *The Life of Devereux Jarratt* (Baltimore: Warner and Hanna, 1806), 12-14, 17, 21; *Virginia Gazette*, December 24, 1736; "Diary of John Harrower," *American Historical Review*, VI (1900-1), 82, 98; *Virginia Gazette* (Purdie), November 22, 1776.

26. Adelaide L. Fries, ed., *Records of the Moravians of North Carolina* (Raleigh: North Carolina Historical Commission, 1922), I, 39; Nannie M. Tilley, "The Industries of Colonial Granville County," *North Carolina Historical Review*, XIII (1921), 281, 287-88; *South Carolina Gazette*, February 26, 1756.

27. John F. D. Smyth, *Tour in the United States of America* (London: Robinson, Robson and Sewell, 1784), I, 10-11; *Maryland Gazette*, April 2, 1761; June 24, 1762; October 12, 1769; November 21, 1771; "Diary of John Harrower," 92, 98; "Journal of a French Traveller," 733-37; *Virginia Gazette* (Purdie and Dixon), April 18, 1766; April 11, 1771; *Antiques*, XLVII (1945), 93-95.

28. George Buckner, Account Book, 1784, Virginia State Library, Richmond; *North Carolina Gazette*, February 12, 1766; *Cape Fear Mercury*, September 22, 1773; May 18, 1774; *Pennsylvania Gazette*, Philadelphia, August 9, 1770.

29. *Virginia Magazine of History and Biography*, VII (1899), 109, 404; XI (1903), 125, 231; XII (1904), 61, 140, 148; XXXI (1923), 249.

30. Robert L. Meriwether, *Expansion of South Carolina, 1729-1765* (Kingsport: Southern Publishers, 1940), 57, 168, 172, 174; Rose, Diary, January 26, 1751.

31. *South Carolina Gazette*, December 22, 1768; March 2, 1769; Samuel Kercheval, *History of the Valley of Virginia* (4th edn.; Strasburg: Shenandoah Printing House, 1925), 247, 268-70.

32. John W. Wayland, ed., *Hopewell Friends History* (Strasburg: Shenandoah Printing House, 1936), 127, 166-69; T. K. Cartmell, *Shenandoah Valley Pioneers and Their Descendants* (Winchester: Eddy Press, 1909), 436-37; Isaac Zane Correspondence, October 11, 1769, 1771-72, *passim*, in Coates and Reynell Papers, Historical Society of Pennsylvania; William Allason, Letter Book, 1770-89, pp. 5, 10, 105, Virginia State Library; *Virginia Gazette* (Dixon and Hunter), December 30, 1775.

33. Robert G. Albion and Leonidas Dodson, eds., *Philip Vickers Fithian: Journal, 1775-1776* (Princeton: Princeton University Press, 1934), 14-15; 30; Freeman H. Hart, *Valley of Virginia in the American Revolution* (Chapel Hill: University of North Carolina Press, 1942), 15, 25; Zane Correspondence, 1766-70; *Virginia Magazine of History and Biography*, XXXVIII (1930), 52; Carl and Jessica Bridenbaugh, *Rebels and Gentlemen: Philadelphia in the Age of Franklin* (New York: Reynal and Hitchcock, 1942), 24.

34. *Records of the Moravians of North Carolina*, I, 80, 83, 103, 129, 148, 156, 172.

35. *Ibid.*, I, 59; II, 605.

36. *Ibid.*, I, 282, 314, 343-44; II, 531, 601-2, 609, 690, 728, 764-65, 771, 810, 822, 830, 883.

37. *Ibid.*, I, 149, 157, 172, 180, 237, 250, 269, 374; II, 762, 775, 815, 884.

38. *Ibid.*, II, 883.

39. "Journal of a French Traveller," 744; *American Husbandry*, 184.

40. *Virginia Gazette* (Purdie and Dixon), November 19, 1772; January 28, December 2, 1773.

41. *Maryland Gazette*, July 19, 1734; February 7, March 6, 1760.

42. *Maryland Gazette*, August 6, 1767.

43. Mason, *John Norton & Sons*, 371.

Notes to Chapter II

1. J. Hector St. John Crèvecoeur, *Letters from an American Farmer* (New York: A. and C. Boni, 1925), 50-56.

2. *New Jersey Archives*, 1st ser., V (1882), 205-8.

3. Anne Bezanson, Robert D. Gray, and Miriam Hussey, *Prices in Colonial Pennsylvania* (Philadelphia: University of Pennsylvania Press, 1935), 267; Rolla M. Tryon, *Household Manufactures in the United States, 1684-1860* (Chicago: University of Chicago Press, 1917), 76, 91; Edmund B. O'Callaghan, ed., *Documentary History of the State of New York* (Albany: Weed, Parsons and Company, 1849-51), I, 734; *New York Post Boy*, January 13, 1772.

4. James P. Baxter, ed., *Documentary History of the State of Maine*, Maine Historical Society, *Collections* (Portland: Le Favor-Tower, 1907), 2d ser., X, 122; Tryon, *Household Manufactures*, 76, 80, 103-4.

5. *Hampshire Gazette*, Northampton, Mass., September 3, 1788.

6. Tench Coxe, *View of the United States of America* (London: J. Johnson, 1795), 443.

7. Carl Bridenbaugh, "The New England Town: A Way of Life," American Antiquarian Society, *Proceedings*, LVI (1946), 21-24, Bridenbaugh, *Rebels and Gentlemen*, 8-9.

8. William Douglass, *A Summary, Historical and Political, of the . . . British Settlements in North America* (Boston: Rogers and Fowle, 1747-52), II, 333; Crèvecoeur, *Letters*, 101; "Journal of a French Traveller," 79.

9. Bridenbaugh, "New England Town," 3-6.

10. *Boston Gazette*, November 6, 1758; *Independent Advertiser*, Boston, March 13, 1749; Penrose R. Hoopes, *Connecticut Clockmakers of the Eighteenth Century* (New York: Dodd, Mead and Company, 1930), 48-49.

11. J. Frederick Kelly, *Early Connecticut Meeting Houses* (New York: Columbia University Press, 1948), I, xxxiii-xxxiv, 161; *Diary of*

Joshua Hempstead (New London: New London County Historical Society, 1901), I; *Boston News Letter*, July 19, 1764.

12. *Boston Gazette,* June 5, 1738; December 11, 1753; July 29, 1765; March 12, 1770; *Connecticut Gazette*, New Haven, August 12, 1764; Hoopes, *Connecticut Clockmakers*, 122-24.

13. *Boston Gazette,* May 23, 1757; January 4, 1760; Aaron M. Stein, "The Chapins and Connecticut Valley Chippendale," *Antiquarian*, XVI (1931), 21-23.

14. Hoopes, *Connecticut Clockmakers*, 3-5, 50-58, 59-61, 126-27; *Boston Evening Post*, December 4, 1767; *Connecticut Courant*, Hartford, December 1, 1772.

15. *Newport Mercury*, October 1, 1764; *Boston News Letter*, October 1, 1764; *Providence Gazette*, November 10, 1770; William D. Miller, "Samuel Casey, Silversmith," Rhode Island Historical Society, *Collections*, XXI (1928), 1-8; William D. Miller, *The Silversmiths of Little Rest* (Kingston: privately printed, 1928).

16. George M. Curtis, *Early Silver of Connecticut and Its Makers* (Meriden: International Silver Company, 1916), 46-47, 49, 83; *Connecticut Courant*, January 1, 1771; February 9, November 2, 1773; March 24, May 31, 1774; *Boston Gazette*, April 18, 1763.

17. *Boston News Letter*, March 17, 1763; July 25, 1765; May 27, 1773; *Boston Gazette*, March 4, 1755; *Boston Evening Post*, April 26, 1762.

18. *Connecticut Courant*, August 5, 16, 1765; August 1, 1768; July 7, August 14, 1769; June 2, 16, 1772; May 3, November 18, 1774.

19. *New Hampshire Gazette*, Portsmouth, January 5, 1770; *Virginia Gazette*, November 24, 1752; *Boston Gazette*, September 4, 1753; May 26, 1755; July 28, 1760; January 31, 1763; February 11, 1765; *Boston News Letter*, April 4, 1760; Charles M. Stow, "A Massachusetts Glass Factory," *Antiquarian*, XIII (1929), 27, 66, 86; *Boston Post Boy*, January 18, 1762; Albert Bushnell Hart, ed., *Commonwealth History of Massachusetts* (New York: States History Company, 1928), II, 411 (chart).

20. Arthur C. Bining, *British Regulation of the Colonial Iron Industry* (Philadelphia: University of Pennsylvania Press, 1933), 14, 126-27; *Boston Gazette*, October 24, 1737; August 17, 1767.

21. Bining, *Colonial Iron Industry*, 14, 23, 27, 73, 91, 92; *Connecticut Courant*, September 8, 1766.

22. *Connecticut Courant*, January 1, 1765; April 2, 1770; January 1, 1771; November 30, December 30, 1773.

23. *Boston News Letter*, July 19, 1764; Frances M. Caulkins, *History of Norwich* (Hartford: the author, 1866), 361, 607-8; *Connecticut Courant*, July 14, 1766; February 23, 1767; *New York Weekly Mercury*, June 10, 1771; *Norwich Packet*, September 15, 1774.

24. Caulkins, *Norwich*, 371, 385, 608; *New York Weekly Mercury*, June 10, 1771.

25. *Norwich Packet*, December 2, 9, 1773; Peter Force, ed., *American Archives* (Washington: Clarke and Force, 1837-53), 4th ser., II, 575; Caulkins, *Norwich*, 359, 360, 367, 371-72, 385, 389, 606-8; Hoopes, *Connecticut Clockmakers*, 83-87; Curtis, *Early Silver*, 83.

26. *Connecticut Courant*, July 20, 1767; October 23, 1769; January 29, October 9, 1770; April 23, 30, June 4, December 17, 1771; April 21, October 10, 1772; April 20, December 26, 1773; January 18, November 7, 1774.

27. Alonzo Lewis and James R. Newhall, *History of Lynn* (Lynn: G. C. Herbert, 1890), I, 90, 299, 324, 328, 334-35; *Boston Gazette*, October 21, 1764 (italics mine); January 11, 1768; *Newport Mercury*, January 25, 1768; *New Hampshire Gazette*, July 20, 1770; June 5, 1772.

28. Joseph W. Roe, *Connecticut Inventors*, Connecticut Tercentenary Commission, *Publications* (New Haven: Yale University Press, 1934), XXXIII, 9.

29. Harry J. Carman and Rexford G. Tugwell, eds., Jared Eliot, *Essays upon Field Husbandry in New England* (New York: Columbia University Press, 1934), lv-lvi, 167, 172, 173, 180, 187.

30. Eliot, *Field Husbandry*, xlix, 116-20; George C. Groce, Jr., "Benjamin Gale," *New England Quarterly*, X (1927), 697, 708.

31. *Pennsylvania Chronicle*, Philadelphia, August 8, 1768; Lawrence C. Wroth, *Abel Buell of Connecticut* (New Haven: Acorn Club, 1926), 28-29.

32. Wroth, *Abel Buell*, 5-8, 10, 34-45; Franklin B. Dexter, ed., *Itineraries of Ezra Stiles* (New Haven: Yale University Press, 1915), 448-49, 476, 494; B. Gale to T. Bond, 1769, American Philosophical Society Archives, Philadelphia; *Early Proceedings of the American Philosophical Society* (Philadelphia: the Society, 1884), XXII, 17, 39; Isabel S. Calder, ed., *Letters and Papers of Ezra Stiles* (New Haven: Yale University Library, 1933), 17.

33. *Connecticut Courant*, December 12, 1768; July 3, 1769; August 16, 1774; *Boston News Letter*, September 7, 1769; *Boston Gazette*, June 10, 1771; Hoopes, *Connecticut Clockmakers*, 70-72; Massachusetts Historical Society, *Collections*, 1st ser., IX (1804), 264-66.

34. B. Gale to Silas Deane, November 9, 1775; Connecticut Historical Society, *Collections*, II (1870), 315-17, 322, 333, 358; Edward H. Tatum, Jr., ed., *The American Journal of Ambrose Serle* (San Marino: Huntington Library, 1940), 56; Groce, "Benjamin Gale," 709.

35. Bertha S. Fox, "Provost William Smith and His Land Investments," *Pennsylvania History*, VIII (1941), 200-2; *Pennsylvania Chronicle*, March 27, 1769.

36. *Pennsylvania Archives* (Harrisburg: Commonwealth of Pennsylvania, 1897), 3d ser., XIV, 334-45.

37. *Pennsylvania Gazette*, October 7, 1762; "Journal of a French Traveller," 78; *Some Cursory Remarks Made By James Birket in His Voyage to North America, 1750-1751* (New Haven: Yale University Press, 1916), 68; Andrew Burnaby, *Travels through the Middle Settlements in North America* (London: T. Payne, 1775), 81-82.

38. Joseph M. Levering, *History of Bethlehem, Pennsylvania, 1741-1892* (Bethlehem: Times Publishing Company, 1903), 225, 257, 291, 344, 379; *Pennsylvania Archives*, 3d ser., XIX, 23-27.

39. Levering, *Bethlehem*, 171, 289-90, 363-64; Raymond Walters, *Bethlehem Long Ago and Today* (Bethlehem: Carey Printing Company, 1923), 34.

40. Schoepf, *Travels*, I, 20-22; *Pennsylvania Archives*, 3d ser., XXI, 3-10.

41. *Maryland Gazette*, May 20, 1773; Albion and Dodson, *Journal of Fithian*, 9.

42. Carl Bridenbaugh, ed., *Gentleman's Progress: The Itinerarium of Dr. Alexander Hamilton, 1744* (Chapel Hill: University of North Carolina Press, 1948), 31; *American Weekly Mercury*, Philadelphia, September 26, 1723; September 5, 1734; *Pennsylvania Gazette*, August 2, 1739; August 15, 1745; January 17, 1765; *New York Evening Post*, October 15, 1750; *Pennsylvania Journal*, Philadelphia, May 6, 1756; *Pennsylvania Chronicle*, July 20, 1772.

43. *New England Weekly Journal*, Boston, March 19, 1733; *Pennsylvania Gazette*, November 15, 1764; August 29, 1765; September 9, 1772; *Pennsylvania Journal*, March 12, 1772; *New York Weekly Mercury*, June 29, 1772.

44. Benjamin F. Stevens, *Facsimiles of MSS in European Archives Relating to America, 1773-1783* (London: Malby and Sons, 1889-95), XXIV, No. 2,086; *Pennsylvania Archives,* 3d ser., XVII; Bezanson, Gray, and Hussey, *Prices in Colonial Pennsylvania,* 46; William Winterbotham, *An Historical, Geographical, Commercial, and Philosophical View of the United States* (London: J. Ridgeway, 1795), II, 466-67; J. Leander Bishop, *History of American Manufacturers from 1608 to 1860* (Philadelphia: Edward Young and Company, 1861-64), I, 111, 142.

45. *Pennsylvania Gazette,* March 26, 1772; *Pennsylvania Chronicle,* February 15, 1768, Postscript.

46. Arthur C. Bining, *Pennsylvania Iron Manufacture in the Eighteenth Century* (Harrisburg: Pennsylvania Historical Commission, 1938), 180, 187-89; Bining, *Colonial Iron Industry,* 26-31; C. S. Boyer, *Early Forges and Furnaces in New Jersey* (Philadelphia: University of Pennsylvania Press, 1931).

47. George Simpson Eddy, *Account Books Kept by Benjamin Franklin, 1739-1747* (New York: privately printed, 1928-29), I, 30; II, 16-18.

48. Stevens, *Facsimiles,* XXIV, No. 2,086; Lyman H. Weeks, *History of the Paper Manufacture in the United States, 1690-1916* (New York: Lockwood Company, 1916), 1-42; *American Weekly Mercury,* July 10, 1729; *New York Gazette,* April 7, 1735; *New York Weekly Mercury,* May 18, 1772; Joseph Richardson to John Paschall, March 1, 1757, Richardson Letter Book, 1702-57, Historical Society of Pennsylvania; Julius F. Sachse, "The Ephrata Paper Mill," Lancaster County Historical Society, *Papers,* I (1896), 323-28.

49. Frederick W. Hunter, *Stiegel Glass* (Boston: Houghton, Mifflin Company, 1914), 157-61; Caspar Wistar, Receipt Book, July 29, 1747, Historical Society of Pennsylvania.

50. *Pennsylvania Gazette,* November 23, December 7, 14, 1752; September 28, 1769; *Pennsylvanische Staatsbote,* Philadelphia, September 30, 1765; *Lancastersche Zeitung,* July 28, August 11, 1752; *New York Journal,* August 17, September 28, Supp., 1769; *Pennsylvania Chronicle,* July 31, 1769; *Pennsylvania Packet,* Philadelphia, August 7, 1775; *Pennsylvania Journal,* October 11, 1780.

51. *American Husbandry,* 509, 512, 513.

52. Clarence E. Carter, ed., *The Correspondence of General Thomas Gage* (New Haven: Yale University Press, 1931-33), II, 616.

Notes to Chapter III

1. *New York Post Boy*, March 19, 1753.

2. *New York Post Boy*, January 5, 1756.

3. *New York Weekly Mercury*, February 15, 1762; *South Carolina Gazette*, August 6, 1772.

4. Coxe, *View of the United States*, 443.

5. Edmund B. O'Callaghan, ed., *Documents relative to the Colonial History of New York* (Albany: Weed, Parsons and Company, 1856-87), IV, 322; *New York Weekly Mercury*, July 4, 1768; December 12, 1774; *New York Post Boy*, December 30, 1754.

6. *Boston Gazette*, August 1, 1763; May 5, 1766; *Boston Post Boy*, October 18, 1773; *Boston Weekly Advertiser*, April 9, 1759.

7. *An Extract of the Journal of Mr. Commissary Von Reck and of the Reverend Mr. Bolzius* (London: M. Downing, 1734), 26-27; *South Carolina Gazette*, February 28, May 8, 1736; January 29, Supp.; October 14, 21, 1756; May 3, 1770.

8. *Pennsylvania Archives*, 3d ser., XIV; Minutes of the Taylor's Company of Philadelphia, Instituted and Begun the 20th day of August, 1771, Historical Society of Pennsylvania; *Pennsylvania Gazette*, July 31, 1766; May 14, December 30, 1772.

9. *New York Weekly Mercury*, August 21, 1769; *Weyman's New York Gazette*, June 23, 1766; *Pennsylvania Gazette*, August 28, 1766; *South Carolina Gazette*, May 14, 1744.

10. *New York Post Boy*, January 16, December 10, 1744; *South Carolina Gazette*, November 15, 1760; November 16, 30, 1769; *Boston News Letter*, September 27, 1770; *Pennsylvania Gazette*, June 25, 1772; *Pennsylvania Journal*, July 17, 1766.

11. *New England Courant*, Boston, April 20, 1724; Colonial Records of Rhode Island (MS), V, 312, Rhode Island Archives, Providence; *Journal of John Lees of Quebec, Merchant* (Detroit: Speaker-Hines Press, 1911), 12.

12. *Boston Post Boy*, June 2, 9, 1760; March 22, 1762; January 17, February 7, 1763; *Boston Gazette*, March 28, 1774.

13. *South Carolina Gazette*, December 8, 1746; April 16, 1754; June 5, 1755; June 16, August 11, 1758; January 14, 1764; April 2, 1772; *South Carolina Gazette and Country Journal*, Charles Town, August 1, 1769.

14. *New York Weekly Mercury*, October 21, 1765; June 24, 1771;

April 12, 1773; *Albany Gazette*, February 24, 1772; *New York Post Boy*, February 18, 1744/5; March 14, 1757; "Journal of a French Traveller," 82.

15. *Pennsylvania Chronicle*, March 21, December 19, 1768; *Correspondence of General Gage*, II, 616.

16. *Boston News Letter*, October 18, 1764; Channing-Ellery Papers, I, 17, Rhode Island Historical Society; New-York Historical Society, *Collections*, 1885, pp. 55-238; *Pennsylvania Archives*, 3d ser., XIV.

17. Nehemiah Allen, Account Books, I-II, Historical Society of Pennsylvania.

18. R. W. Symonds prints important trade statistics in "The English Export Trade in Furniture to Colonial America," *Antiques*, XXVIII (1935), 214-17; XXVIII (1935), 156-59; see also an analysis by Edwin J. Hipkiss, "Merely a Pair of Chairs," Boston Museum of Fine Arts, *Bulletin*, XLII (1944), 56-59.

19. Treasury 1, Bundle 406, folio 30, Public Record Office, Library of Congress Transcripts; *Pennsylvania Gazette*, September 23, 1742; Paul H. Burroughs, "Two Centuries of Massachusetts Furniture," *American Collector*, VI (1937), 4-5, 11-13; William M. Hornor, *The Blue Book of Philadelphia Furniture* (Philadelphia: n.p., 1935), 191; Mabel M. Swan, "The Goddards and Townsends, Joiners," *Antiques*, XLIX (1946), 229, 231; George C. Mason, *Reminiscences of Newport* (Newport: C. E. Hammett, 1884), 49-50.

20. Hornor, *Philadelphia Furniture*, 191, 291-97; Harrold E. Gillingham, "The Philadelphia Windsor-Chair and Its Journeyings," *Pennsylvania Magazine of History and Biography*, LV (1931), 310-11; *South Carolina Gazette*, June 23, 1766; *Rivington's New York Gazetteer*, February 17, August 25, 1774; *New York Weekly Mercury*, August 8, 1774.

21. Hornor, *Philadelphia Furniture*, 2-5; *Pennsylvania Archives*, 3d ser., XIV; Bridenbaugh, *Gentleman's Progress*, 18.

22. Hornor, *Philadelphia Furniture*, 5-39; *South Carolina Gazette*, March 22, 1740.

23. *Pennsylvania Chronicle*, September 14, 1767; August 14, 1769; *Maryland Gazette*, October 5, 1769; David Evans, Day Book, 1774-1781, Historical Society of Pennsylvania; Hornor, *Philadelphia Furniture*, 90-93, 153-65; *Pennsylvania Packet*, January 30, 1775.

24. William M. Hornor, "William Savery," *Antiquarian*, XVI (1930), 32; David Evans, Day Book.

25. Hornor, *Philadelphia Furniture*, 74-77.

26. Abraham Redwood, Letter Book, I, 55, Newport Historical Society; Ward Papers, July 1, 1746, Rhode Island Historical Society; Swan, "Goddards and Townsends," 228-29.

27. Job Townsend, Jr., Ledger, 1750-1779; Vernon Papers, April 29, 1765, both in Newport Historical Society; Metropolitan Museum of Art, *The American Wing* (New York: the Museum, 1942), 118-19, 121, 123.

28. Moses Brown, Miscellaneous Letters, Rhode Island Historical Society; Vernon Papers, April 29, 1765; Edwin J. Hipkiss, *Eighteenth Century American Arts. The M. and M. Carolik Collection* (Boston: Museum of Fine Arts, 1941), x, 30, 32, 56, 64, 68, 98.

29. *American Weekly Mercury*, May 28, 1730; *Pennsylvania Chronicle*, December 7, 1767; October 30, 1769; October 22, 1770; March 4, 1771; October 24, 1772; Bining, *Pennsylvania Iron Manufacture*, 103, 188; *Pennsylvania Packet*, January 18, 1773, Supp.; *New York Weekly Mercury*, July 18, 1768; *New York Post Boy*, February 11, 1771.

30. Israel Acrelius, *History of New Sweden*, Historical Society of Pennsylvania, *Memoirs*, XI (1876), 7, 170; *Maryland Gazette*, December 11, 1760; H. L. Whittlesey, "Josiah Hornblower," *Dictionary of American Biography*, IX, 231-32; William Nelson, *Josiah Hornblower and the First Steam Engine in America* (Newark: Daily Advertiser Printing House, 1883); *New York Weekly Journal*, November 5, 1739; *New York Weekly Mercury*, March 22, 1762; *Pennsylvania Gazette*, November 15, 1764; *Pennsylvania Journal*, January 21, 1765.

31. *Pennsylvania Archives*, 3d ser., XIV.

32. *Boston Gazette*, March 12, 1770; *Boston Post Boy*, June 21, 1773; *New York Post Boy*, May 6, July 1, 1745; *New York Evening Post*, May 26, 1746; *New York Weekly Mercury*, May 27, 1754; *Pennsylvania Journal*, March 19, 1761; *Pennsylvanische Staatsbote*, June 30, 1772; *South Carolina Gazette*, January 4, 1734/5; Bridenbaugh, *Rebels and Gentlemen*, 319-21, 351-53; Saul K. Padover, ed., *The Complete Jefferson* (New York: Duell, Sloan and Pearce, 1943), 611-12.

33. Joseph Richardson, Account Book, 1733-1739; Letter Book, 1732-1757, both in Historical Society of Pennsylvania; *New York Weekly Mercury*, January 3, 1763; April 20, 1767; January 24, July 18, 1774; Hermann F. Clarke, *John Coney, Silversmith* (Boston: Houghton, Mifflin Company, 1932); Hollis French, *Jacob Hurd and His Sons, Silversmiths*

(Cambridge, Mass.: Walpole Society, 1939); John M. Phillips, *American Silver* (New York: Chanticleer Press, 1949), 11-23, 62-88.

34. Hunter, *Stiegel Glass*, 157-58; *Pennsylvania Gazette*, November 23, 1752; *New York Post Boy*, September 17, 1750; October 13, 1760; *New York Weekly Mercury*, March 18, 1765; *New York Journal and General Advertiser*, August 17, 1769, Supp.

35. *New York Weekly Mercury*, September 2, 1765; *Boston Gazette*, August 22, 1774; February 6, 1775.

36. *Pennsylvania Chronicle*, August 26, 1771; *Pennsylvania Gazette*, September 26, 1771; *Pennsylvania Packet*, March 2, 1772; March 13, 1773; *Early Proceedings of the American Philosophical Society*, 82-83.

37. *New York Weekly Mercury*, August 1, 1774; *Rivington's New York Gazetteer*, February 16, 1775.

38. *Boston News Letter*, October 5, 1758; *Boston Weekly Advertiser*, August 13, 1759.

39. *Boston Gazette*, April 13, 1761; March 28, 1763; August 17, 1767; January 24, 1770; *New Hampshire Gazette*, March 3, 1769.

40. *Boston Post Boy*, April 11, 1743; *New York Post Boy*, May 25, 1747; Treasury 1, Bundle 406, folio 30, P.R.O., Library of Congress Transcripts; *South Carolina Gazette*, August 3, 1765; *Maryland Gazette*, April 18, 1765.

41. *American Weekly Mercury*, May 8, 1729; *Pennsylvania Gazette*, August 1, 1751; February 14, 1765; *Maryland Gazette*, July 16, 1767; *New York Post Boy*, February 23, 1764; August 13, 1767; *New York Weekly Mercury*, September 28, 1767; *New York Journal and General Advertiser*, June 4, 1772.

42. Douglass, *Summary*, I, 539-40.

43. Lord John Sheffield, *Observations on the Commerce of the American States* (London: J. Debrett, 1784), 96; Acrelius, *New Sweden*, 143; *Pennsylvania Archives*, 3d ser., XIV.

44. George F. Dow, *The Sailing Ships of New England* (Salem: Marine Research Society, 1928), 3d ser., 10-15; for a ship built in seventy-three days in wartime, see *Pennsylvania Gazette*, June 24, 1762.

45. *Boston Evening Post*, September 7, 1741; *New Hampshire Gazette*, September 22, 1769; "Journal of a French Traveller," 79; *South Carolina Gazette*, February 24, June 23, 1757; November 14, 1771; *Pennsylvania Archives*, 3d ser., XIV.

46. John Banister, Account Book, 1739-1744, pp. 241-44, Newport Historical Society; see also the account books of James West, John Rey-

nell, and Joshua Humphreys at the Historical Society of Pennsylvania; Carl Bridenbaugh, *Peter Harrison: First American Architect* (Chapel Hill: University of North Carolina Press, 1949), 10-12.

47. Compiled from "Burghers and Freemen of New York," New-York Historical Society, *Collections*, 1885.

48. *Pennsylvania Archives*, 3d ser., XIV.

Notes to Chapter IV

1. Lawrence C. Wroth, *The Colonial Printer* (Portsmouth: Southworth Anthoensen Press, 1938), is the best single study of a craft.

2. Bridenbaugh, *Rebels and Gentlemen*, 76.

3. *Maryland Gazette*, November 1, 1753; *South Carolina Gazette*, November 15, 1752; *Pennsylvania Journal*, January 19, 1758; October 18, 1759; May 11, September 14, 1774; *Pennsylvania Packet*, May 23, December 5, 1774; *Pennsylvania Evening Post*, Philadelphia, May 11, June 29, 1775.

4. Meriwether, *Expansion of South Carolina*, 46-47; *American Collector*, VII (1939), 6-7.

5. Leonardo da Vinci, *Paragone: A Comparison of the Arts* (Oxford: Oxford University Press, 1949).

6. *Letters & Papers of John Singleton Copley and Henry Pelham*, Massachusetts Historical Society, *Collections*, LXXI, 65-66.

7. *New York Evening Post*, September 1, 1746; *Maryland Gazette*, October 12, 1752.

8. *Maryland Gazette*, March 17, 1753; *American Magazine or Monthly Chronicle for the British Colonies* (September, 1758), 607-8.

9. *Maryland Gazette*, January 21, 1762; May 12, 1763; February 9, 1764.

10. *Maryland Gazette*, September 8, 15, 22, October 6, 13, 20, 27, November 3, 1774.

11. *South Carolina Gazette*, December 16, 1756; February 2, 1765; *Boston Post Boy*, April 26, 1762; July 4, 1763; *Pennsylvania Chronicle*, July 13, 1767; *New York Post Boy*, June 6, 1765, Supp.; November 30, 1767; *Pennsylvania Gazette*, October 19, 1769; *Pennsylvania Packet*, May 29, 1775; *Pennsylvania Journal*, April 10, 1776; *Boston News Letter*, September 23, 1762; March 17, 1768.

12. Bridenbaugh, *Rebels and Gentlemen*, 203; *New York Weekly Mercury*, March 11, 1765; *Boston Gazette*, June 20, 1763; *Maryland*

Gazette, November 29, 1745; December 16, 1746; *New York Journal,* August 6, 1767.

13. *Boston News Letter,* April 3, 1729; *Massachusetts Gazette,* Boston, June 27, 1768; *New York Weekly Mercury,* December 27, 1756; *South Carolina Gazette,* August 6, 1772.

14. *South Carolina Gazette,* November 18, 1751; *Boston Post Boy,* June 22, 1767; *New York Post Boy,* August 5, 1771.

15. *Newport Mercury,* April 25, 1763; *South Carolina Gazette,* January 11, 1739; July 29, 1756, Supp.; *Maryland Gazette,* April 26, September 27, 1759; *Virginia Gazette* (Rind), September 2, 1773; *Providence Gazette,* August 24, 1765; *Maryland Journal,* Baltimore, May 10, 1775.

16. *South Carolina and American General Gazette,* Charleston, December 5, 1766.

17. *Maryland Gazette,* January 13, 1757; *South Carolina Gazette,* March 27, May 12, 1757; *North Carolina Gazette,* April 15, 1757; *Virginia Gazette,* April 22, 1757.

18. *Connecticut Courant,* June 3, 1765; *Maryland Gazette,* March 21, 1771; Frank R. Lewis, "Benjamin Franklin and the Society of Arts," *Pennsylvania History,* VI (1939), 19.

19. Franklin B. Dexter, ed., *Literary Diary of Ezra Stiles* (New York: Charles Scribner's Sons, 1901), I, 229.

20. William G. Saltonstall, *Ports of the Piscataqua* (Cambridge: Harvard University Press, 1941), 20-21, 29-31, 48; Sheffield, *Observations,* 96.

21. Saltonstall, *Ports of the Piscataqua,* 51-53; *New Hampshire Gazette,* April 26, 1774.

22. *New Hampshire Gazette,* January 15, 1762; August 12, 1768; September 22, 1769; Saltonstall, *Ports of the Piscataqua,* 52, 171-73.

23. Mabel M. Swan, "Coastwise Cargoes of Venture Furniture," *Antiques,* L (1949), 279; *North Carolina Magazine,* New Bern, November 16, 1764; *New Hampshire Gazette,* March 31, August 4, October 20, 1769; November 16, 1770; April 26, May 31, June 21, July 6, August 2, 1771; May 7, 1773; November 18, 1774.

24. *New Hampshire Gazette,* January 15, 1762; May 5, 1769; March 1, 8, 1771; May 28, December 17, 1773; *Freeman's Journal,* Portsmouth, August 24, 1776.

25. *New Hampshire Gazette,* October 25, 1765; January 31, 1772; January 29, 1773; February 17, 1775.

26. Gertrude S. Kimball, *Providence in Colonial Times* (Boston: Houghton, Mifflin Company, 1912), 244, 246, 276-77.

27. *Boston Chronicle,* May 24, 1770; *Commerce of Rhode Island,* Massachusetts Historical Society, *Collections,* XLIX, I, 88-92, 97-100; George F. Dow, *Whaling Ships and Whaling* (Salem: Marine Research Society, 1925), 35; Moses Brown Papers: Miscellaneous Letters, 1760, L60M, Rhode Island Historical Society.

28. Kimball, *Providence,* 249; Bridenbaugh, *Peter Harrison: First American Architect,* 11.

29. *Providence Gazette,* December 18, 1762; June 6, September 26, 1772; February 21, October 20, 1775; *Newport Mercury,* June 22, 1767.

30. Irving W. Lyon, *Colonial Furniture of New England* (Boston: Houghton, Mifflin Company, 1891), appendix; George Whipple, Account Book, 1764-1814, pp. 7-8, Institute of Early American History and Culture, Williamsburg, Va.

31. *Providence Gazette,* March 4, 1769; *Boston Chronicle,* February 5, 1770.

32. Lancaster County Historical Society, *Papers and Addresses,* XXVII (1923), 46; *Pennsylvania Archives,* 3d ser., XVII, 454-55.

33. *Ibid.,* 454-55; *Pennsylvania Gazette,* June 14, 1770; "Journal of a French Traveller," 80.

34. John G. W. Dillin, *The Kentucky Rifle* (Washington: National Rifle Association, 1924), 3, 7, 11-15, 17, 20, 21; *Pennsylvania Archives,* 3d ser., XVII, 454-55; *Papers and Addresses,* IX (1904), 67; XI (1907), 303, 305-6, 310-15; XXVII (1923), 91, 96; Meriwether, *Expansion of South Carolina,* 169; information communicated by Dr. Brooke Hindle; American Philosophical Society, *Transactions,* I (1771), 289.

35. *Pennsylvania Gazette,* February 26, 1750; John Omwake, *The Conestoga Six-Horse Bell Teams of Eastern Pennsylvania* (Cincinnati: Elbert and Richardson Company, 1930), 15-20.

36. *Pennsylvania Archives,* 3d ser., XVII, 654-65; *New York Post Boy,* April 9, 1774; Crèvecoeur, *Letters,* 81-82.

37. *Virginia Gazette,* July 22, 1737; October 30, 1738; May 15, 1752; *Virginia Gazette* (Purdie and Dixon), June 11, July 30, 1772; *Virginia Magazine of History and Biography,* XLIX (1941), 103-24; Rutherford Goodwin, *The William Parks Paper Mill at Williamsburg* (Lexington: Washington and Lee Press, 1939), 16.

38. *Maryland Gazette*, December 13, 1749; July 11, 1754; October 9, 1755; August 11, 1757; April 27, 1758; May 17, 1759; August 21, 1760; February 21, March 7, April 25, June 27, 1765; September 25, 1766; April 21, 1774.

39. E. Milby Burton, *South Carolina Silversmiths 1690-1860* (Charleston: Charleston Museum, 1942), 12-210; *South Carolina Gazette*, August 1, 1740; August 26, 1756; November 22, 1760; February 16, 1763; October 19, 31, 1765; June 27, 1768; October 25, 1773; *American Husbandry*, 312-13.

40. *South Carolina Gazette*, January 7, 1751; August 23, 1760; November 10, 1766; *South Carolina and American General Gazette*, August 14, 1769; Jennie H. Rose, "Thomas Elfe, Cabinet-Maker," *Antiques*, XXV (1934), 147-49; Rose, "Pre-Revolutionary Cabinet-Makers of Charleston," *Antiques*, XXIII (1933), 126-28, 184-85; *Statutes at Large of South Carolina*, III, 583.

41. Hipkiss, *Eighteenth Century American Arts*, x, xiii.

Notes to Chapter V

1. *New York Weekly Mercury*, January 30, 1769; *New York Post Boy*, January 10, 1757; Robert Anderson, Account Book, 1808-1812, p. 44, Virginia Historical Society, Colonial Williamsburg Transcript.

2. Herbert Heaton, *Economic History of Europe* (New York: Harper and Brothers, 1936), 337.

3. "Accounts of Losses, Miscellaneous Papers," *Twenty-Ninth Report of the Record Commissioners of the City of Boston* (Boston: the City, 1900), 5, 7-8, 72; Newport Town Council Records, IX, 379-80.

4. *Pennsylvania Archives*, 3d ser., XIV.

5. Clarke, *John Coney*, 14-15.

6. *New York Colonial Documents*, VIII, 888-89.

7. "Indentures of Apprentices, 1718-1727," New-York Historical Society, *Collections*, 1909, pp. 113-14, 122, 127, 130.

8. "Indentures of Apprentices," 113.

9. William L. Saunders, *Colonial Records of North Carolina* (Raleigh: P. M. Hale, 1886), I, 407, 577; *Boston Post Boy*, May 9, 1763; Vestry Minutes, St. Philip's Parish, Charleston, I, 71, 94, 121, 140, 158; II, 17.

10. *Two Centuries of Nazareth* (Nazareth: Nazareth Item Publishing Company, 1940), 31.

11. *New England Weekly Journal*, January 11, 1737; I. N. Phelps

Stokes, *Iconography of Manhattan Island* (New York: R. H. Dodd, 1922), IV, 489.

12. *Albany Gazette*, December 2, 1771; *Massachusetts Gazette*, April 10, 1769; *Boston Post Boy*, June 15, 1761; *Boston Gazette*, July 18, 1763; *New York Journal*, March 16, 1775.

13. *New England Courant*, March 5, 1722; *New York Post Boy*, January 3, 1765; St. Philip's Vestry Minutes, I, 158.

14. *Virginia Gazette*, June 13, 1728; April 16, 1767; *New York Post Boy*, August 5, 1771.

15. New-York Historical Society, *Collections*, 1884, pp. 464-65; John R. Bartlett, ed., *Records of the Colony of Rhode Island and Providence Plantation* (Providence: Knowles and Anthony, 1858), III, 544-46; William W. Hening, *The Statutes at Large: Being a Collection of all the Laws of Virginia* (Richmond: Franklin Press, 1819), V, 588; Public Records of South Carolina, XX, 498.

16. *New York Colonial Documents*, VIII, 888-89; *Maryland Gazette*, October 18, 1770.

17. *New York Post Boy*, April 18, 1757; October 29, 1760; *New York Weekly Mercury*, November 25, 1754; March 22, 1756; December 24, 1759; *Connecticut Courant*, 1771-1773, *passim*.

18. *Virginia Gazette* (Purdie and Dixon), January, 1771-December, 1773; *South Carolina Gazette*, June 30, 1758; *South Carolina Historical and Genealogical Magazine*, XXVI (1925), 27.

19. *New York Post Boy*, February 1, 1768; *South Carolina Gazette*, March 7, 1768; *Weyman's New York Gazette*, October 8, 1764.

20. *South Carolina Historical and Genealogical Magazine*, XXXV (1934), 15; *South Carolina Gazette*, June 30, 1758; *North Carolina Gazette*, November 15, 1751; *Georgia Historical Quarterly*, XVI (1932), 80, 84-85; *Albany Gazette*, February 17, 1772.

21. *New York Post Boy*, April 23, 1744; *Connecticut Courant*, March 20, 1775.

22. *New York Post Boy*, March 19, 1753.

23. *New York Gazette*, November 7, 1737; *American Husbandry*, 110, 510; Crèvecoeur, *Letters*, 76; Carl Bridenbaugh, ed., Patrick M'Robert, *Tour Through Part of the North Provinces of America*, . . . *1774-1775* (Philadelphia: Historical Society of Pennsylvania, 1935), 9-10, 14, 31; *New York Weekly Mercury*, August 7, 1758.

24. Hugh Jones, *Present State of Virginia*, 38; *William and Mary College Quarterly*, 1st ser., XXI (1912), 93; *Virginia Gazette* (Rind),

November 24, 1768; March 9, 1769; April 19, 1770; Marcus W. Jernegan, *Laboring and Dependent Classes in Colonial America* (Chicago: University of Chicago Press, 1931), chapter on "Slavery and the Beginnings of Industrialism."

25. Public Records of South Carolina, XXIV, 315-16.

26. *Virginia Magazine of History and Biography*, II (1895), 429; *Virginia County Records: Spotsylvania*, I, 308.

27. Peletiah Webster, "Journal of a Voyage to Charlestown," Southern History Association, *Publications*, II (1898), 135; *South Carolina Gazette*, December 7, 1747; February 29, 1748; March 15, 1770; *South Carolina and American General Gazette*, January 13, 1772; Burton, *South Carolina Silversmiths*, 52, 208-9.

28. Commons Journal, South Carolina, 1743-1744, XIX, 144, 159, 332-34; Council Journal, 1744, pp. 6-9; Snowden, "Labor Organizations in South Carolina," 1-7; Richard B. Morris, *Government and Labor in Early America* (New York: Columbia University Press, 1946), 184-85.

29. *South Carolina Gazette*, May 13, 1751; May 8, 1755, Supp.; August 26, 1756; May 17, 1773.

30. Bridenbaugh, *Cities in the Wilderness*, 200-1, 359; Morris, *Government and Labor*, 183; *New York Evening Post*, April 8, 1751; *New Hampshire Gazette*, August 12, 1768; Charles W. Brewster, *Rambles about Portsmouth* (Portsmouth: C. W. Brewster and Son, 1859), I, 208.

31. *Maryland Gazette*, January 27, 1757; April 16, 1761; August 6, 1764; March 21, 1765; M'Robert, *Tour*, 31; *Pennsylvania Journal*, August 1, 1771; *Pennsylvania Packet*, June 21, 1773.

32. *Maryland Gazette*, March 10, 1757; April 16, 1761; January 5, August 2, 1764; April 2, 1772.

33. *South Carolina Gazette*, November 9, 1734; March 22, 1740; *South Carolina Gazette and Country Journal*, April 15, 1766; March 24, 1767; *Pennsylvania Chronicle*, July 13, 1767; *Maryland Gazette*, April 9, 1767; January 19, 1774.

34. Bridenbaugh, *Cities in the Wilderness*, 198-99, 355; Beverley McAnear, "The Place of the Freeman in Old New York," *New York History*, XXI (1940), 418-30.

35. *Minutes of the Common Council of the City of Philadelphia* (Philadelphia: Crissy and Markley, 1847), 34, 145-47.

36. *An Act to Incorporate the Carpenter's Company of the City and County of Philadelphia* (Philadelphia: T. E. Chapman, 1857), 3, 14, 21;

New England Courant, December 7, 1724; *Boston News Letter,* February 19, 1741; December 31, 1747.

37. George W. Edwards, *New York as an Eighteenth-Century Municipality* (New York: Columbia University Press, 1917), 89-90; *New York Weekly Mercury,* August 7, 1758.

38. Bridenbaugh, *Rebels and Gentlemen,* 198; *New York Weekly Mercury,* November 18, 1771; Minutes of the Cordwainer's Fire Company; Minutes of the Taylor's Company, Historical Society of Pennsylvania.

39. Bridenbaugh, *Cities in the Wilderness,* 49-52, 201-3, 356.

40. *Connecticut Courant,* February 2, 23, March 2, 9, 1767; *Boston News Letter,* March 29, 1750.

41. *Virginia Gazette,* December 9, 1737; *South Carolina Gazette,* June 4, 1741; July 19, 1742; *Boston Gazette,* April 18, 1774.

42. *Boston Gazette,* April 11, 1774; *South Carolina Gazette,* March 12, 1737; May 17, 1773; *Maryland Gazette,* July 5, 12, 19, 1764; July 23, November 5, 1772; *Cape Fear Mercury,* January 13, 1773; *South Carolina Gazette and Country Journal,* June 3, 1766.

43. *Connecticut Courant,* March 20, 1775.

44. *Maryland Gazette,* May 19, 1768, Supp.

45. *New Hampshire Gazette,* January 6, March 17, 1769.

46. *New Hampshire Gazette,* March 24, 1769.

47. *Boston News Letter,* February 9, 1769; *New Hampshire Gazette,* April 14, 1769.

48. *New Hampshire Gazette,* April 21, 1769.

49. *New Hampshire Gazette,* July 14, August 18, September 1, 1769.

50. *New Hampshire Gazette,* January 12, February 2, May 8, 1770.

51. *New Hampshire Gazette,* June 29, 1770; *New York Journal,* August 23, 1770; *New York Post Boy,* December 23, 1771.

52. *New Hampshire Gazette,* December 27, 1771; May 22, 1772; May 6, 1774; April 21, 1775.

53. *Connecticut Courant,* February 2, 1767.

54. Wilbur C. Plummer, "Consumer Credit in Colonial Philadelphia," *Pennsylvania Magazine of History and Biography,* LXVI (1942), 390-94; *Virginia Gazette* (Purdie and Dixon), December 31, 1772; Bridenbaugh, *Cities in the Wilderness,* 344.

55. Plummer, "Consumer Credit in Philadelphia," 408-9.

Notes to Chapter VI

1. N. Bailey, comp., *Dictionarium Britannicum* (London: T. Cox, 1730); Bridenbaugh, *Gentleman's Progress*, 31.

2. Frederick B. Tolles, *Meeting House and Counting House: The Quaker Merchants of Colonial Philadelphia* (Chapel Hill: University of North Carolina Press, 1948), 117.

3. *Act to Incorporate the Carpenter's Company*; Bridenbaugh, *Rebels and Gentlemen*, 351-53.

4. *Copley-Pelham Letters*, 48, 68, 92n., 106-7, 134.

5. Record Commissioners of the City of Boston, *Sixteenth Report* (Boston: Rockwell and Churchill, 1886), 19, 35, 50, 70, 82; *Twenty-Third Report* (1893), 2.

6. Record Commissioners of the City of Boston, *Eighteenth Report* (Boston: Rockwell and Churchill, 1887), 64, 71; *Sixteenth Report*, 135; *Twenty-Ninth Report*, 320; *Boston Post Boy*, August 26, 1771.

7. *Eighteenth Report*, 72, 111, 130, 136, 151, 217; *Twenty-Third Report*, 132; Edward A. Jones, *Loyalists of Massachusetts* (London: St. Catherine Press, 1930), 226-27; *Boston Gazette*, September 21, 1772.

8. Isaac Q. Leake, *Memoir of the Life and Times of General John Lamb* (Albany: J. Munsell, 1857); *Dictionary of American Biography*, X, 555-56.

9. *Dictionary of American Biography*, XV, 637-38.

10. *Virginia Gazette* (Purdie and Dixon), September 3, 24, October 1, 1772.

11. Samuel G. Drake, *History and Antiquities of Boston* (Boston: L. Stevens, 1856), 544; "Journal of Josiah Quincy, jr.," Massachusetts Historical Society, *Proceedings*, XLIX (1915-16), 444n.; Lawrence S. Mayo, ed., Thomas Hutchinson, *The History of the Colony and Province of Massachusetts-Bay* (Cambridge: Harvard University Press, 1936), III, 87, 88; *New York Weekly Mercury*, October 10, 1763.

12. William Henry Drayton, *The Letters of Freeman* (London: printed in the year 1771), 60-61; "Journal of Josiah Quincy," 455.

13. Barbara M. Parker and Anne B. Wheeler, *John Singleton Copley* (Boston: Museum of Fine Arts, 1938), plates 4, 10, 26, 44, 45, 61, 63.

14. *Boston Gazette*, September 24, 1764.

15. Bridenbaugh, *Rebels and Gentlemen*, 20; *Pennsylvania Magazine of History and Biography*, XXIX (1905), 457; XVII (1893), 1, 274; *Boston Evening Post*, November 10, 1740.

16. *Pennsylvania Magazine of History and Biography*, XVII (1893), 267; *New York Post Boy*, August 31, 1747, Supp.; June 14, 1750; April 20, 1752; *New York Weekly Mercury*, August 13, 1753; February 16, 1756.

17. *New York Weekly Mercury*, October 10, 1763.

18. *New York Weekly Mercury*, May 10, 1762.

19. Bridenbaugh, *Rebels and Gentlemen*, 143-44; *New York Weekly Mercury*, May 8, 1766; May 3, 1773; *New York Post Boy*, February 1, 1768.

20. *New York Post Boy*, January 13, 1746; *New York Evening Post*, May 27, 1751.

21. *Boston News Letter*, November 9, 1738; November 9, 1758; May 14, 1761; *Boston Gazette*, April 2, 1769; *Newport Mercury*, May 22, 1759; October 24, November 7, December 26, 1763; Bridenbaugh, *Rebels and Gentlemen*, 37-40; *South Carolina Gazette*, December 31, 1744; June 16, 1766; *South Carolina Gazette and Country Journal*, May 28, 1771.

22. *South Carolina Gazette and Country Journal*, May 31, 1768; *Boston Post Boy*, May 30, 1743; George W. McCreary, *The Ancient and Honorable Mechanics Company of Baltimore* (Baltimore: Kohn and Pollock, 1901), 13, 26; Bridenbaugh, *Rebels and Gentlemen*, 86-91.

23. Stokes, *Iconography of Manhattan Island*, IV, 536.

24. Albert E. McKinley, *Suffrage Franchise in the American Colonies* (Philadelphia: University of Pennsylvania, 1905), 155-58, 160-61, 212, 217-18, 221, 288-93.

25. Charles M. Andrews, "Boston Merchants and the Non-Importation Movement," Colonial Society of Massachusetts, *Publications*, XIX (1917), 189-91; Arthur M. Schlesinger, *Colonial Merchants and the American Revolution* (New York: Columbia University Press, 1917), 56-59; Charles F. Adams, ed., *The Works of John Adams* (Boston: Little, Brown and Company, 1856), X, 260.

26. Plummer, "Consumer Credit in Philadelphia," 405-9; *New York Post Boy*, December 26, 1765; *New York Weekly Mercury*, December 25, 1769; Bridenbaugh, *Rebels and Gentlemen*, 250-52; *Pennsylvania Chronicle*, January 22, 1770; *Boston News Letter*, February 25, March 3, 1768; *Connecticut Courant*, 1766-67; *Newport Mercury*, June 25, 1764.

27. Samuel E. Morison, *Sources and Documents Illustrating the American Revolution* (Oxford: Clarendon Press, 1929), 165-76.

28. Arthur M. Schlesinger, "Colonial Newspapers and the Stamp Act," *New England Quarterly*, VIII (1935), 63-83; David D. Wallace, *Life of Henry Laurens* (New York: G. P. Putnam's Sons, 1915), 154-62.

29. *Boston Gazette*, September 23, 1765; McCreary, *Ancient and Honorable Mechanics Company of Baltimore*, 14-15, 18, 19, 25.

30. *Boston News Letter*, July 7, 1748; Esther Forbes, *Paul Revere and the World He Lived In* (Boston: Houghton, Mifflin Company, 1942), 91-202; Papers relating to New England: Chalmers Papers, Sparks MSS, XII, 2, Houghton Library, Harvard University; Lawrence H. Gipson, *Jared Ingersoll* (New Haven: Yale University Press, 1918), 270.

31. Carl L. Becker, *History of Political Parties in the Province of New York, 1760-1776* (Madison: University of Wisconsin, 1909), 41-51.

32. George P. Anderson, "Ebenezer Mackintosh: Stamp Act Rioter and Patriot," and "A Note on Ebenezer Mackintosh," Colonial Society of Massachusetts, *Publications*, XXVI (1924-26), 15-64, 180-210, 348-61; Joseph Johnson, *Traditions and Reminiscences Chiefly of the American Revolution in the South* (Charleston: Walker and James, 1851), 30-34; *South Carolina Gazette*, July 31, 1762; June 16, November 12, December 29, 1768.

33. Bridenbaugh, *Cities in the Wilderness*, 70, 223-24, 382-84, 388-89; *Boston Gazette*, November 2, 1767.

34. *Boston Chronicle*, November 7, 1768; *Boston Gazette*, June 27, 1774; *Connecticut Courant*, May 26, 1766; July 2, 1770; *Newport Mercury*, November 7, 1768.

35. *Connecticut Courant*, January 21, 1765; May 21, 1770; April 20, 1773; October 24, 1774; *Maryland Gazette*, February 15, September 12, 1765; *South Carolina Gazette*, May 3, 1770; *Boston Gazette*, February 6, 1775.

36. *Pennsylvania Magazine of History and Biography*, XIX (1895), 531-32.

37. William R. Smith, *South Carolina as a Royal Province* (New York: The Macmillan Company, 1903), 351; *South Carolina Gazette*, June 1, 1769; Schlesinger, *Colonial Merchants*, 140-47, 206.

INDEX

New England, 48, 110, 111
northern colonies, 44-46
southern colonies, 22
Metalworkers of Philadelphia, 85
Mills
middle colonies, 58-59
southern colonies, 19-20, 21, 24
See also Merchant mills; Paper mills
Millwrights, southern colonies, 19
Moore, Robert, 104
Moravian settlements
apprentices, 131
North Carolina, 26-29
Pennsylvania, 55-56
Morgan, Thomas, 142
Moses boats, 38
Mullam, Robert, 142

Nail industry, 48
Needles, 88
Negro craftsmen, 10, 138-41
carpenters, 11, 15
coopers, 13-14
ironworkers, 17-18
Neilson, George, 122
Newspapers, 98-99
New Hampshire, 110
role in Revolution, 174, 176
women publishers, 107
Nicholson, Francis, 168-69
Niles, Nathaniel, 48
Nonimportation agreements and crafts, 97-98
Norman, John, 99
Northern colonies
conditions favoring crafts, 33, 36
population, 33-34

See also Middle colonies; New England
Norwich, Conn., 47-48
Novelty trades, 104

Offley, Daniel, 84
Organ builders, 56
Orr, Hugh, 52

Paddock, Adino, 43, 90, 158-60
Painters. *See* Artists
Palmer, Joseph, 44
Paper mills
middle colonies, 61-62
New England, 47
Virginia, 121
Paschall, Stephen, 84
Pastorius, Francis Daniel, 54
Pateshall, Richard, 168
Pattison, Edward, 49
Payments
in kind or service, 9, 71, 82, 111, 153-54
slow collections, 9, 31, 121
Peale, Charles Willson, 12, 102-3, 149, 157, 180
Pennsylvania rifle, 117-18
Pewterers, 111, 114
"Philadelphia Brass Buttons," 87-88
Philadelphia, Pa., 125-26
Philadelphia-trained craftsmen, 142
Philadelphia Wagon Road, 23
Philips, David, 145
Plantation crafts, 10, 13-14, 15
Plumb, August, 43
Pooley, A., 100-1
Population figures on colonies, 6, 7, 66
Porteus, James, 144
Portsmouth, N.H., 108-12
Potash, making of, 104-5

A CATALOG OF SELECTED
DOVER BOOKS
IN ALL FIELDS OF INTEREST

A CATALOG OF SELECTED DOVER
BOOKS IN ALL FIELDS OF INTEREST

100 BEST-LOVED POEMS, Edited by Philip Smith. "The Passionate Shepherd to His Love," "Shall I compare thee to a summer's day?" "Death, be not proud," "The Raven," "The Road Not Taken," plus works by Blake, Wordsworth, Byron, Shelley, Keats, many others. 96pp. 5³⁄₁₆ x 8¼. 0-486-28553-7

100 SMALL HOUSES OF THE THIRTIES, Brown-Blodgett Company. Exterior photographs and floor plans for 100 charming structures. Illustrations of models accompanied by descriptions of interiors, color schemes, closet space, and other amenities. 200 illustrations. 112pp. 8⅜ x 11. 0-486-44131-8

1000 TURN-OF-THE-CENTURY HOUSES: With Illustrations and Floor Plans, Herbert C. Chivers. Reproduced from a rare edition, this showcase of homes ranges from cottages and bungalows to sprawling mansions. Each house is meticulously illustrated and accompanied by complete floor plans. 256pp. 9⅜ x 12¼.
0-486-45596-3

101 GREAT AMERICAN POEMS, Edited by The American Poetry & Literacy Project. Rich treasury of verse from the 19th and 20th centuries includes works by Edgar Allan Poe, Robert Frost, Walt Whitman, Langston Hughes, Emily Dickinson, T. S. Eliot, other notables. 96pp. 5³⁄₁₆ x 8¼. 0-486-40158-8

101 GREAT SAMURAI PRINTS, Utagawa Kuniyoshi. Kuniyoshi was a master of the warrior woodblock print — and these 18th-century illustrations represent the pinnacle of his craft. Full-color portraits of renowned Japanese samurais pulse with movement, passion, and remarkably fine detail. 112pp. 8⅜ x 11. 0-486-46523-3

ABC OF BALLET, Janet Grosser. Clearly worded, abundantly illustrated little guide defines basic ballet-related terms: arabesque, battement, pas de chat, relevé, sissonne, many others. Pronunciation guide included. Excellent primer. 48pp. 4³⁄₁₆ x 5¾.
0-486-40871-X

ACCESSORIES OF DRESS: An Illustrated Encyclopedia, Katherine Lester and Bess Viola Oerke. Illustrations of hats, veils, wigs, cravats, shawls, shoes, gloves, and other accessories enhance an engaging commentary that reveals the humor and charm of the many-sided story of accessorized apparel. 644 figures and 59 plates. 608pp. 6⅛ x 9¼.
0-486-43378-1

ADVENTURES OF HUCKLEBERRY FINN, Mark Twain. Join Huck and Jim as their boyhood adventures along the Mississippi River lead them into a world of excitement, danger, and self-discovery. Humorous narrative, lyrical descriptions of the Mississippi valley and memorable characters. 224pp. 5³⁄₁₆ x 8¼. 0-486-28061-6

ALICE STARMORE'S BOOK OF FAIR ISLE KNITTING, Alice Starmore. A noted designer from the region of Scotland's Fair Isle explores the history and techniques of this distinctive, stranded-color knitting style and provides copious illustrated instructions for 14 original knitwear designs. 208pp. 8⅜ x 10⅞. 0-486-47218-3

Browse over 9,000 books at www.doverpublications.com

ALICE'S ADVENTURES IN WONDERLAND, Lewis Carroll. Beloved classic about a little girl lost in a topsy-turvy land and her encounters with the White Rabbit, March Hare, Mad Hatter, Cheshire Cat, and other delightfully improbable characters. 42 illustrations by Sir John Tenniel. 96pp. 5³⁄₁₆ x 8¼.   0-486-27543-4

AMERICA'S LIGHTHOUSES: An Illustrated History, Francis Ross Holland. Profusely illustrated fact-filled survey of American lighthouses since 1716. Over 200 stations — East, Gulf, and West coasts, Great Lakes, Hawaii, Alaska, Puerto Rico, the Virgin Islands, and the Mississippi and St. Lawrence Rivers. 240pp. 8 x 10¾.
0-486-25576-X

AN ENCYCLOPEDIA OF THE VIOLIN, Alberto Bachmann. Translated by Frederick H. Martens. Introduction by Eugene Ysaye. First published in 1925, this renowned reference remains unsurpassed as a source of essential information, from construction and evolution to repertoire and technique. Includes a glossary and 73 illustrations. 496pp. 6½ x 9¼.   0-486-46618-3

ANIMALS: 1,419 Copyright-Free Illustrations of Mammals, Birds, Fish, Insects, etc., Selected by Jim Harter. Selected for its visual impact and ease of use, this outstanding collection of wood engravings presents over 1,000 species of animals in extremely lifelike poses. Includes mammals, birds, reptiles, amphibians, fish, insects, and other invertebrates. 284pp. 9 x 12.   0-486-23766-4

THE ANNALS, Tacitus. Translated by Alfred John Church and William Jackson Brodribb. This vital chronicle of Imperial Rome, written by the era's great historian, spans A.D. 14-68 and paints incisive psychological portraits of major figures, from Tiberius to Nero. 416pp. 5³⁄₁₆ x 8¼.   0-486-45236-0

ANTIGONE, Sophocles. Filled with passionate speeches and sensitive probing of moral and philosophical issues, this powerful and often-performed Greek drama reveals the grim fate that befalls the children of Oedipus. Footnotes. 64pp. 5³⁄₁₆ x 8 ¼.   0-486-27804-2

ART DECO DECORATIVE PATTERNS IN FULL COLOR, Christian Stoll. Reprinted from a rare 1910 portfolio, 160 sensuous and exotic images depict a breathtaking array of florals, geometrics, and abstracts — all elegant in their stark simplicity. 64pp. 8⅜ x 11.   0-486-44862-2

THE ARTHUR RACKHAM TREASURY: 86 Full-Color Illustrations, Arthur Rackham. Selected and Edited by Jeff A. Menges. A stunning treasury of 86 full-page plates span the famed English artist's career, from *Rip Van Winkle* (1905) to masterworks such as *Undine, A Midsummer Night's Dream,* and *Wind in the Willows* (1939). 96pp. 8⅜ x 11.
0-486-44685-9

THE AUTHENTIC GILBERT & SULLIVAN SONGBOOK, W. S. Gilbert and A. S. Sullivan. The most comprehensive collection available, this songbook includes selections from every one of Gilbert and Sullivan's light operas. Ninety-two numbers are presented uncut and unedited, and in their original keys. 410pp. 9 x 12.
0-486-23482-7

THE AWAKENING, Kate Chopin. First published in 1899, this controversial novel of a New Orleans wife's search for love outside a stifling marriage shocked readers. Today, it remains a first-rate narrative with superb characterization. New introductory Note. 128pp. 5³⁄₁₆ x 8¼.   0-486-27786-0

BASIC DRAWING, Louis Priscilla. Beginning with perspective, this commonsense manual progresses to the figure in movement, light and shade, anatomy, drapery, composition, trees and landscape, and outdoor sketching. Black-and-white illustrations throughout. 128pp. 8⅜ x 11.   0-486-45815-6

THE BATTLES THAT CHANGED HISTORY, Fletcher Pratt. Historian profiles 16 crucial conflicts, ancient to modern, that changed the course of Western civilization. Gripping accounts of battles led by Alexander the Great, Joan of Arc, Ulysses S. Grant, other commanders. 27 maps. 352pp. 5⅜ x 8½. 0-486-41129-X

BEETHOVEN'S LETTERS, Ludwig van Beethoven. Edited by Dr. A. C. Kalischer. Features 457 letters to fellow musicians, friends, greats, patrons, and literary men. Reveals musical thoughts, quirks of personality, insights, and daily events. Includes 15 plates. 410pp. 5⅜ x 8½. 0-486-22769-3

BERNICE BOBS HER HAIR AND OTHER STORIES, F. Scott Fitzgerald. This brilliant anthology includes 6 of Fitzgerald's most popular stories: "The Diamond as Big as the Ritz," the title tale, "The Offshore Pirate," "The Ice Palace," "The Jelly Bean," and "May Day." 176pp. 5⅜ x 8½. 0-486-47049-0

BESLER'S BOOK OF FLOWERS AND PLANTS: 73 Full-Color Plates from Hortus Eystettensis, 1613, Basilius Besler. Here is a selection of magnificent plates from the *Hortus Eystettensis,* which vividly illustrated and identified the plants, flowers, and trees that thrived in the legendary German garden at Eichstätt. 80pp. 8⅜ x 11.
0-486-46005-3

THE BOOK OF KELLS, Edited by Blanche Cirker. Painstakingly reproduced from a rare facsimile edition, this volume contains full-page decorations, portraits, illustrations, plus a sampling of textual leaves with exquisite calligraphy and ornamentation. 32 full-color illustrations. 32pp. 9⅜ x 12¼. 0-486-24345-1

THE BOOK OF THE CROSSBOW: With an Additional Section on Catapults and Other Siege Engines, Ralph Payne-Gallwey. Fascinating study traces history and use of crossbow as military and sporting weapon, from Middle Ages to modern times. Also covers related weapons: balistas, catapults, Turkish bows, more. Over 240 illustrations. 400pp. 7¼ x 10¼. 0-486-28720-3

THE BUNGALOW BOOK: Floor Plans and Photos of 112 Houses, 1910, Henry L. Wilson. Here are 112 of the most popular and economic blueprints of the early 20th century — plus an illustration or photograph of each completed house. A wonderful time capsule that still offers a wealth of valuable insights. 160pp. 8⅜ x 11.
0-486-45104-6

THE CALL OF THE WILD, Jack London. A classic novel of adventure, drawn from London's own experiences as a Klondike adventurer, relating the story of a heroic dog caught in the brutal life of the Alaska Gold Rush. Note. 64pp. 5³⁄₁₆ x 8¼.
0-486-26472-6

CANDIDE, Voltaire. Edited by Francois-Marie Arouet. One of the world's great satires since its first publication in 1759. Witty, caustic skewering of romance, science, philosophy, religion, government — nearly all human ideals and institutions. 112pp. 5³⁄₁₆ x 8¼. 0-486-26689-3

CELEBRATED IN THEIR TIME: Photographic Portraits from the George Grantham Bain Collection, Edited by Amy Pastan. With an Introduction by Michael Carlebach. Remarkable portrait gallery features 112 rare images of Albert Einstein, Charlie Chaplin, the Wright Brothers, Henry Ford, and other luminaries from the worlds of politics, art, entertainment, and industry. 128pp. 8⅜ x 11. 0-486-46754-6

CHARIOTS FOR APOLLO: The NASA History of Manned Lunar Spacecraft to 1969, Courtney G. Brooks, James M. Grimwood, and Loyd S. Swenson, Jr. This illustrated history by a trio of experts is the definitive reference on the Apollo spacecraft and lunar modules. It traces the vehicles' design, development, and operation in space. More than 100 photographs and illustrations. 576pp. 6¾ x 9¼. 0-486-46756-2

Browse over 9,000 books at www.doverpublications.com

A CHRISTMAS CAROL, Charles Dickens. This engrossing tale relates Ebenezer Scrooge's ghostly journeys through Christmases past, present, and future and his ultimate transformation from a harsh and grasping old miser to a charitable and compassionate human being. 80pp. 5³⁄₁₆ x 8¼. 0-486-26865-9

COMMON SENSE, Thomas Paine. First published in January of 1776, this highly influential landmark document clearly and persuasively argued for American separation from Great Britain and paved the way for the Declaration of Independence. 64pp. 5³⁄₁₆ x 8¼. 0-486-29602-4

THE COMPLETE SHORT STORIES OF OSCAR WILDE, Oscar Wilde. Complete texts of "The Happy Prince and Other Tales," "A House of Pomegranates," "Lord Arthur Savile's Crime and Other Stories," "Poems in Prose," and "The Portrait of Mr. W. H." 208pp. 5³⁄₁₆ x 8¼. 0-486-45216-6

COMPLETE SONNETS, William Shakespeare. Over 150 exquisite poems deal with love, friendship, the tyranny of time, beauty's evanescence, death, and other themes in language of remarkable power, precision, and beauty. Glossary of archaic terms. 80pp. 5³⁄₁₆ x 8¼. 0-486-26686-9

THE COUNT OF MONTE CRISTO: Abridged Edition, Alexandre Dumas. Falsely accused of treason, Edmond Dantès is imprisoned in the bleak Chateau d'If. After a hair-raising escape, he launches an elaborate plot to extract a bitter revenge against those who betrayed him. 448pp. 5³⁄₁₆ x 8¼. 0-486-45643-9

CRAFTSMAN BUNGALOWS: Designs from the Pacific Northwest, Yoho & Merritt. This reprint of a rare catalog, showcasing the charming simplicity and cozy style of Craftsman bungalows, is filled with photos of completed homes, plus floor plans and estimated costs. An indispensable resource for architects, historians, and illustrators. 112pp. 10 x 7. 0-486-46875-5

CRAFTSMAN BUNGALOWS: 59 Homes from "The Craftsman," Edited by Gustav Stickley. Best and most attractive designs from Arts and Crafts Movement publication — 1903–1916 — includes sketches, photographs of homes, floor plans, descriptive text. 128pp. 8¼ x 11. 0-486-25829-7

CRIME AND PUNISHMENT, Fyodor Dostoyevsky. Translated by Constance Garnett. Supreme masterpiece tells the story of Raskolnikov, a student tormented by his own thoughts after he murders an old woman. Overwhelmed by guilt and terror, he confesses and goes to prison. 480pp. 5³⁄₁₆ x 8¼. 0-486-41587-2

THE DECLARATION OF INDEPENDENCE AND OTHER GREAT DOCUMENTS OF AMERICAN HISTORY: 1775-1865, Edited by John Grafton. Thirteen compelling and influential documents: Henry's "Give Me Liberty or Give Me Death," Declaration of Independence, The Constitution, Washington's First Inaugural Address, The Monroe Doctrine, The Emancipation Proclamation, Gettysburg Address, more. 64pp. 5³⁄₁₆ x 8¼. 0-486-41124-9

THE DESERT AND THE SOWN: Travels in Palestine and Syria, Gertrude Bell. "The female Lawrence of Arabia," Gertrude Bell wrote captivating, perceptive accounts of her travels in the Middle East. This intriguing narrative, accompanied by 160 photos, traces her 1905 sojourn in Lebanon, Syria, and Palestine. 368pp. 5⅜ x 8¼. 0-486-46876-3

A DOLL'S HOUSE, Henrik Ibsen. Ibsen's best-known play displays his genius for realistic prose drama. An expression of women's rights, the play climaxes when the central character, Nora, rejects a smothering marriage and life in "a doll's house." 80pp. 5³⁄₁₆ x 8¼. 0-486-27062-9

DOOMED SHIPS: Great Ocean Liner Disasters, William H. Miller, Jr. Nearly 200 photographs, many from private collections, highlight tales of some of the vessels whose pleasure cruises ended in catastrophe: the *Morro Castle, Normandie, Andrea Doria, Europa,* and many others. 128pp. 8⅞ x 11¾. 0-486-45366-9

THE DORÉ BIBLE ILLUSTRATIONS, Gustave Doré. Detailed plates from the Bible: the Creation scenes, Adam and Eve, horrifying visions of the Flood, the battle sequences with their monumental crowds, depictions of the life of Jesus, 241 plates in all. 241pp. 9 x 12. 0-486-23004-X

DRAWING DRAPERY FROM HEAD TO TOE, Cliff Young. Expert guidance on how to draw shirts, pants, skirts, gloves, hats, and coats on the human figure, including folds in relation to the body, pull and crush, action folds, creases, more. Over 200 drawings. 48pp. 8¼ x 11. 0-486-45591-2

DUBLINERS, James Joyce. A fine and accessible introduction to the work of one of the 20th century's most influential writers, this collection features 15 tales, including a masterpiece of the short-story genre, "The Dead." 160pp. 5³⁄₁₆ x 8¼. 0-486-26870-5

EASY-TO-MAKE POP-UPS, Joan Irvine. Illustrated by Barbara Reid. Dozens of wonderful ideas for three-dimensional paper fun — from holiday greeting cards with moving parts to a pop-up menagerie. Easy-to-follow, illustrated instructions for more than 30 projects. 299 black-and-white illustrations. 96pp. 8⅜ x 11. 0-486-44622-0

EASY-TO-MAKE STORYBOOK DOLLS: A "Novel" Approach to Cloth Dollmaking, Sherralyn St. Clair. Favorite fictional characters come alive in this unique beginner's dollmaking guide. Includes patterns for Pollyanna, Dorothy from *The Wonderful Wizard of Oz,* Mary of *The Secret Garden,* plus easy-to-follow instructions, 263 black-and-white illustrations, and an 8-page color insert. 112pp. 8¼ x 11. 0-486-47360-0

EINSTEIN'S ESSAYS IN SCIENCE, Albert Einstein. Speeches and essays in accessible, everyday language profile influential physicists such as Niels Bohr and Isaac Newton. They also explore areas of physics to which the author made major contributions. 128pp. 5 x 8. 0-486-47011-3

EL DORADO: Further Adventures of the Scarlet Pimpernel, Baroness Orczy. A popular sequel to *The Scarlet Pimpernel,* this suspenseful story recounts the Pimpernel's attempts to rescue the Dauphin from imprisonment during the French Revolution. An irresistible blend of intrigue, period detail, and vibrant characterizations. 352pp. 5³⁄₁₆ x 8¼. 0-486-44026-5

ELEGANT SMALL HOMES OF THE TWENTIES: 99 Designs from a Competition, Chicago Tribune. Nearly 100 designs for five- and six-room houses feature New England and Southern colonials, Normandy cottages, stately Italianate dwellings, and other fascinating snapshots of American domestic architecture of the 1920s. 112pp. 9 x 12. 0-486-46910-7

THE ELEMENTS OF STYLE: The Original Edition, William Strunk, Jr. This is the book that generations of writers have relied upon for timeless advice on grammar, diction, syntax, and other essentials. In concise terms, it identifies the principal requirements of proper style and common errors. 64pp. 5⅜ x 8½. 0-486-44798-7

THE ELUSIVE PIMPERNEL, Baroness Orczy. Robespierre's revolutionaries find their wicked schemes thwarted by the heroic Pimpernel — Sir Percival Blakeney. In this thrilling sequel, Chauvelin devises a plot to eliminate the Pimpernel and his wife. 272pp. 5³⁄₁₆ x 8¼. 0-486-45464-9

AN ENCYCLOPEDIA OF BATTLES: Accounts of Over 1,560 Battles from 1479 B.C. to the Present, David Eggenberger. Essential details of every major battle in recorded history from the first battle of Megiddo in 1479 B.C. to Grenada in 1984. List of battle maps. 99 illustrations. 544pp. 6½ x 9¼. 0-486-24913-1

ENCYCLOPEDIA OF EMBROIDERY STITCHES, INCLUDING CREWEL, Marion Nichols. Precise explanations and instructions, clearly illustrated, on how to work chain, back, cross, knotted, woven stitches, and many more — 178 in all, including Cable Outline, Whipped Satin, and Eyelet Buttonhole. Over 1400 illustrations. 219pp. 8⅜ x 11¼. 0-486-22929-7

ENTER JEEVES: 15 Early Stories, P. G. Wodehouse. Splendid collection contains first 8 stories featuring Bertie Wooster, the deliciously dim aristocrat and Jeeves, his brainy, imperturbable manservant. Also, the complete Reggie Pepper (Bertie's prototype) series. 288pp. 5⅜ x 8½. 0-486-29717-9

ERIC SLOANE'S AMERICA: Paintings in Oil, Michael Wigley. With a Foreword by Mimi Sloane. Eric Sloane's evocative oils of America's landscape and material culture shimmer with immense historical and nostalgic appeal. This original hardcover collection gathers nearly a hundred of his finest paintings, with subjects ranging from New England to the American Southwest. 128pp. 10⅝ x 9.
0-486-46525-X

ETHAN FROME, Edith Wharton. Classic story of wasted lives, set against a bleak New England background. Superbly delineated characters in a hauntingly grim tale of thwarted love. Considered by many to be Wharton's masterpiece. 96pp. 5³⁄₁₆ x 8¼.
0-486-26690-7

THE EVERLASTING MAN, G. K. Chesterton. Chesterton's view of Christianity — as a blend of philosophy and mythology, satisfying intellect and spirit — applies to his brilliant book, which appeals to readers' heads as well as their hearts. 288pp. 5⅜ x 8½.
0-486-46036-3

THE FIELD AND FOREST HANDY BOOK, Daniel Beard. Written by a co-founder of the Boy Scouts, this appealing guide offers illustrated instructions for building kites, birdhouses, boats, igloos, and other fun projects, plus numerous helpful tips for campers. 448pp. 5³⁄₁₆ x 8¼. 0-486-46191-2

FINDING YOUR WAY WITHOUT MAP OR COMPASS, Harold Gatty. Useful, instructive manual shows would-be explorers, hikers, bikers, scouts, sailors, and survivalists how to find their way outdoors by observing animals, weather patterns, shifting sands, and other elements of nature. 288pp. 5⅜ x 8½. 0-486-40613-X

FIRST FRENCH READER: A Beginner's Dual-Language Book, Edited and Translated by Stanley Appelbaum. This anthology introduces 50 legendary writers — Voltaire, Balzac, Baudelaire, Proust, more — through passages from *The Red and the Black, Les Misérables, Madame Bovary,* and other classics. Original French text plus English translation on facing pages. 240pp. 5⅜ x 8½. 0-486-46178-5

FIRST GERMAN READER: A Beginner's Dual-Language Book, Edited by Harry Steinhauer. Specially chosen for their power to evoke German life and culture, these short, simple readings include poems, stories, essays, and anecdotes by Goethe, Hesse, Heine, Schiller, and others. 224pp. 5⅜ x 8½. 0-486-46179-3

FIRST SPANISH READER: A Beginner's Dual-Language Book, Angel Flores. Delightful stories, other material based on works of Don Juan Manuel, Luis Taboada, Ricardo Palma, other noted writers. Complete faithful English translations on facing pages. Exercises. 176pp. 5⅜ x 8½. 0-486-25810-6

FIVE ACRES AND INDEPENDENCE, Maurice G. Kains. Great back-to-the-land classic explains basics of self-sufficient farming. The one book to get. 95 illustrations. 397pp. 5⅜ x 8½. 0-486-20974-1

FLAGG'S SMALL HOUSES: Their Economic Design and Construction, 1922, Ernest Flagg. Although most famous for his skyscrapers, Flagg was also a proponent of the well-designed single-family dwelling. His classic treatise features innovations that save space, materials, and cost. 526 illustrations. 160pp. 9⅜ x 12¼.
0-486-45197-6

FLATLAND: A Romance of Many Dimensions, Edwin A. Abbott. Classic of science (and mathematical) fiction — charmingly illustrated by the author — describes the adventures of A. Square, a resident of Flatland, in Spaceland (three dimensions), Lineland (one dimension), and Pointland (no dimensions). 96pp. 5³⁄₁₆ x 8¼.
0-486-27263-X

FRANKENSTEIN, Mary Shelley. The story of Victor Frankenstein's monstrous creation and the havoc it caused has enthralled generations of readers and inspired countless writers of horror and suspense. With the author's own 1831 introduction. 176pp. 5³⁄₁₆ x 8¼. 0-486-28211-2

THE GARGOYLE BOOK: 572 Examples from Gothic Architecture, Lester Burbank Bridaham. Dispelling the conventional wisdom that French Gothic architectural flourishes were born of despair or gloom, Bridaham reveals the whimsical nature of these creations and the ingenious artisans who made them. 572 illustrations. 224pp. 8⅜ x 11. 0-486-44754-5

THE GIFT OF THE MAGI AND OTHER SHORT STORIES, O. Henry. Sixteen captivating stories by one of America's most popular storytellers. Included are such classics as "The Gift of the Magi," "The Last Leaf," and "The Ransom of Red Chief." Publisher's Note. 96pp. 5³⁄₁₆ x 8¼. 0-486-27061-0

THE GOETHE TREASURY: Selected Prose and Poetry, Johann Wolfgang von Goethe. Edited, Selected, and with an Introduction by Thomas Mann. In addition to his lyric poetry, Goethe wrote travel sketches, autobiographical studies, essays, letters, and proverbs in rhyme and prose. This collection presents outstanding examples from each genre. 368pp. 5⅜ x 8½. 0-486-44780-4

GREAT EXPECTATIONS, Charles Dickens. Orphaned Pip is apprenticed to the dirty work of the forge but dreams of becoming a gentleman — and one day finds himself in possession of "great expectations." Dickens' finest novel. 400pp. 5³⁄₁₆ x 8¼.
0-486-41586-4

GREAT WRITERS ON THE ART OF FICTION: From Mark Twain to Joyce Carol Oates, Edited by James Daley. An indispensable source of advice and inspiration, this anthology features essays by Henry James, Kate Chopin, Willa Cather, Sinclair Lewis, Jack London, Raymond Chandler, Raymond Carver, Eudora Welty, and Kurt Vonnegut, Jr. 192pp. 5⅜ x 8½. 0-486-45128-3

HAMLET, William Shakespeare. The quintessential Shakespearean tragedy, whose highly charged confrontations and anguished soliloquies probe depths of human feeling rarely sounded in any art. Reprinted from an authoritative British edition complete with illuminating footnotes. 128pp. 5³⁄₁₆ x 8¼. 0-486-27278-8

THE HAUNTED HOUSE, Charles Dickens. A Yuletide gathering in an eerie country retreat provides the backdrop for Dickens and his friends — including Elizabeth Gaskell and Wilkie Collins — who take turns spinning supernatural yarns. 144pp. 5⅜ x 8½. 0-486-46309-5

HEART OF DARKNESS, Joseph Conrad. Dark allegory of a journey up the Congo River and the narrator's encounter with the mysterious Mr. Kurtz. Masterly blend of adventure, character study, psychological penetration. For many, Conrad's finest, most enigmatic story. 80pp. 5$\frac{3}{16}$ x 8$\frac{1}{4}$. 0-486-26464-5

HENSON AT THE NORTH POLE, Matthew A. Henson. This thrilling memoir by the heroic African-American who was Peary's companion through two decades of Arctic exploration recounts a tale of danger, courage, and determination. "Fascinating and exciting." — *Commonweal*. 128pp. 5$\frac{3}{8}$ x 8$\frac{1}{2}$. 0-486-45472-X

HISTORIC COSTUMES AND HOW TO MAKE THEM, Mary Fernald and E. Shenton. Practical, informative guidebook shows how to create everything from short tunics worn by Saxon men in the fifth century to a lady's bustle dress of the late 1800s. 81 illustrations. 176pp. 5$\frac{3}{8}$ x 8$\frac{1}{2}$. 0-486-44906-8

THE HOUND OF THE BASKERVILLES, Arthur Conan Doyle. A deadly curse in the form of a legendary ferocious beast continues to claim its victims from the Baskerville family until Holmes and Watson intervene. Often called the best detective story ever written. 128pp. 5$\frac{3}{16}$ x 8$\frac{1}{4}$. 0-486-28214-7

THE HOUSE BEHIND THE CEDARS, Charles W. Chesnutt. Originally published in 1900, this groundbreaking novel by a distinguished African-American author recounts the drama of a brother and sister who "pass for white" during the dangerous days of Reconstruction. 208pp. 5$\frac{3}{8}$ x 8$\frac{1}{2}$. 0-486-46144-0

THE HUMAN FIGURE IN MOTION, Eadweard Muybridge. The 4,789 photographs in this definitive selection show the human figure — models almost all undraped — engaged in over 160 different types of action: running, climbing stairs, etc. 390pp. 7$\frac{7}{8}$ x 10$\frac{5}{8}$. 0-486-20204-6

THE IMPORTANCE OF BEING EARNEST, Oscar Wilde. Wilde's witty and buoyant comedy of manners, filled with some of literature's most famous epigrams, reprinted from an authoritative British edition. Considered Wilde's most perfect work. 64pp. 5$\frac{3}{16}$ x 8$\frac{1}{4}$. 0-486-26478-5

THE INFERNO, Dante Alighieri. Translated and with notes by Henry Wadsworth Longfellow. The first stop on Dante's famous journey from Hell to Purgatory to Paradise, this 14th-century allegorical poem blends vivid and shocking imagery with graceful lyricism. Translated by the beloved 19th-century poet, Henry Wadsworth Longfellow. 256pp. 5$\frac{3}{16}$ x 8$\frac{1}{4}$. 0-486-44288-8

JANE EYRE, Charlotte Brontë. Written in 1847, *Jane Eyre* tells the tale of an orphan girl's progress from the custody of cruel relatives to an oppressive boarding school and its culmination in a troubled career as a governess. 448pp. 5$\frac{3}{16}$ x 8$\frac{1}{4}$. 0-486-42449-9

JAPANESE WOODBLOCK FLOWER PRINTS, Tanigami Kônan. Extraordinary collection of Japanese woodblock prints by a well-known artist features 120 plates in brilliant color. Realistic images from a rare edition include daffodils, tulips, and other familiar and unusual flowers. 128pp. 11 x 8$\frac{1}{4}$. 0-486-46442-3

JEWELRY MAKING AND DESIGN, Augustus F. Rose and Antonio Cirino. Professional secrets of jewelry making are revealed in a thorough, practical guide. Over 200 illustrations. 306pp. 5$\frac{3}{8}$ x 8$\frac{1}{2}$. 0-486-21750-7

JULIUS CAESAR, William Shakespeare. Great tragedy based on Plutarch's account of the lives of Brutus, Julius Caesar and Mark Antony. Evil plotting, ringing oratory, high tragedy with Shakespeare's incomparable insight, dramatic power. Explanatory footnotes. 96pp. 5$\frac{3}{16}$ x 8$\frac{1}{4}$. 0-486-26876-4

THE JUNGLE, Upton Sinclair. 1906 bestseller shockingly reveals intolerable labor practices and working conditions in the Chicago stockyards as it tells the grim story of a Slavic family that emigrates to America full of optimism but soon faces despair. 320pp. 5³⁄₁₆ x 8¼. 0-486-41923-1

THE KINGDOM OF GOD IS WITHIN YOU, Leo Tolstoy. The soul-searching book that inspired Gandhi to embrace the concept of passive resistance, Tolstoy's 1894 polemic clearly outlines a radical, well-reasoned revision of traditional Christian thinking. 352pp. 5³⁄₁₆ x 8¼. 0-486-45138-0

THE LADY OR THE TIGER?: and Other Logic Puzzles, Raymond M. Smullyan. Created by a renowned puzzle master, these whimsically themed challenges involve paradoxes about probability, time, and change; metapuzzles; and self-referentiality. Nineteen chapters advance in difficulty from relatively simple to highly complex. 1982 edition. 240pp. 5⅜ x 8½. 0-486-47027-X

LEAVES OF GRASS: The Original 1855 Edition, Walt Whitman. Whitman's immortal collection includes some of the greatest poems of modern times, including his masterpiece, "Song of Myself." Shattering standard conventions, it stands as an unabashed celebration of body and nature. 128pp. 5³⁄₁₆ x 8¼. 0-486-45676-5

LES MISÉRABLES, Victor Hugo. Translated by Charles E. Wilbour. Abridged by James K. Robinson. A convict's heroic struggle for justice and redemption plays out against a fiery backdrop of the Napoleonic wars. This edition features the excellent original translation and a sensitive abridgment. 304pp. 6⅛ x 9¼. 0-486-45789-3

LILITH: A Romance, George MacDonald. In this novel by the father of fantasy literature, a man travels through time to meet Adam and Eve and to explore humanity's fall from grace and ultimate redemption. 240pp. 5⅜ x 8½. 0-486-46818-6

THE LOST LANGUAGE OF SYMBOLISM, Harold Bayley. This remarkable book reveals the hidden meaning behind familiar images and words, from the origins of Santa Claus to the fleur-de-lys, drawing from mythology, folklore, religious texts, and fairy tales. 1,418 illustrations. 784pp. 5⅜ x 8½. 0-486-44787-1

MACBETH, William Shakespeare. A Scottish nobleman murders the king in order to succeed to the throne. Tortured by his conscience and fearful of discovery, he becomes tangled in a web of treachery and deceit that ultimately spells his doom. 96pp. 5³⁄₁₆ x 8¼. 0-486-27802-6

MAKING AUTHENTIC CRAFTSMAN FURNITURE: Instructions and Plans for 62 Projects, Gustav Stickley. Make authentic reproductions of handsome, functional, durable furniture: tables, chairs, wall cabinets, desks, a hall tree, and more. Construction plans with drawings, schematics, dimensions, and lumber specs reprinted from 1900s *The Craftsman* magazine. 128pp. 8⅛ x 11. 0-486-25000-8

MATHEMATICS FOR THE NONMATHEMATICIAN, Morris Kline. Erudite and entertaining overview follows development of mathematics from ancient Greeks to present. Topics include logic and mathematics, the fundamental concept, differential calculus, probability theory, much more. Exercises and problems. 641pp. 5⅜ x 8½. 0-486-24823-2

MEMOIRS OF AN ARABIAN PRINCESS FROM ZANZIBAR, Emily Ruete. This 19th-century autobiography offers a rare inside look at the society surrounding a sultan's palace. A real-life princess in exile recalls her vanished world of harems, slave trading, and court intrigues. 288pp. 5⅜ x 8½. 0-486-47121-7

Browse over 9,000 books at www.doverpublications.com

THE METAMORPHOSIS AND OTHER STORIES, Franz Kafka. Excellent new English translations of title story (considered by many critics Kafka's most perfect work), plus "The Judgment," "In the Penal Colony," "A Country Doctor," and "A Report to an Academy." Note. 96pp. 5³⁄₁₆ x 8¼. 0-486-29030-1

MICROSCOPIC ART FORMS FROM THE PLANT WORLD, R. Anheisser. From undulating curves to complex geometrics, a world of fascinating images abound in this classic, illustrated survey of microscopic plants. Features 400 detailed illustrations of nature's minute but magnificent handiwork. The accompanying CD-ROM includes all of the images in the book. 128pp. 9 x 9. 0-486-46013-4

A MIDSUMMER NIGHT'S DREAM, William Shakespeare. Among the most popular of Shakespeare's comedies, this enchanting play humorously celebrates the vagaries of love as it focuses upon the intertwined romances of several pairs of lovers. Explanatory footnotes. 80pp. 5³⁄₁₆ x 8¼. 0-486-27067-X

THE MONEY CHANGERS, Upton Sinclair. Originally published in 1908, this cautionary novel from the author of *The Jungle* explores corruption within the American system as a group of power brokers joins forces for personal gain, triggering a crash on Wall Street. 192pp. 5⅜ x 8½. 0-486-46917-4

THE MOST POPULAR HOMES OF THE TWENTIES, William A. Radford. With a New Introduction by Daniel D. Reiff. Based on a rare 1925 catalog, this architectural showcase features floor plans, construction details, and photos of 26 homes, plus articles on entrances, porches, garages, and more. 250 illustrations, 21 color plates. 176pp. 8⅜ x 11. 0-486-47028-8

MY 66 YEARS IN THE BIG LEAGUES, Connie Mack. With a New Introduction by Rich Westcott. A Founding Father of modern baseball, Mack holds the record for most wins — and losses — by a major league manager. Enhanced by 70 photographs, his warmhearted autobiography is populated by many legends of the game. 288pp. 5⅜ x 8½. 0-486-47184-5

NARRATIVE OF THE LIFE OF FREDERICK DOUGLASS, Frederick Douglass. Douglass's graphic depictions of slavery, harrowing escape to freedom, and life as a newspaper editor, eloquent orator, and impassioned abolitionist. 96pp. 5³⁄₁₆ x 8¼. 0-486-28499-9

THE NIGHTLESS CITY: Geisha and Courtesan Life in Old Tokyo, J. E. de Becker. This unsurpassed study from 100 years ago ventured into Tokyo's red-light district to survey geisha and courtesan life and offer meticulous descriptions of training, dress, social hierarchy, and erotic practices. 49 black-and-white illustrations; 2 maps. 496pp. 5⅜ x 8½. 0-486-45563-7

THE ODYSSEY, Homer. Excellent prose translation of ancient epic recounts adventures of the homeward-bound Odysseus. Fantastic cast of gods, giants, cannibals, sirens, other supernatural creatures — true classic of Western literature. 256pp. 5³⁄₁₆ x 8¼. 0-486-40654-7

OEDIPUS REX, Sophocles. Landmark of Western drama concerns the catastrophe that ensues when King Oedipus discovers he has inadvertently killed his father and married his mother. Masterly construction, dramatic irony. Explanatory footnotes. 64pp. 5³⁄₁₆ x 8¼. 0-486-26877-2

ONCE UPON A TIME: The Way America Was, Eric Sloane. Nostalgic text and drawings brim with gentle philosophies and descriptions of how we used to live — self-sufficiently — on the land, in homes, and among the things built by hand. 44 line illustrations. 64pp. 8⅜ x 11. 0-486-44411-2

ONE OF OURS, Willa Cather. The Pulitzer Prize–winning novel about a young Nebraskan looking for something to believe in. Alienated from his parents, rejected by his wife, he finds his destiny on the bloody battlefields of World War I. 352pp. 5¾₆ x 8¼. 0-486-45599-8

ORIGAMI YOU CAN USE: 27 Practical Projects, Rick Beech. Origami models can be more than decorative, and this unique volume shows how! The 27 practical projects include a CD case, frame, napkin ring, and dish. Easy instructions feature 400 two-color illustrations. 96pp. 8¼ x 11. 0-486-47057-1

OTHELLO, William Shakespeare. Towering tragedy tells the story of a Moorish general who earns the enmity of his ensign Iago when he passes him over for a promotion. Masterly portrait of an archvillain. Explanatory footnotes. 112pp. 5¾₆ x 8¼. 0-486-29097-2

PARADISE LOST, John Milton. Notes by John A. Himes. First published in 1667, *Paradise Lost* ranks among the greatest of English literature's epic poems. It's a sublime retelling of Adam and Eve's fall from grace and expulsion from Eden. Notes by John A. Himes. 480pp. 5¾₆ x 8¼. 0-486-44287-X

PASSING, Nella Larsen. Married to a successful physician and prominently ensconced in society, Irene Redfield leads a charmed existence — until a chance encounter with a childhood friend who has been "passing for white." 112pp. 5⅜ x 8½. 0-486-43713-2

PERSPECTIVE DRAWING FOR BEGINNERS, Len A. Doust. Doust carefully explains the roles of lines, boxes, and circles, and shows how visualizing shapes and forms can be used in accurate depictions of perspective. One of the most concise introductions available. 33 illustrations. 64pp. 5⅜ x 8½. 0-486-45149-6

PERSPECTIVE MADE EASY, Ernest R. Norling. Perspective is easy; yet, surprisingly few artists know the simple rules that make it so. Remedy that situation with this simple, step-by-step book, the first devoted entirely to the topic. 256 illustrations. 224pp. 5⅜ x 8½. 0-486-40473-0

THE PICTURE OF DORIAN GRAY, Oscar Wilde. Celebrated novel involves a handsome young Londoner who sinks into a life of depravity. His body retains perfect youth and vigor while his recent portrait reflects the ravages of his crime and sensuality. 176pp. 5¾₆ x 8¼. 0-486-27807-7

PRIDE AND PREJUDICE, Jane Austen. One of the most universally loved and admired English novels, an effervescent tale of rural romance transformed by Jane Austen's art into a witty, shrewdly observed satire of English country life. 272pp. 5¾₆ x 8¼. 0-486-28473-5

THE PRINCE, Niccolò Machiavelli. Classic, Renaissance-era guide to acquiring and maintaining political power. Today, nearly 500 years after it was written, this calculating prescription for autocratic rule continues to be much read and studied. 80pp. 5¾₆ x 8¼. 0-486-27274-5

QUICK SKETCHING, Carl Cheek. A perfect introduction to the technique of "quick sketching." Drawing upon an artist's immediate emotional responses, this is an extremely effective means of capturing the essential form and features of a subject. More than 100 black-and-white illustrations throughout. 48pp. 11 x 8¼. 0-486-46608-6

RANCH LIFE AND THE HUNTING TRAIL, Theodore Roosevelt. Illustrated by Frederic Remington. Beautifully illustrated by Remington, Roosevelt's celebration of the Old West recounts his adventures in the Dakota Badlands of the 1880s, from roundups to Indian encounters to hunting bighorn sheep. 208pp. 6¼ x 9¼. 0-486-47340-6

Browse over 9,000 books at www.doverpublications.com

THE RED BADGE OF COURAGE, Stephen Crane. Amid the nightmarish chaos of a Civil War battle, a young soldier discovers courage, humility, and, perhaps, wisdom. Uncanny re-creation of actual combat. Enduring landmark of American fiction. 112pp. 5³⁄₁₆ x 8¼. 0-486-26465-3

RELATIVITY SIMPLY EXPLAINED, Martin Gardner. One of the subject's clearest, most entertaining introductions offers lucid explanations of special and general theories of relativity, gravity, and spacetime, models of the universe, and more. 100 illustrations. 224pp. 5⅜ x 8½. 0-486-29315-7

REMBRANDT DRAWINGS: 116 Masterpieces in Original Color, Rembrandt van Rijn. This deluxe hardcover edition features drawings from throughout the Dutch master's prolific career. Informative captions accompany these beautifully reproduced landscapes, biblical vignettes, figure studies, animal sketches, and portraits. 128pp. 8⅜ x 11. 0-486-46149-1

THE ROAD NOT TAKEN AND OTHER POEMS, Robert Frost. A treasury of Frost's most expressive verse. In addition to the title poem: "An Old Man's Winter Night," "In the Home Stretch," "Meeting and Passing," "Putting in the Seed," many more. All complete and unabridged. 64pp. 5³⁄₁₆ x 8¼. 0-486-27550-7

ROMEO AND JULIET, William Shakespeare. Tragic tale of star-crossed lovers, feuding families and timeless passion contains some of Shakespeare's most beautiful and lyrical love poetry. Complete, unabridged text with explanatory footnotes. 96pp. 5³⁄₁₆ x 8¼. 0-486-27557-4

SANDITON AND THE WATSONS: Austen's Unfinished Novels, Jane Austen. Two tantalizing incomplete stories revisit Austen's customary milieu of courtship and venture into new territory, amid guests at a seaside resort. Both are worth reading for pleasure and study. 112pp. 5⅜ x 8½. 0-486-45793-1

THE SCARLET LETTER, Nathaniel Hawthorne. With stark power and emotional depth, Hawthorne's masterpiece explores sin, guilt, and redemption in a story of adultery in the early days of the Massachusetts Colony. 192pp. 5³⁄₁₆ x 8¼.
0-486-28048-9

THE SEASONS OF AMERICA PAST, Eric Sloane. Seventy-five illustrations depict cider mills and presses, sleds, pumps, stump-pulling equipment, plows, and other elements of America's rural heritage. A section of old recipes and household hints adds additional color. 160pp. 8⅜ x 11. 0-486-44220-9

SELECTED CANTERBURY TALES, Geoffrey Chaucer. Delightful collection includes the General Prologue plus three of the most popular tales: "The Knight's Tale," "The Miller's Prologue and Tale," and "The Wife of Bath's Prologue and Tale." In modern English. 144pp. 5³⁄₁₆ x 8¼. 0-486-28241-4

SELECTED POEMS, Emily Dickinson. Over 100 best-known, best-loved poems by one of America's foremost poets, reprinted from authoritative early editions. No comparable edition at this price. Index of first lines. 64pp. 5³⁄₁₆ x 8¼. 0-486-26466-1

SIDDHARTHA, Hermann Hesse. Classic novel that has inspired generations of seekers. Blending Eastern mysticism and psychoanalysis, Hesse presents a strikingly original view of man and culture and the arduous process of self-discovery, reconciliation, harmony, and peace. 112pp. 5³⁄₁₆ x 8¼. 0-486-40653-9

SKETCHING OUTDOORS, Leonard Richmond. This guide offers beginners step-by-step demonstrations of how to depict clouds, trees, buildings, and other outdoor sights. Explanations of a variety of techniques include shading and constructional drawing. 48pp. 11 x 8¼. 0-486-46922-0

SMALL HOUSES OF THE FORTIES: With Illustrations and Floor Plans, Harold E. Group. 56 floor plans and elevations of houses that originally cost less than $15,000 to build. Recommended by financial institutions of the era, they range from Colonials to Cape Cods. 144pp. 8⅜ x 11. 0-486-45598-X

SOME CHINESE GHOSTS, Lafcadio Hearn. Rooted in ancient Chinese legends, these richly atmospheric supernatural tales are recounted by an expert in Oriental lore. Their originality, power, and literary charm will captivate readers of all ages. 96pp. 5⅜ x 8½. 0-486-46306-0

SONGS FOR THE OPEN ROAD: Poems of Travel and Adventure, Edited by The American Poetry & Literacy Project. More than 80 poems by 50 American and British masters celebrate real and metaphorical journeys. Poems by Whitman, Byron, Millay, Sandburg, Langston Hughes, Emily Dickinson, Robert Frost, Shelley, Tennyson, Yeats, many others. Note. 80pp. 5³⁄₁₆ x 8¼. 0-486-40646-6

SPOON RIVER ANTHOLOGY, Edgar Lee Masters. An American poetry classic, in which former citizens of a mythical midwestern town speak touchingly from the grave of the thwarted hopes and dreams of their lives. 144pp. 5³⁄₁₆ x 8¼. 0-486-27275-3

STAR LORE: Myths, Legends, and Facts, William Tyler Olcott. Captivating retellings of the origins and histories of ancient star groups include Pegasus, Ursa Major, Pleiades, signs of the zodiac, and other constellations. "Classic." — *Sky & Telescope.* 58 illustrations. 544pp. 5⅜ x 8½. 0-486-43581-4

THE STRANGE CASE OF DR. JEKYLL AND MR. HYDE, Robert Louis Stevenson. This intriguing novel, both fantasy thriller and moral allegory, depicts the struggle of two opposing personalities — one essentially good, the other evil — for the soul of one man. 64pp. 5³⁄₁₆ x 8¼. 0-486-26688-5

SURVIVAL HANDBOOK: The Official U.S. Army Guide, Department of the Army. This special edition of the Army field manual is geared toward civilians. An essential companion for campers and all lovers of the outdoors, it constitutes the most authoritative wilderness guide. 288pp. 5³⁄₁₆ x 8¼. 0-486-46184-X

A TALE OF TWO CITIES, Charles Dickens. Against the backdrop of the French Revolution, Dickens unfolds his masterpiece of drama, adventure, and romance about a man falsely accused of treason. Excitement and derring-do in the shadow of the guillotine. 304pp. 5³⁄₁₆ x 8¼. 0-486-40651-2

TEN PLAYS, Anton Chekhov. *The Sea Gull, Uncle Vanya, The Three Sisters, The Cherry Orchard,* and *Ivanov,* plus 5 one-act comedies: *The Anniversary, An Unwilling Martyr, The Wedding, The Bear,* and *The Proposal.* 336pp. 5³⁄₁₆ x 8¼. 0-486-46560-8

THE FLYING INN, G. K. Chesterton. Hilarious romp in which pub owner Humphrey Hump and friend take to the road in a donkey cart filled with rum and cheese, inveighing against Prohibition and other "oppressive forms of modernity." 320pp. 5⅜ x 8½. 0-486-41910-X

THIRTY YEARS THAT SHOOK PHYSICS: The Story of Quantum Theory, George Gamow. Lucid, accessible introduction to the influential theory of energy and matter features careful explanations of Dirac's anti-particles, Bohr's model of the atom, and much more. Numerous drawings. 1966 edition. 240pp. 5⅜ x 8½. 0-486-24895-X

TREASURE ISLAND, Robert Louis Stevenson. Classic adventure story of a perilous sea journey, a mutiny led by the infamous Long John Silver, and a lethal scramble for buried treasure — seen through the eyes of cabin boy Jim Hawkins. 160pp. 5³⁄₁₆ x 8¼. 0-486-27559-0

Browse over 9,000 books at www.doverpublications.com

THE TRIAL, Franz Kafka. Translated by David Wyllie. From its gripping first sentence onward, this novel exemplifies the term "Kafkaesque." Its darkly humorous narrative recounts a bank clerk's entrapment in a bureaucratic maze, based on an undisclosed charge. 176pp. 5 3/16 x 8 1/4. 0-486-47061-X

THE TURN OF THE SCREW, Henry James. Gripping ghost story by great novelist depicts the sinister transformation of 2 innocent children into flagrant liars and hypocrites. An elegantly told tale of unspoken horror and psychological terror. 96pp. 5 3/16 x 8 1/4. 0-486-26684-2

UP FROM SLAVERY, Booker T. Washington. Washington (1856-1915) rose to become the most influential spokesman for African-Americans of his day. In this eloquently written book, he describes events in a remarkable life that began in bondage and culminated in worldwide recognition. 160pp. 5 3/16 x 8 1/4. 0-486-28738-6

VICTORIAN HOUSE DESIGNS IN AUTHENTIC FULL COLOR: 75 Plates from the "Scientific American – Architects and Builders Edition," 1885-1894, Edited by Blanche Cirker. Exquisitely detailed, exceptionally handsome designs for an enormous variety of attractive city dwellings, spacious suburban and country homes, charming "cottages" and other structures — all accompanied by perspective views and floor plans. 80pp. 9 1/4 x 12 1/4. 0-486-29438-2

VILLETTE, Charlotte Brontë. Acclaimed by Virginia Woolf as "Brontë's finest novel," this moving psychological study features a remarkably modern heroine who abandons her native England for a new life as a schoolteacher in Belgium. 480pp. 5 3/16 x 8 1/4. 0-486-45557-2

THE VOYAGE OUT, Virginia Woolf. A moving depiction of the thrills and confusion of youth, Woolf's acclaimed first novel traces a shipboard journey to South America for a captivating exploration of a woman's growing self-awareness. 288pp. 5 3/16 x 8 1/4. 0-486-45005-8

WALDEN; OR, LIFE IN THE WOODS, Henry David Thoreau. Accounts of Thoreau's daily life on the shores of Walden Pond outside Concord, Massachusetts, are interwoven with musings on the virtues of self-reliance and individual freedom, on society, government, and other topics. 224pp. 5 3/16 x 8 1/4. 0-486-28495-6

WILD PILGRIMAGE: A Novel in Woodcuts, Lynd Ward. Through startling engravings shaded in black and red, Ward wordlessly tells the story of a man trapped in an industrial world, struggling between the grim reality around him and the fantasies his imagination creates. 112pp. 6 1/8 x 9 1/4. 0-486-46583-7

WILLY POGÁNY REDISCOVERED, Willy Pogány. Selected and Edited by Jeff A. Menges. More than 100 color and black-and-white Art Nouveau–style illustrations from fairy tales and adventure stories include scenes from Wagner's "Ring" cycle, *The Rime of the Ancient Mariner, Gulliver's Travels,* and *Faust.* 144pp. 8 3/8 x 11. 0-486-47046-6

WOOLLY THOUGHTS: Unlock Your Creative Genius with Modular Knitting, Pat Ashforth and Steve Plummer. Here's the revolutionary way to knit — easy, fun, and foolproof! Beginners and experienced knitters need only master a single stitch to create their own designs with patchwork squares. More than 100 illustrations. 128pp. 6 1/2 x 9 1/4. 0-486-46084-3

WUTHERING HEIGHTS, Emily Brontë. Somber tale of consuming passions and vengeance — played out amid the lonely English moors — recounts the turbulent and tempestuous love story of Cathy and Heathcliff. Poignant and compelling. 256pp. 5 3/16 x 8 1/4. 0-486-29256-8